RURAL CHANGE IN IRELAND

RURAL CHANGE IN IRELAND

Edited by

John Davis

The Institute of Irish Studies
The Queen's University of Belfast

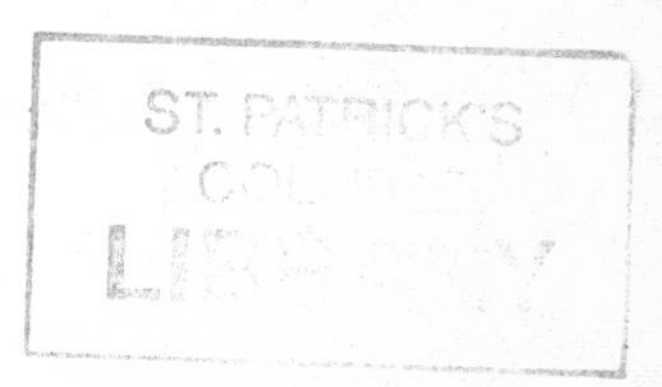

First published in 1999
The Institute of Irish Studies
The Queen's University of Belfast

British Library Cataloguing-in-Publication Data.
A catalogue record for this book is available from the British Library.

ISBN 0 85389 744 1 hbk
ISBN 0 85389 734 4 pbk

Typeset in Palatino 10pt by Book Production Services, London.

Printed by W & G Baird Ltd, Antrim

Contents

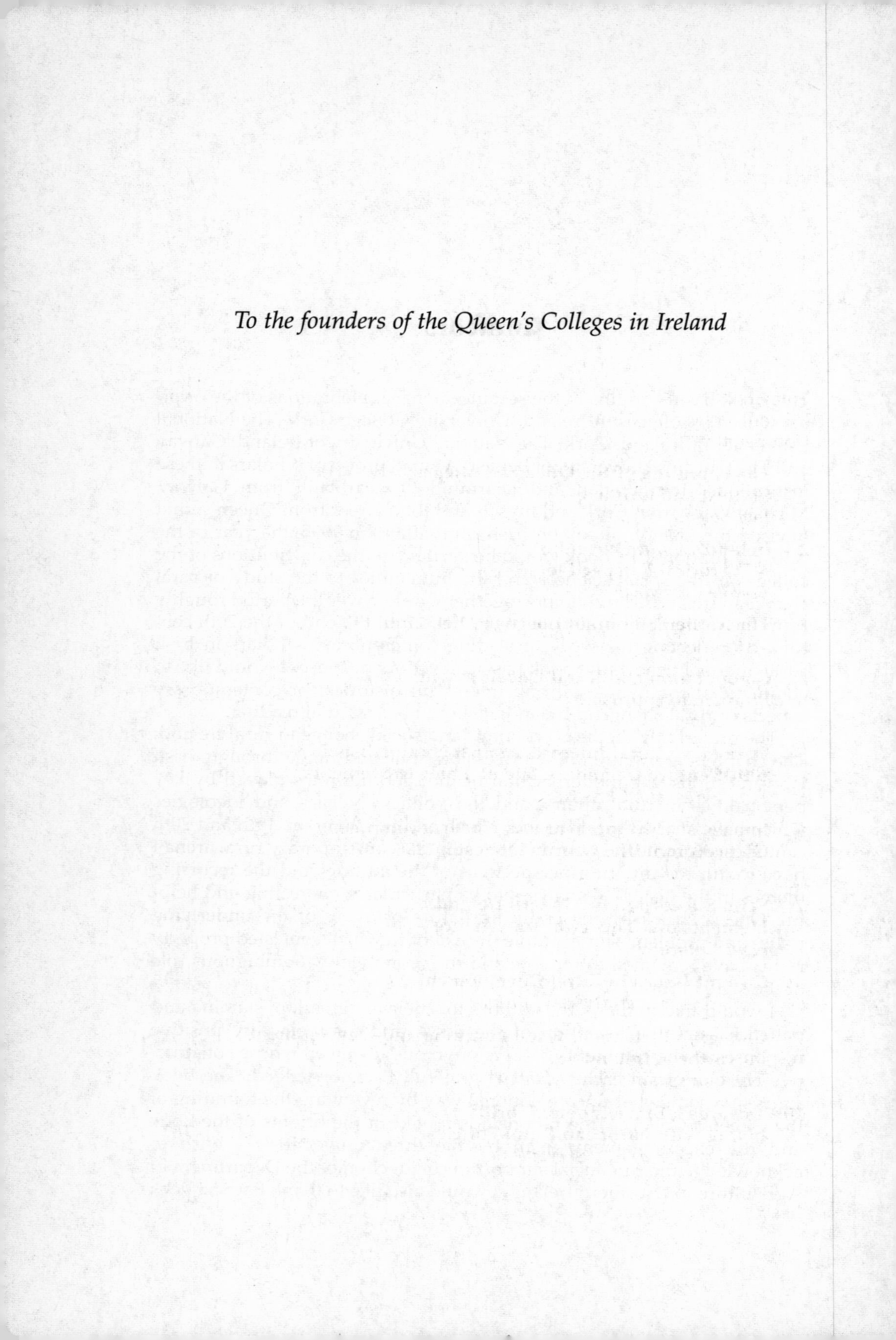

To the founders of the Queen's Colleges in Ireland

Foreword

This book has its origins in the sesquicentenary celebrations of the original Queen's Colleges in Ireland; University College Cork (The National University of Ireland, Cork) The National University of Ireland, Galway and The Queen's University of Belfast. A small group of scholars in these institutions, Tom Boylan and Diarmuid Ó Cearbhaill from Galway, Michael Ward from Cork and myself and John Greer from Queen's, first devised the idea of a book on Irish rural affairs in 1995, the year of the '150' celebrations: the book would be a tribute to the contributions of the colleges in the social sciences and the humanities to the study of rural change in Ireland. The chapters together would cover the period roughly from the formation of the colleges in 1845 until the end of the 20th century. By reflecting the work of leading contemporary scholars in Irish rural affairs, I believe the book has achieved its purpose. I would like to commend it to anyone with an interest in historical or contemporary aspects of rural change in Ireland; it should be essential reading.

The underlying theme is economic and social change in rural Ireland. The chapters are written in an accessible style and range through, Irish land questions, the modernisation of the diet, the roles played by key personalities in rural affairs, and the politics, policies and ideologies which have shaped rural Ireland, North and South, in the 19th and 20th centuries. As someone with an interest in the contemporary rural arena I have found the differing perspectives of the authors and the recurring themes in the historical analyses to be particularly interesting and helpful. One is struck by the enduring nature of many of the underlying issues and problems; for example the extent to which contested property rights have remained to the fore and the prominent yet ambiguous role of the state in rural affairs.

I would like to thank the authors for their imagination, stamina and patience since the inception of the book; and for their very positive responses to the comments of an anonymous reviewer, whose constructive critique on an earlier draft is gratefully acknowledged. The book starts in a somewhat unconventional way by reviewing the founding of the Queen's Colleges: the rationale is rooted in the origins of the book and the encouragement given by the three universities; I wish to acknowledge their financial support in conjunction of the Department of Agriculture for Northern Ireland. I would also like to thank Patricia Lock of the Gibson Institute of Rural Studies in Queen's for her painstaking work on the first drafts, and Catherine McColgan and Margaret McNulty of the Institute of Irish Studies for their help in making the book ready for publication.

The emergence of the book is tinged with considerable sadness. Shortly after he produced the first draft of chapter 6, Vincent Tucker, tragically, died in a car accident: he was a fine scholar and is sadly missed by his colleagues. An appreciation of his life and work follows this foreword.

John Davis

Vincent Tucker: A Tribute

Vincent started his academic career at UCC, in 1981, with the newly-born Centre for Co-operative Studies. He was in the final stages of writing his doctoral thesis on the Glencolumbkille Community Co-operative in County Donegal. As we in the centre grappled with the problem of defining and clarifying the nature of co-operatives, Vincent challenged our basic assumption and nudged our deliberations into new levels of creativity.

To our work in the centre, he brought his vast experience of different cultures and peoples. His multi-disciplinary intellectual training helped him to integrate everyday concerns with a theoretical conceptualisation which lacked arrogance and did not slavishly follow the accepted tenets of any single discipline. Confronted by good sparring partners, Vincent thrived in the cut and thrust of passionate debate. Each meeting was a real education, following Freire's *conscientization* approach, of which Vincent was a gifted exponent. For many of us, this experience proved to be our real university education.

Vincent made a huge contribution with publications and teaching in the Centre for Co-operative Studies, before moving on, on completion of his doctoral studies, to the Department of Social Theory and Institutions. He was quickly promoted to a statutory position and took his turn as a head of department. His anthropological training and his unusual ability to identify the historical roots of current problems enabled him to make a major contribution to the development of his department.

Given Vincent's doctoral studies and his prolific commentary on rural society and the role of co-operatives, it was no surprise that he was chosen to contribute to the book on rural change in Ireland to mark the 150th anniversary of our universities. Tragically, he was never to see it in print as an untimely accident, on a wintry country road, took his life as he drove in the role of a good Samaritan to visit an elderly relative. This was very much in Vincent's character as he was forever involved in promoting social causes and the betterment of humanity. This was not mere intellectual posturing, however, as he practised what he preached in his everyday, personal dealings with people.

Vincent was a warm, affectionate, larger than life man, who approached issues with an infectious enthusiasm. He regularly challenged conventional notions of *leaders* and *leadership* and his own life embodied the alternative, co-operative leadership he advocated so eloquently – a leadership which starts from urgent problems and involves people experiencing these problems in the design of their own collective solutions.

While Vincent is sorely missed here in the Centre for Co-operative Studies, his work continues to inspire not only those who knew him but all who read the works he has left behind. We hope that the growing realisation of the significance of Vincent's legacy to us all will, in time, be some comfort to his wife, Kathleen, and his children, Aíne and Oisín. His family, in turn, were always an immense support and source of inspiration to Vincent in all his life's endeavours.

Ar dheis Dé go raibh a anam dilis.

Denis IF Lucey, Michael Ward, Bob Briscoe,
Centre for Co-operative Studies, University College Cork

Contributors

Tom Boylan is Professor of Economics and Dean of Research in the National University of Ireland, Galway. His research interests are in growth and development, economic methodology and the history of economic thought.

Mary Cawley is a senior lecturer in the Department of Geography, National University of Ireland, Galway. Her research interests are in the social and economic geography of rural areas, especially aspects of population change and the diversification of the rural economy.

Leslie Clarkson is Professor Emeritus of Social History and former senior pro vice-chancellor, The Queen's University of Belfast. His current research interests are in the history of the Irish diet, 1500–1920, and in Irish historical demography.

Chris Curtin is Professor of Political Science and Sociology at the National University of Ireland, Galway. His research interests include rural and community development, regional and local politics and Mexican politics and society.

John Davis is Head of Agricultural and Food Economics and former director of the Institute of Rural Studies at The Queen's University of Belfast. His research interests include regional agricultural and rural policy evaluation and the rural reform process in China.

John Greer is a senior lecturer in the School of Environmental Planning at The Queen's University of Belfast. His research interests include the spatial planning aspects of rural development and the effects of rural planning policy on rural areas.

Michael J Keane is an associate professor in the Department of Economics, National University of Ireland, Galway. His research interests include the economics of tourism, territorial economic dynamics and social entrepreneurship.

Liam Kennedy is Professor of Economic and Social History at The Queen's University of Belfast. His research interests include the Irish rural economy in the 19th and 20th centuries.

Carla King lectures in history at St Patrick's College, Dublin. Her research interests include the role of Horace Plunkett in the co-operative movement; this work has involved collaboration with the Centre for Co-operative Studies, National University of Ireland, University College Cork.

Michael Murray is a senior lecturer in the School of Public Policy, Economics and Law, at the University of Ulster. His research interests include community-led rural development, partnership governance, and town and country planning policies.

Gearóid Ó Tuathaigh is Professor of History and former dean of arts and vice-president of the National University of Ireland, Galway. His research interests are in 19th and 20th century British and Irish history.

Sally Shortall is a reader in sociology at The Queen's University of Belfast. Her research interests include the role of women in rural development and the factors contributing to social exclusion in rural areas.

Vincent Tucker lectured in the Department of Social Theory and Institutions, University College Cork, until his untimely death in 1997. His research interests included the role of co-operatives in development and identifying the historical roots of current development problems.

Tony Varley lectures in political science and sociology at the National University of Ireland, Galway. His research interests include rural and agricultural development, community development and agrarian politics.

Chapter 1

The Founding of the Queen's Colleges: Context and Origins

Tom Boylan

The crisis in the Irish rural economy and society at the time of the founding of the Queen's Colleges underlined the need to expand university education in Ireland. Although not the primary reason for their establishment, the desperate problems in the rural economy at the time served to foreshadow the great contributions which the Colleges would make ultimately, through their teaching and research, to the development of rural Ireland. The documenting of these achievements is far beyond the scope of any single chapter, or even book. This chapter, therefore, provides a brief contextual account of the circumstances surrounding the establishment of the Queen's Colleges against the background of 19th-century Irish economy and society.

The two most significant developments in Irish education during the course of the 19th century were the creation of a national system of primary education in the early 1830s, and the establishment of the Queen's Colleges at Belfast, Cork, and Galway in the mid 1840s. The former amounted to what was to be a major experiment in a state-supported system of non-denominational national education, which preceded the introduction of a similar system in Britain by a period of 40 years.[1] The establishment of the Queen's Colleges, which was followed shortly afterwards by the creation of their degree-granting institution, the Queen's University, represented the provision of an additional set of university institutions in Ireland. Prior to the establishment of the Queen's Colleges, the provision of university education in Ireland was the sole preserve of the University of Dublin, which had become synonymous with Trinity

College Dublin.[2] The decision to establish the Queen's Colleges at this time was not an isolated event. It was an integral part of an elaborate policy of conciliation, implemented by Sir Robert Peel to counteract Daniel O'Connell's campaign for repeal of the union between Great Britain and Ireland.

Through a striking coincidence of historical events, the second half of the 1840s, from the passing of the Colleges (Ireland) Act in July 1845 which established the Queen's Colleges to the arrival of the first students in 1849, coincided almost exactly with the cataclysmic events of the Great Famine. The latter event is generally taken as the critical watershed in the economic and social history of 19th-century Ireland. In terms of their timing the Queen's Colleges were clearly destined to become an integral part of post-Famine Ireland. Notwithstanding the centrality of the Great Famine, from an economic perspective there is considerable continuity in the economic dimensions of the 'Irish question' during the course of the 19th century. The 'Irish question' was a persistent and enduring issue in British politics and public debate throughout the 19th century: it presented not only formidable economic problems, but was also characterised by deeply divisive political, social, and religious dimensions. From an economic perspective the distinguished historian of economic thought, Jacob Viner, encapsulated the complexity of the situation when he stated that, 'the "Irish problem" had many facets, but for the economist it was primarily the problem of Irish poverty'.[3] It is hard to dispute Viner's reading of the situation and it is certainly substantiated when one examines the writings of contemporary political economists in the 19th century in relation to their diagnosis of and prescriptions for the problems of the Irish situation.

At the beginning of the 19th century the Irish economy could look back to a period of successful economic expansion in both agriculture and industry. By the middle of the century, however, the industrial base had suffered substantial decline, while the agricultural economy had experienced extended periods of difficult adjustments which culminated in its near collapse during the years of the Great Famine. The adjustments occurring in the agricultural economy were in general terms concerned with the implications of the rapid growth in population in the decades preceding the Famine relative to the corresponding growth in the means of supporting and employing this population. The increase in population in the pre-Famine economy was dramatic, rising from under 5 million in 1791 to over 8 million in 1841, two-thirds of which in 1841 obtained their living from agricultural activity. Up to the mid 1840s, agriculture carried the responsibility of supporting the expanding population, but in many areas of the country, with increasing difficulty.[4]

Agricultural output increased in this period, but the standard of living of many of those employed in it declined. The nexus of mechanisms which contributed to this situation was complex, but included the dynamics of market behaviour for agricultural produce, the changing conditions of cultivation and land tenure, along with the growing pressure of population. The dynamics of Irish agriculture in the pre-Famine economy followed what is now a clearly identified pattern of change which reflected these critical factors. In the early years of the 19th century the high prices for grain crops led to a substantial expansion of tillage, which was extremely labour intensive. Against the background of a rapidly expanding population a ready supply of cheap labour was available to farmers, sustained through the provision of small patches of land, on which a crop of potatoes, adequate to their needs, could be cultivated. Landlords and their agents were not opposed to such sub-division and resulting fragmentation of holdings, since it simultaneously facilitated the subsistence of a cheap labour force without substantially impinging on the supply of land available for the cultivation of profitable rent-yielding grain crops.[5]

This structure of production and social formation within the agricultural economy facilitated the expanding population. The most vulnerable class in this arrangement was the newly-emergent class of cottier labourers. With the ensuing slump in the prices of wheat and other grain crops following the cessation of the Napoleonic Wars, the central axis of this system of production was removed with major implications for the different classes within the agricultural economy. The larger farmers had the capacity to meet the new situation, albeit with some adjustments, but for many small farmers the situation proved extremely difficult; they were either driven heavily into debt in an attempt to sustain their situation or else began to lose their hold on the land.[6] The cottier and labourer class fared worse, in that they met increasing resistance on the part of landlords and large farmers to allow subsistence plots to impinge on profitable land. In this situation an increasing proportion of the agricultural population came to depend on the potato crop as their only means of subsistence. Insights into the increasing dependence on the potato as the staple diet were indicated by the partial failures of that crop in the earlier part of the century, particularly in 1817, 1821, and 1831, but did not prepare either the population at large or government of the day for the catastrophe that followed the failure of the potato crop in 1845 and again in 1846, the details of which have been the subject of extensive recent publications.[7]

Post-Famine Ireland was dominated in one form or another by adjustments to changes, a number of which had emerged prior to the Famine, but were now forcefully brought to the foreground of public policy debate. Many of the most distinguished members of the Queen's Colleges were to make major contributions to these debates, particularly in the areas of law, political economy, social policy, along with agricultural science and its applications.[8] In the immediate aftermath of the Famine, the government of Lord John Russell was committed to the view that a necessary and urgent requirement of Irish economic recovery was to replace the existing class of landlords, who were deemed to be both inefficient and dilatory in their managerial responsibilities, with a new and improving breed of proprietors. This shift was greatly facilitated by the fact that many of the existing landlord class had been driven into bankruptcy by the Famine which had burdened them with increased poor rates at a time when they experienced increasing difficulties in collecting their rents. The government solution to the problem of bankrupt estates was contained in the Encumbered Estates Act of 1849, which conducted the rapid sale and transfer of these properties through a special court.[9] While the Encumbered Estates Court addressed the problem of bankruptcy for the landlord class, at the other extreme small tenants and labourers were offered little beyond poor relief. The solution to the problem for this social class emerged, ostensibly in the form of voluntary emigration, assisted for a period by elaborate schemes of subsidised migration.[10] Emigration had emerged prior to the Famine, but the scale of the movement in the post-Famine period was unprecedented, with more than 1 million people emigrating between 1851 and 1860. The incidence of post-Famine adjustment fell disproportionately on the small tenants and cottiers and these constituted the majority of those who emigrated.[11]

For those who remained, mostly the larger farmers, conditions unquestionably improved over the 30–year period from the 1850s. The movement of prices in this period clearly indicated a continuing shift from grain crops to livestock production, and the response was rapid and extensive. As a system of production it was labour displacing rather than labour intensive and neither did it generate great pressures for improved efficiency. Depressions in the value of agricultural output in the 1860s and again in the late 1870s endangered profitability in agriculture and in these years problems of rent arrears emerged for tenant farmers with the ensuing threat of evictions.[12] While evictions were not widespread the landlord-tenant relationships were embittered and demands for 'fair rents' and 'fixity of tenure' emerged. The resulting agitation resulted in Gladstone's first land act of 1870, which was passed in the face of bitter opposition from landed interests in the British parliament. Gladstone believed, at least for a period, that he had solved the Irish agrarian problem. The act was in practice a very limited affair which was exposed in the light of the depression in the late 1870s.[13] The formation in 1879 of the Irish National Land League launched the systematic agitation for land reform, which had as its short-term objectives the protection of tenants against eviction and rent increases and a long-term aim of converting the tenants into owners of their own land. As a result of their campaign and the pressure it exerted in Ireland, and in Westminster through the Irish members of parliament, a number of land acts were passed between 1881 and 1903, which conceded tenant security, rents fixed by law, and finally peasant proprietorship, an issue which had emerged in the 1860s.[14]

The effects of these legislative changes on the performance of the agricultural economy have been contested in recent historical research. The leitmotif of revisionist Irish economic history for the last few decades has been self-consciously aimed at correcting various populist-nationalist misconceptions about historical grievances, with particular attention being paid to the historiography of the Famine.[15] The centrality of providing a solution to the land question as the key to Irish economic development does not occupy the privileged position in recent historical research as that accorded to it by contemporary writers in the 19th century. In any event the central thrust of historical research indicates that the shift in the structure of ownership did not generate major changes in agricultural methods or growth in output.

Development in other sectors, particularly industry, did not compensate for the lacklustre performance in agriculture. While there was overall growth in the post-Famine economy, it was highly uneven both sectorally and spatially and ultimately insufficient to provide even the reduced population with adequate employment at reasonable levels of income. Manufacturing industry became increasingly concentrated in the north-eastern part of the country, particularly in Belfast. The growth of ship-building and engineering in that city sustained an increasing population, from 100,000 in 1850 to 400,000 in 1914. Similar-sized cities elsewhere in the country, such as Dublin and Cork, generated nothing comparable to Belfast by way of industrial activity, remaining essentially dominated by commerce and the professions. The contributing factors to this spatial configuration of industrial development in the post-Famine economy of the 19th century have been interrogated in considerable detail by historians and economic historians and a number of hypotheses currently compete for acceptability as an explanation to this historical pattern of development. Explanations currently on offer range from the paucity of physical resources through to the weakness of financial resources to the lack of local entrepreneurial capacities.[16] Whatever the explanation, the concentration of manufacturing industry in the north-east contributed to an accentuation of the differences that already existed within Irish society. In addition to the religious differences between the Protestant majority in Ulster and the Catholic majority in the rest of the country were added differences in economic perspective and vested interest. The former were concerned with maintaining the union with Great Britain, based on a policy regime of free trade, to ensure the availability of the necessary imports such as raw materials and access to the major markets in Great Britain, while the latter were more concerned with reacquiring the proprietorship of their land, and fostering the objective of national independence and providing protection for the home market. It was against this background of a deeply divided society in political, religious, economic and social terms, that the Queen's Colleges were established. This decision was deeply motivated by political considerations and the colleges, once established, had to contend with the opposing forces that constituted the social and political structure of 19th-century Ireland.

The problem which Robert Peel sought to solve by the establishment of the Queen's Colleges, the inadequate provision of higher education in Ireland, had a long history and involved not only issues of education but also of religion, politics, and economics. It was a source of profound periodic disturbance in Irish public debate, as it was in Anglo-Irish relations throughout the 19th century. The university question in Ireland emerged in the last quarter of the 18th century. At this time, the only university institution was the University of Dublin, centred on its single constituent college, Trinity College, whose role was to provide a supply of clergy to the established church. Trinity College was overwhelmingly Anglican, its students drawn from the Church of Ireland, whose members comprised the bulk of the landed aristocracy and professions and were dominant socially and politically throughout the 19th century. Admission to the college was never formally denied to either Catholics or Protestant dissenters, but they were in effect legally excluded. During the course of the 1780s, public debate in Ireland centred on a number of possible solutions which were put forward for consideration. These included: the 'opening' of Trinity College to Catholics and Protestant dissenters, by the abolition of religious tests; the establishment of a new college or colleges within the University of Dublin; and the foundation of new university institutions independent of the existing university. In the event, nothing was to emerge from the deliberations of the 1780s.[17] However, in the following decade, under the impetus of external events, a number of important developments were to take place.

The external events included the French Revolution and the ensuing war between Great Britain and the new revolutionary regime. One of the results of the French Revolution was the closing down of the Irish colleges in France and Flanders, which had been the principal locations for the education of the Irish Catholic clergy. With the closure of these colleges the Irish bishops regarded the continued education of Irish clerical students on the Continent with grave apprehension, fearing that students would be exposed to the prevailing revolutionary ideas. The government was equally anxious to inhibit the importation of revolutionary notions into Ireland. With an impressive display of declared common purpose and tactical manoeuvrings, the government and hierarchy forged a mutually acceptable solution. This came in the form of a number of major concessions to Catholics. The first was contained in a section of the Catholic Relief Act of 1793, which legally permitted Catholics to enter and graduate from Trinity College. Given the restrictions surrounding this concession however, the Catholic hierarchy did not view it as a solution to the problem of educating the Catholic clergy. They pressed for the establishment of a special seminary which would be, for all practical purposes, under their exclusive control. The government, for their own strategic reasons, based primarily on their desire to secure the services of the Catholic clergy in maintaining the established order, granted permission for the foundation of a college at Maynooth, to be supported by an annual grant from parliament. Maynooth became, within a short time, one of the most powerful national institutions in Ireland.[18]

The Protestant dissenters, mainly Presbyterian, comprised of middle-class tenant farmers, businessmen, industrialists, and shopkeepers, concentrated geographically in Ulster, and now motivated as a result of the establishment of Maynooth College, demanded a similar arrangement for the education of their clergy. Traditionally, the Ulster Presbyterians had maintained strong cultural links with Scotland, and many of their clergy were educated there. Politically, however, they were out of favour with the government of the day as a result of their espousal of radical and republican principles and hence continued demands for a second university in Ulster fell on unresponsive ears. A plan for a more broadly-based university in Ulster, which was to be accessible to all Protestant denominations, including Anglicans and dissenters, and to be financed from a bequest from Lord Rokeby, a former primate, was unequivocally rejected by parliament in London in 1799. This, in effect, marked the end of an important decade in the history of Irish university education, for the problem would not receive any further serious attention, at Westminster at least, until the 1840s.[19]

It would be a mistake however, to assume that the intervening period, from the close of the 18th century to the 1840s, was a period of inactivity with respect to higher education issues. On the contrary it was a period of intense agitation, which was to bear fruit by the mid 1840s. In Ulster the Presbyterians, whose demands had been firmly rejected by parliament, established a college in Belfast, the Belfast Academical Institution, which opened in 1814 and went a considerable distance in satisfying their educational needs. Its establishment was the result of the combined efforts of the local commercial and industrial interests who were anxious to provide in Belfast, the focal point of Ulster and Irish Presbyterianism, a centre of education at school and university level for both their clergy and laity. The institution was, in effect, free from religious tests, being founded on the principle that secular education could be distinguished from religious education and that students of whatever religious denominations should receive their secular education in common. For over 30 years the Belfast Academical Institution contributed greatly to solving the practical difficulties of providing university education for Ulster Presbyterians. But it suffered from two major difficulties: an inadequate level of financial support from the state, and the emergence of an internal controversy between orthodox and non-subscribing Presbyterians. It was the latter problem which finally led orthodox Presbyterians to sever their connections with the institution in 1844, by which time in July of that year, Peel announced in parliament his intention to introduce legislation on the Irish university question.[20]

Peel's decision to introduce legislation on the university question was the result of agitation for educational provision, particularly for the Catholic laity, which had greatly intensified during the 1840s. This pressure was provided by the leadership of Thomas Wyse, MP, a major figure in Irish educational reform in the 19th century.[21] It was this agitation, rather than events in Ulster, which finally provoked Peel into addressing the question of university education in Ireland. Wyse, who belonged to the Catholic upper class, was an enthusiastic supporter of O'Connell in the struggle for Catholic emancipation. When emancipation was granted in 1829 he was one of the first Catholics to enter the Westminster parliament. He immediately committed himself to achieving a number of major reforms in Ireland, especially in the area of education. His plan for reform embraced all three levels, primary, secondary, and higher education. By the end of 1830, Wyse had presented a scheme for a national system of education in Ireland, which, though rejected, exerted a decisive influence on the scheme introduced the following year by Stanley, the Irish chief secretary, on behalf of Grey's Whig administration. In 1835 Wyse introduced his second education bill, this time dealing with secondary and higher education. The government of the day, under Lord Melbourne, appointed a select committee, with Wyse as chairman. This committee reported in 1838, and in an impressive document, written by Wyse, they provided the government with an elaborate blueprint for the future of Irish education.[22] It included a proposal for five different levels of schools, including the establishment of four provincial colleges. A central concern of the proposed scheme was the emphasis on the provision of education for the middle classes. This argument was predicated on the premise that the upper classes were catered for by the University of Dublin, while the lower classes had available, by this time, the state-financed national school scheme, but that the middle classes were largely neglected by the state. It was to rectify this deficiency that the Wyse committee proposed the establishment of county secondary schools, or academies, and in particular the provision of the provincial colleges. The publication of the Wyse committee's report gave rise to considerable agitation, particularly in Munster centred on Cork and later in Limerick, between 1838 and 1840. By this time the administration of Lord Melbourne was in retreat and the Munster college movement, as it was known, was a spent force by the time parliament was dissolved in June 1841. Notwithstanding the government's overall lack of response to the Wyse committee's report, it did provide the basis for educational reform in the 19th century, with its principle of mixed or united education, its advocacy of hierarchical structure, and its emphasis on providing an integrated structure of education for the whole country. These principles were not lost on Peel's administration when it addressed the issue of higher education in the mid 1840s.

The major problem which faced the government in 1845 was the higher education of the Catholic laity. Peel's motivation in pursuing educational reform was based on his fear of losing the support of the middle and upper classes among the Roman Catholics, whose loyalty he wished to retain, at what some members of his administration regarded as too high a price.[23] Peel embarked on a policy of conciliation for Ireland, which consisted of a number of measures including a substantial increase in the financial grant to Maynooth College,[24] but the centrepiece was unquestionably the establishment of three new colleges at Belfast, Cork, and Galway. The bill to enact this development received a first reading in May 1845, a second reading was carried by a large majority later that month, and following a number of amendments at the committee stage, the bill was passed in the house of commons on 10 July 1845. The bill passed through all its stages without a division in the house of lords, and received the royal assent on 31 July 1845 as the Queen's Colleges (Ireland) Act.[25]

From the outset it was clearly envisaged by the Peel administration that the Queen's Colleges at Cork and Galway were intended mainly for Catholics, while the Queen's College at Belfast would cater primarily for Presbyterians. Nevertheless, the issue of the denominational status of the new colleges remained to be resolved, an issue which exerted a profound influence on the Queen's Colleges in their early years. The problem, as perceived by the administration, centred on the fact that the legally-established religion was not that of the majority of the people. However, a similar problem had been encountered and resolved at the primary school level in the previous decade through the provision of a system of national schools based on the principle of mixed secular education, and separate religious instruction, for the children of all denominations. The working of that system was deemed sufficiently satisfactory, in the specificity of the prevailing circumstances, to justify its extension into higher education. In addition to enlisting the national school model in support of their scheme, the administration pointed to the experience of the Scottish universities, and to University College London. Consequently, the Queen's Colleges, which were incorporated in December 1845, were to be undenominational and free from all religious tests. They were forbidden to use their endowments from public sources to fund theological teaching, though private endowment for such teaching on a voluntary basis was permitted. The Queen's Colleges scheme was completed in 1850 by the establishment of a new university, the Queen's University in Ireland. The Queen's University, after consideration of different organisational models, was established within a federal structure and designated as a teaching university in that only students educated in one of its three colleges could obtain its degrees. It exercised a powerful control over the colleges and maintained a high and consistent standard of instruction.

The reception which the new colleges received in Ireland was an extremely mixed one, extending from enthusiastic support to relentless hostility. The scheme, originally conceived by Peel as a conciliatory measure, became a source of controversy and contention. It is impossible to understand the history of the Queen's Colleges, their acceptability in Irish society, or their role in Irish education, without an appreciation of the reactions of the different social and religious groupings to the founding of the colleges. In Britain the college scheme provoked little reaction. In Ireland opinions differed sharply. The supporters of the principle of mixed education, mainly non-subscribing Presbyterians, enthusiastically supported the measure. Nationalist opinion was divided. Daniel O'Connell, representing one strand of this thinking, condemned the measure when he spoke of the 'godless colleges,' echoing the militant Tory, Sir Robert Inglis, who had earlier denounced the bill as 'a gigantic scheme of godless education'.[26] In contrast, the Young Ireland movement welcomed the colleges. They viewed them as promoting and facilitating two of their most desired objectives; an educated and independent-minded laity and union between Irishmen of different religions. The Catholic hierarchy was also divided. One section, a minority, led by the primate, Dr Murray of Dublin, was prepared to give the colleges a fair chance. The other section, led by Archbishop MacHale of Tuam, was utterly opposed to the scheme. It was under the influence of MacHale that the hierarchy, withholding their outright condemnation at the beginning, insisted that certain amendments be made to the scheme if their co-operation was to be secured. These included, among other things: that a fair proportion of the professors and other officers would be Catholics and approved by the bishops; that all officers should be appointed by a board of trustees, which should include the Catholic prelates of the province, and should have the power to dismiss any officer convicted of undermining the faith or morals of students; and that Catholic chaplains should be appointed at suitable salaries to supervise the religious and moral instruction of Catholic students.[27]

These demands would have effectively undermined the scheme of mixed education, and were rejected by Peel's administration. The struggle between the hierarchy and the administration which followed was a protracted affair and involved missions to Rome by both sides. The hierarchy, under MacHale's leadership, triumphed and three papal rescripts in 1847, 1848, and 1850 – the latter coinciding with a national episcopal synod in Thurles – formally condemned the Queen's Colleges, and warned the laity to avoid the colleges as subversive to their faith and morals.[28] Thereafter the hierarchy acted in union against the colleges and set about establishing a university of their own, which emerged in 1854 as the Catholic University, with John Henry Newman as its first rector. The bishops' hostility to the Queen's Colleges had a blighting effect on their development, particularly in Cork and Galway, and these colleges, while far from being failures, nevertheless did not succeed in realising their potential or the purpose of their foundation.

In Belfast the position was different, but even there the creation of alternative institutions to the Queen's College was not avoided. The essential difference between Belfast and the rest of the country was that the population from which potential university students could be drawn was almost totally Protestant, and the Presbyterian church, which was comparable in influence to the Catholic church in the rest of the country, saw its way to co-operate with the Queen's College in Belfast. However, the General Assembly of the Presbyterian church, whose main concern was the education of its clergy, did not present a totally unified front on the question. Notwithstanding the establishment of a Presbyterian theological college at Belfast in 1853, which worked in harmony with the Queen's College, a minority in the General Assembly insisted on establishing a completely independent college in Ulster to provide instruction in arts and theology and to be totally under their control. This they did in 1865 in Derry, with the help of a sizeable bequest from a Mrs Magee, when they established a college named in her honour.[29] Queen's College Belfast, in contrast to those at Cork and Galway, and in the different circumstances of Ulster, was immediately successful and shortly after its opening had as many students as Cork and Galway combined. It was in these difficult and complex circumstances that the Queen's Colleges were launched.

The next 50 years were to prove just as turbulent as the years of their launching, and the Irish university question was to remain a continuing source of grievance to Roman Catholics and an unsettling issue for successive British administrations. Major re-organisational arrangements were to follow, with the abolition of the Queen's University and the incorporation of the colleges into the Royal University in 1879. In the early 20th century the Queen's Colleges of Cork and Galway were incorporated into the National University of Ireland under new legislation in 1908, while the Queen's College Belfast became the autonomous Queen's University of Belfast.[30] With respect to the National University of Ireland this remained the situation until recent legislation, enacted in 1997, altered the status of the constituent colleges (which now include those at Dublin, Cork, Galway, and Maynooth) to that of effectively autonomous universities. The institution of the National University of Ireland has, however, been retained as a corporate entity linked to considerations such as ensuring an institutional identity and historical continuity between the participating institutions.

Since their foundation, and more particularly in the course of this century, the Queen's Colleges have provided a significant contribution to the development of Irish rural society and its economy. These contributions have been reflected in both the teaching commitment of the members of the colleges across a number of faculties along with the fundamental and applied research endeavours of the colleges in areas of central concern to the development of the rural economy. In addition, the provision of extension and outreach-educational services in the form of specific educational programmes and adult education in general has been an integral part of the contribution of the colleges to rural society. Many of the major developments in the agricultural sector, in addition to those in the agri-processing and food industries have been initiated as the result of the application of research emanating from the colleges. More recently, in the face of rapidly changing circumstances in both the technological, economic, and social environments, the rural economy and the larger rural society are experiencing a relentless process of fundamental change and restructuring. This has led to a number of innovative responses on the part of the colleges in their respective regions, again reflected in the provision of new teaching programmes and extension services; and now greatly assisted by the application of new communication technologies which facilitate the provision of distance education to what is, in particular circumstances, an extremely dispersed rural population. The provision of education to this population will provide a crucial test case of the capacity of the new information technologies to overcome the difficulties of dispersal. This issue is illustrative of the new challenges facing both rural society and the universities.

While a modern university institution has many and varied constituencies with claims on its resources and services, the rural economy and the larger rural society, in both Northern Ireland and the Republic of Ireland, have been well served by the original Queen's Colleges and their successors. While the systematic chronicle of the contribution of the Queen's Colleges and their successors to rural society remains an untold story, when that story is told it will be seen to have been an impressive achievement in which the original Queens Colleges and now the University institutions at Belfast, Cork, and Galway may take justifiable pride.

Notes

1. The most extended treatment of this topic is contained in the excellent study by DH Akenson, *The Irish education experiment: the national system of education in the nineteenth century* (London, 1970).
2. There are a number of histories of Trinity College, including: William Urwick, *The early history of Trinity College Dublin 1591–1660* (London, 1892); Constantia Maxwell, *A history of Trinity College, Dublin 1591–1892* (Dublin, 1946); HL Murphy, *A history of Trinity College Dublin from its foundation to 1702* (Dublin, 1951); RB McDowell and DA Webb, *Trinity College, Dublin 1592–1952: an academic history* (Cambridge, 1982); JV Luce, *Trinity College Dublin: the first 400 Years* (Dublin, 1992).
3. Quoted in Foreword of RDC Black, *Economic thought and the Irish question 1817–1870* (Cambridge, 1960) p v.
4. Gearóid Ó Tuathaigh, *Ireland before the Famine 1798–1848* (Dublin, 1972, reissued 1990). This outstanding monograph is a marvel of precision and com-

prehensiveness in its treatment of this period. A more recent general coverage is provided in Cormac Ó Gráda, *Ireland: a new economic history 1780–1939* (Oxford, 1994).

5. The dynamics of the pre-Famine agricultural economy have been the subject of extensive recent research. A seminal text which generated a great deal of this research was RD Crotty, *Irish agricultural production: its volume and structure* (Cork, 1966). For an extended account of the more recent research on this topic see Ó Gráda, *Ireland: a new economic history*, chapters 4–7.
6. Ó Tuathaigh, *Ireland before the Famine*, pp 135–6.
7. The Great Famine has in recent years been the subject of very extensive research, much of it related to the 150th commemoration. Prior to this recent resurgence of interest there was, as recently noted by Lee, 'extraordinarily little scholarly writing about the Famine until roughly a generation age' (JJ Lee, in *Famine 150: commemorative lecture series*, Cormac Ó Grada (ed) (Dublin, 1997) p 159). In the 19th century three major works appeared on the Famine: John Mitchel, *The last conquest of ireland (perhaps)* (Dublin, 1861); Fr John O'Rourke, *The history of the Great Famine of 1847, with notices of earlier famines* (Dublin, 1875); WP O'Brien, *The Great Famine in Ireland and a retrospect of the fifty years 1845–95* (London, 1896). The next 60 years was characterised by a dearth of material until the publication of the first academic history of the Famine by R Dudley Edwards and T Desmond Williams (eds), *The Great Famine: studies in Irish history, 1845–52* (Dublin, 1956), reissued in 1994 with a new introduction and bibliography by Cormac Ó Gráda. A more popular work on the Famine was Cecil Woodham-Smith, *The Great Hunger: Ireland 1845–1859* (London, 1962). These two works were, until recently, the two standard works on the Famine. Since the early 1980s this lack of material has been replaced by a rapidly expanding volume of publications including: Joel Mokyr, *Why Ireland starved* (London, 1983); Cormac Ó Gráda, *Ireland before and after the Famine: explorations in economic history, 1800–1925* (Manchester, 1988, 2nd rev, ed 1993); Mary Daly, *The Famine in Ireland* (Dundalk, 1986); Cormac Ó Grada, *The Great Irish Famine* (London, 1989); EM Crawford (ed), *Famine: the Irish experience 900–1900: subsistence crises and famines in Ireland* (Edinburgh, 1989); Austin Bourke, *'The visitation of God'? The potato and the Great Irish Famine* (Dublin, 1993); Christine Kinealy, *This great calamity: the Irish Famine 1845–52* (Dublin, 1994); Austin Bourke, *A death-dealing famine: the great hunger in Ireland* (London, 1997); Cathal Póirtéir (ed) *The Great Irish Famine* (Dublin, 1995); RJ Scully, *The end of hidden Ireland: rebellion, famine, and emigration* (Oxford, 1995); Chris Morash and Richard Hayes (eds) *Fearful realities: new perspectives on the Famine* (Dublin, 1996); DA Kerr, *'A nation of beggars'? Priests, people and politics in Famine Ireland 1846–1852* (Oxford, 1994); DA Kerr, *The Catholic church and the Famine* (Dublin, 1996). For a very recent and extremely valuable overview on the extensive literature on the Famine see Graham Davis, 'The historiography of the Irish Famine,' in Patrick O'Sullivan (ed), *The meaning of the Famine* (London, 1997), pp 15–39.
8. For a discussion on the contribution of one distinguished political economist on the land issue, see TA Boylan and TP Foley, 'John Elliot Cairnes, John Stuart Mill and Ireland: some problems for political economy,' *Hermathena*, no CXXXV (Winter 1983) pp 96–119. Reprinted in *Economists and the Irish economy: from the eighteenth century to the present day*, (ed) AE Murphy

(Dublin, 1984) pp 96–119. For a more general discussion on the contribution of members of the Queen's Colleges to 19th-century political economy see TA Boylan and TP Foley, *Political economy and colonial Ireland: the propagation and ideological function of economic discourse in the nineteenth century* (London, 1992) chapter 3. The latter part of the present chapter draws heavily from chapter 3 of this work.

9. JJ Lee, *The modernisation of Irish society 1848–1918* (Dublin, 1973) pp 36–9.
10. RDC Black, *Economic thought and the Irish question*, chapter VII. See also chapter XXVIII, 'Emigration, 1801–70' by David Fitzpatrick in *A new history of Ireland, V: Ireland under the Union, 1801–70*, (ed) WE Vaughan (Oxford, 1989).
11. Ó Gráda, *Ireland: a new economic history*, chapter 9.
12. Lee, *The modernisation of Irish society*, chapter 3; Ó Gráda, *Ireland: a new economic history*, chapters 10–11.
13. WE Vaughan, 'Ireland c. 1870,' chapter XXXII in *A new history of Ireland*, V, (ed) WE Vaughan (Oxford, 1989); A Warren, 'Gladstone, land and social reconstruction in Ireland, 1881–1887, *Parliamentary History*, ii (1983) pp 153–73.
14. ED Steele, *Irish land and British politics: tenant-right and nationality, 1865–1870* (Cambridge, 1974); Barbara Solow, *The land question and the Irish economy*, 1870–1903, (Cambridge, Mass, 1971); Paul Bew, *Land and the national question in Ireland 1858–82* (Dublin, 1978); Philip Bull, *Land, politics and nationalism: A study of the Irish land question* (Dublin, 1996).
15. For two recent works which address the issues of revisionism see Ciaran Brady (ed) *Interpreting Irish history: the debate on historical revisionism 1938–1994* (Dublin, 1994); DG Boyce and Alan O'Day (eds) *The making of modern Irish history: revisionism and the revisionist controversy* (London, 1996).
16. Ó Tuathaigh, *Ireland before the Famine*, chapter 4; JJ Lee, *The modernization of Irish society*, chapter 1; E O'Malley, 'The decline of Irish industry in the nineteenth century' in *The Economic and Social Review*, vol 13, no 1 (1981) pp 21–42; E O'Malley, *Industry and economic development: the challenge for the latecomer* (Dublin, 1989); Ó Gráda, *Ireland: a new economic history*, chapter 13.
17. TW Moody, 'The Irish university question of the nineteenth century' in *History*, vol 42 (1958), pp 90–109.
18. R O'Connell, 'The political background to the establishment of Maynooth College' *Irish Ecclesiastical Record*, vol 85 (1956) pp 325–34, 406–15; vol 86 (1956) pp 1–16.
19. TW Moody and JC Beckett, *Queen's Belfast 1845–1949: the history of a university*, 2 vols (London, 1959), vol 1, pp xli–xliv.
20. Ibid, pp xliv–liii.
21. See entry for Wyse in *Dictionary of national biography*.
22. Moody and Beckett, *Queen's Belfast 1845-1949: the history of a university*, vol 1, pp xli–xliv.
23. RB McDowell, *Public opinion and government policy in Ireland, 1800–46* (London, 1952).
24. John Healy, *Maynooth College: its centenary history* (Dublin, 1895); the most recent history coinciding with the bicentennial of the college is PJ Corish, *Maynooth College, 1795–1995* (Dublin, 1995).
25. Ó Tuathaigh, *Ireland before the Famine*, pp 107–8.
26. *Hansard*, 3rd series, vol LXXX, cols 1155–8 (30 May 1845).

27. Beckett, *The making of modern Ireland 1603–1923*, 2nd edn (London, 1981) p 331.
28. WJ Hegerty, 'The Irish hierarchy and the Queen's Colleges (1845–1850)', *Cork University Record*, vol 5 (1945) pp 20–33.
29. TW Moody, 'The Irish university question of the nineteenth century,' pp 98–9.
30. The histories of the individual Queen's Colleges provide the requisite historical background. See Moody and Beckett, *Queen's Belfast 1845–1949: the history of a university*, 2 vols (London, 1959); JA Murphy, *The College: a history of Queen's/University College Cork, 1845–1995* (Cork, 1995); TA Boylan and TP Foley (eds), *From Queen's College to National University: essays towards an academic history of Queen's/University College Galway, 1845–1995* (forthcoming).

Chapter 2

Ireland's Land Questions: A Historical Perspective

Gearóid Ó Tuathaigh

In recent years the debate generated by the sesquicentenary commemoration of the Great Irish Famine has often echoed to the sound of recriminations, with demands from many Irish nationalists for some public expression of remorse and gestures of atonement from the British royal family. No less thunderous, at times, has been the din of ideological battle between revisionists, traditionalists and post-revisionists among the historians and cultural critics writing on Ireland's past. In all of the rich excitement of these debates one familiar motif has made regular appearances, namely, the 'Irish land question'. Its most familiar guise is in formulations such as the following: the Famine occurred because so many of the Irish poor were vulnerable as exclusively potato-eaters; their number and their vulnerability were, in turn, rooted in a population-resource dilemma that was rooted in a larger and more complex issue, called 'the Irish land question'.

The use of this phrase, 'the Irish land question', deserves a moment's attention. In fact, it is generally to be found in the literature as an aspect of a larger issue – 'the Irish question' – in 19th and early 20th-century British politics. That is to say, 'the Irish land question' in recent centuries has generally made its appearance as a central aspect of the analysis of the core political-constitutional issue in the relationship between Ireland and Britain during the period of the Union, 1801–1920. The central political problem or challenge, as defined by successive British governments and by the thinking classes in Britain, was how to provide in Ireland, government so compellingly good that it would remove those sources of disaffection which were the pernicious well-springs of Irish nationalist (not to say, separatist) sentiment.[2]

There were, it was acknowledged, many different sources for this disaffection. The various elements of the toxic sentiment were interrelated. Disraeli, on the eve of the Famine, summarised the elements as follows: 'Thus you have a starving population, an absentee aristocracy, and an alien church, and in addition, the weakest executive in the world. That is the Irish Question.'[3]

Many other British statesmen and intellectuals also spoke in these terms, and for all of them the Irish land question was part – a central part – of that larger 'Irish question', nationalist disaffection. In this line of reasoning and argument, therefore, the solution of the Irish question (that is, the creation of a general pro-Union sentiment in Ireland) required a solution of the Irish land question.

The terms in which the land question was understood and formulated were significant. The problem was seen overwhelmingly as a politico-legal problem, with an identifiable historical origin. The legal terms of ownership and occupancy of land (legal status and tenurial rights and arrangements) were seen as the nub of the problem. The supposed 'backwardness' of Irish agriculture, the social tensions and sporadic agrarian violence, were all traced, or reduced, to the central problem of a tenantry whose insecurity and exploitation were a disincentive to investment, to long-term thinking or planning, or to social cohesion and contentment. Outside of Ulster, this insecurity of tenure, or otherwise adverse tenurial conditions (the absence of 'tenant-right', however defined), was understood as being underlined by a deep social cleavage – on religious and more broadly cultural grounds – between the landlord class and those at all levels below them in Irish rural society throughout the other three provinces.

It didn't matter that this reading of the situation greatly over-simplified the variety and complexity of relationships in rural society, or that it removed from view much that is of major interest to historians and social scientists in recent decades.[4] What is critical is the fact that this view of the 'land question' was widely shared by most British governments throughout the Union period. They accepted – even where they did not go quite so far as to openly acknowledge – the view of the nationalists that the legacy of the conquest, confiscations and land settlements of the 16th and 17th centuries in Ireland was a rural society over which presided a culturally alienated Protestant landlord class, and, below them, a large (if socially and economically variegated or stratified) Catholic sub-landlord community of occupying tenant-farmers (large and small) and their labourers. The different, not to say competing, interests of these various strata of occupiers below the top layer of landlords were seen, when they were seen at all, as being less significant than the central problem of 'landlord-tenant' relations.

An early intimation of the acceptance of the centrality of this problem (taken in conjunction with Disraeli's intemperate reference to an 'absentee aristocracy') can be found in the terms of reference of the Devon Commission of 1843. In November 1843 (as part of Peel's Irish 'reform' package), a Royal Commission under the Earl of Devon was appointed to enquire into 'the state of law and practice relating to occupation of land in Ireland'. It reported in February 1845, recommending compensation for improvements and various other minor reforms.[5]

The Famine and its horrific aftermath reinforced a negative view of Irish landlords among the British public. More significantly, however, the Famine greatly strengthened the conviction among sections of the intelligentsia that the application of English (regularly described as 'universal') ideas of political economy to Ireland, including the Irish land system, was highly questionable. The full force of the assault on the application of English ideas on political economy to Ireland may not, perhaps, have been felt until the 1860s; and, as this debate has been thoroughly discussed in Boylan and Foley's excellent *Political Economy and Colonial Ireland*, (following on earlier pioneering work by Black and, later, by David Steele and Clive Dewey), we do not need to dwell too long on it here.[6] What the challenge of the post-Famine critique entailed was the promotion of so-called Irish ideas (in preference and contrast to English or indeed 'abstract' ideas) in relation to the absolute right of property ownership, the law of contract (and its inviolability), the general conceptual and cultural nature of landlord-tenant relations in Ireland, and the systems and modalities which, in the light of historical experience, might be acceptable in the regulation of the occupancy of land in Ireland.

That there developed from the 1860s forward a strong 'historicist' dimension to the underlying relativism of this critique (by Cairnes, Mill and others) has been demonstrated by a number of scholars, notably by Clive Dewey. It is clear that, in addition to latitudinal comparisons (with India, in particular) in support of a more relativistic approach to differing English and Irish conditions, a historicist and longitudinal approach began to emphasise an antique Celtic attitude towards land (and the legitimation of its occupancy), in contrast to English contract law on private property. This so-called Celticist view stressed the communal (as against the individualistic), and the consensual or shared (as against the strictly contractual) understanding of rights and obligations in relation to land occupancy.[7]

The precise channels through which this relativism (or, at the least, a disposition to seek 'Irish' solutions to Irish problems) became the dominant attitude among sections of key elites (political and intellectual) in Britain need not concern us here. But the long legislative drive towards an Irish solution to the Irish land problem is now well-documented and understood: from the 1869 and 1870 acts of Gladstone's first ministry, through the 1881 land act (in effect, acknowledging a dual interest – of tenant and landlord – in respect of land occupancy), and on to the succession of land purchase schemes from the early 1880s to 1906, which ultimately resulted in the creation of a peasant-proprietorship system of land occupancy in Ireland. Indeed, the particularity of Irish circumstances and needs was also acknowledged in ways other than by land purchase schemes: the establishment in 1891 of the Congested Districts Board represents an interesting departure into primitive 'regional planning' that has not yet received the attention that it merits.

But, however the changing ideas came to be adopted (or at least deployed) by political leaders in Britain, or whatever their provenance among sections of the intelligentsia in Britain or in Ireland, the strategic need for British statesmen to 'solve' the Irish land question was at all times *political*. Whether with Peel (in setting up the Devon Commission), trying to produce a reform package to trump O'Connell's Repeal campaign, or with Gladstone in the late 1860s, with his post-Fenian mission to 'pacify Ireland', or indeed the later Gladstonian and Conservative governments seeking, in their different ways, to trump the Land League and Parnellism or, later still, to kill home rule with kindness, the objective throughout was to solve the Irish land question in the hope that by so doing a major step (perhaps the decisive step) would be taken towards solving the larger 'Irish question'– the problem of political disaffection and the menace of Irish nationalism.[8]

If the definition of the Irish land question by British statesmen cast it as essentially a landlord-tenant issue rooted in particular historical conditions (frustrated Celtic ideas on communal rights of ownership; an irreconcilable view of the conquest and plantation of the 16th and 17th centuries – on both its legal foundations and on its ethno-cultural complexion), it must be stressed that successive leaders of Irish nationalist movements of the 19th century were in substantial agreement with this formulation of the question. Indeed, in some instances, they were among its prime sponsors. Thus, Daniel O'Connell (himself a rent-receiver, obsessively opposed to agrarian violence and secret societies, and notably unreceptive to radical ideas on land reform or rent or property) could only offer a denunciation of landlord absenteeism (and a tax on absentees) as a contribution to the debate on pre-Famine rural problems and poverty.[9] The well-organised (and O'Connell-approved) anti-tithe agitation of the 1830s was not only an interesting precursor of the later land war of the 1879–82 period, but it also illustrates the way in which political mobilisation for the redress of socio-economic grievances was handled by the bourgeois nationalist leadership in Ireland. The identification of an essentially confessional, multi-class grievance as an issue for mobilisation cleverly built upon the Catholic emancipation model movement of the 1820s and also subsumed, more menacingly, divisive tensions relating to access to land further down the social ladder of rural society.[10]

During the Famine crisis James Fintan Lalor's radical call for land reform turned out, on closer inspection, to be directed principally towards basing the right to occupancy of existing occupiers on communal sanction (the will of the people, but with formal structures and agreements) rather than on existing contract law (based on the flawed rights of ownership gained through earlier conquest and spoliation). But Lalor's solution did not involve any wholesale redistribution of land. It offered no comfort to the utterly landless labourers. Indeed, Lalor saw the land question as the engine of a popular movement for independence, and doubted whether a 'solution' to the land question was possible in Ireland within existing political and constitutional arrangements.[11] The tenant league movement of the 1850s returned to the issues of security of tenure for tenants and their right to some compensation for improvements to their farms undertaken and paid for by themselves.[12]

The Fenians had not so much a programme of land reform as a set of instincts that were loosely Jacobin, in terms of creating an Irish republic of contented small-holders free from British rule. But, as the early work of Paul Bew convincingly showed, the emergence of the Land League in the late 1870s and the early phase of the land war presented the Fenian leaders with a dilemma. What they really wanted was political separation, and they feared any popular enthusiasm for a cause that might distract from or dilute the support needed for this pure revolutionary objective. Yet, a significant cadre of Fenian leaders came to support the Land League struggle on the grounds, first, that there was clearly strong popular support for the land struggle, and, second, that the British government would not concede the demands of the Land League, thus precipitating a political crisis of authority in Ireland which would provide the Fenians with their opportunity to move the separatist issue to the top of the agenda. In sum, the social movement of the land struggle would climax in a constitutional crisis and pave the way for a political revolution.[13]

If many Fenians saw hope for political revolution in the subversive possibilities of land agitation, other nationalist leaders in the home rule ranks feared the exact opposite. John Dillon was not the only home rule leader of the Parnellite period to harbour fears that if the land question were successfully 'solved' by British legislation, the steam might go out of the popular movement for home rule, as farmers might settle back to attend to their 'selfish' interests and no longer trouble themselves with the constitutional status of Ireland.[14] As it happened, both the Fenians and worried home rulers, such as Dillon, were mistaken in their political calculations and expectations. As for Charles Stewart Parnell, he wanted the land question solved in order to remove a cancer of distrust between the bulk of the farmers and the landlord class (his own class), for the most enlightened, courageous and patriotic of whom he envisaged a prominent role as 'natural' leaders in a home rule Ireland. If the land question were solved then there was no reason why 'reconciled' (largely Protestant) landlords could not play a positive role in a home rule Ireland and its institutions.[15] Parnell's successor, John Redmond, was also generally sympathetic to this view. The point to be stressed here, as with earlier leaders, is that the home rule leaders also judged the land question on its fundamental political significance and implications. Whether as a prerequisite or a trigger for, or an impediment to, popular enthusiasm for political sovereignty, most nationalists up to the early 20th century considered the land question in essentially political terms. This gradually ceased to be the case after the substantial body of land-purchase schemes had begun to work their course in the years before 1914.

We have spent some time considering the land question as part of a larger, essentially political, 'Irish question' for British statesmen and Irish nationalist leaders throughout most of the Union period. Not surprisingly, this version is also strongly represented in the historiography concerned with the political dimension of Anglo-Irish relations and with the dynamics of Irish nationalism itself. But, of course, there were others, both in the 19th century and among historians and other scholars of more recent times, who defined the 'Irish land question' in significantly different terms.[16] The economic and social dimensions of Irish land: its use, cultivation and productivity (in addition to issues of ownership and occupancy), were the primary concerns of many reformers of the 19th century, and have been especially the concerns addressed in a growing body of scholarly literature, from economic historians, agriculturalists, agricultural and general economists and other social scientists, in recent decades. The writings of Blacker, Connor, Sharman Crawford and other early 19th-century writer-reformers were primarily concerned with the actual state of Irish agriculture: the implications for land values, incomes and productivity (as well as social harmony and cohesion) of differences in farm structure and size, of methods of farming and husbandry, of land use and the markets for its produce.[17]

Certainly, these reformers were also interested in landlord-tenant relations. They discussed the implications of tenurial arrangements and customs for investment behaviour and improvements in farming and the working of the land. But their questions were formulated primarily in agronomic rather than political terms. They sought to establish whether or not productivity was a function of farm size; they were interested in the diffusion of best practice, in the role of price and market sensitivity in determining land use. It is fair to say that the same 'scientific' concerns (with establishing accurate data on the various aspects of agricultural practices and land use in Ireland) can be found in the Royal Dublin Society county surveys, in such major national surveys as Wakefield, Shaw Mason, Newenham, Lewis and others, as well as in some, at least, of the data collected for parliamentary select committees and royal commissions in the 19th century.[18] To this we must surely add the early pioneering work of the Dublin Statistical Society, later the Statistical and Social Enquiry Society of Ireland.[19]

This is not to pretend that any of these individuals or societies were entirely innocent of ideological commitment. But the questions they sought to put and to answer relating to the Irish land question were not exclusively, and for the most part, not primarily driven by political considerations. A more contentious later example, perhaps, was Horace Plunkett and his co-operative movement, though here also it is true that among the co-operative evangelists were to be found agricultural improvers of very different political allegiances.[20] What is particularly striking, however, is the extraordinary growth – one is justified in talking of an explosion – of scholarship during the past four decades or so on a range of newly-formulated 'Irish land questions', questions that have been formulated overwhelmingly in economic and agronomic terms.

We may trace the origins of this new wave of scholarship to the early work of such social geographers and statisticians as Staehle, Austin Bourke, Cousens, Freeman, McCourt and others,[21] and to the pioneering work in demography and economic history of Ken Connell, Rodney Green, JH Johnson, and Louis Cullen.[22] If one were to point to a significant, if controversial, landmark, one might cite Raymond Crotty's 1966 volume on *Irish Agricultural Production*.[23] Indeed, it would be hard to find a more revealing contrast between the 'old' and the 'new' land questions posed in scholarly literature, than by a comparison of George O'Brien's traditionalist (with strongly legal landlord-tenant perspective) commentary with Crotty's radically different set of land questions for 19th-century Ireland. One is tempted to see this shift in interest and approach as reflecting political and ideological shifts and concerns within the wider Irish society. It is arguable that, at least in the independent Irish state, access to land and land redistribution remained politically sensitive and significant issues right up to the late 1950s, but that from the 1960s onward (with the demise of Clann na Talmhan and the arrival of the Lemass-Whitaker free trade and industrial orientation) this rapidly ceased to be the case.[24] The new Ireland of Lemass would inevitably formulate new questions relating to Irish agriculture and Irish land.

It is worth noting, however, that this inter-generational shift of perspective and of scholarly concern is not an exclusively Irish phenomenon, but has certain parallels across the Atlantic. Thus, for example, it is legitimate to compare Pomfret's *The Struggle for Land in Ireland* (Princeton, 1930) or Palmer's *The Land League Crisis* (Yale, 1940) with the fruits of the post-war period, represented by, for example, Barbara L Solow's *The Land Question and the Irish Economy* (Cambridge, Mass 1971) and the early work of James Donnelly, Jr.[25] The concerns, the sources, the methodology – the whole intellectual process, from assumptions to hypotheses, to investigation and exposition – of the new generation are very different indeed from 'the land question' as understood by

Gladstone or Disraeli. This, of course, only confirms what one would in any case expect to have taken place, namely, that new questions have been generated by the availability of new sources, new developments, methodologies and techniques in various disciplines (eg, the advance of econometrics) and by the growth in the number of scholars working in the field, as well as by the changing political and ideological climate.

Space does not permit – nor, perhaps is it necessary to attempt here – a detailed tracing of the extraordinary growth, in volume and sophistication, in scholarly writing on the Irish land question since the 1970s (in demography, investment behaviour, land use, markets, prices, product choice and range, productivity, efficiency, and various exercises in modelling).[26] But one has only to reflect on the early work of KH Connell and then turn to the most recent cliometric excursi of Joel Mokyr, Cormac Ó Gráda, Kevin O'Rourke and others, to get some sense of the distance that has been travelled by the practitioners of economic history in their reformulation of many of the key questions relating to Irish land use and Irish agriculture, within various comparative frameworks for assessing economic performance.[27] One hastens to add that the new practitioners of the strongly quantitative techniques of economic history regularly carry their own distinctive ideological packs. They are not afraid to address explicitly issues that are fundamentally ideological, political or ethical in nature. Indeed, it is this interaction between econometric techniques of data analysis and contentious political issues (on policy intentions, options and responsibility) that has given a particularly sharp edge to some of the contributions to the debate on the Irish potato famine of the 1840s.[28]

Ideological currents also course through a further category of writings on the Irish land question on which I wish to comment, however briefly. These particular formulations of the land question derive from the perspectives and insights of human or cultural geographers, of anthropologists and of cultural theorists. This rich body of writing generally views the land as a 'habitat', as defined by E Estyn Evans, that is, as a physical site of human settlement. More than that, the land is seen as a site of belonging, in an emotional and an almost metaphysical sense: as the repository of an historical consciousness, and as a key site of the imagination – collective as well as individual. In the Irish case, the land is also represented in some of these writings as a site of conflicting views of belonging, of selective appropriations and expropriations, of landscape and memory and history, as a metaphor for the discussion of relationships of power in Irish history.[29]

The spatial dimension of human settlement, the processes by which physical features of the land become, by dint of human settlement and effort, a living landscape, a human habitat; and the manner in which the physical environment itself (including climate) shapes or influences many aspects of human culture – from individual personality to aspects of work and leisure culture – have been explored in a rich and engrossing literature by human geographers for several decades: the distinguished list of key contributors must include TW Freeman, E Estyn Evans, T Jones Hughes, Frank Mitchell, JH Andrews, and a whole generation of younger scholars, mainly their own disciples, who have further enriched and extended their discipline.[30] The ambition of several younger cultural geographers has gone well beyond the more obvious themes and concerns of human geography in its re-interrogation of the Irish landscape as a human habitat. Of course, geographers have given us valuable longitudinal studies of human settlements, in particular units or structures – the estate, the townland, the parish, the town.[31] There has been excellent mapping of historical data on the distribution of house types and styles, of economic sites (fairs, markets), of animals and different forms of land use and cultivation, of farm implements and folk traditions, and a host of other human activities. The *Atlas of Ireland*, published by the Royal Irish Academy in 1979, illustrates well the progress made in this area. New insights and perspectives on the land and landscape of Ireland, deriving from cultural geography, continue to add complexity and range to our 'Irish land questions', as the more recent *Atlas of the Irish Rural Landscape* demonstrates so triumphantly.[32]

But beyond even these exciting new directions of enquiry, cultural scholars (including the human geographers) have in recent decades begun to address the more problematic but immensely challenging area of the land and landscape in the context of cultural conflict. For example, questions have been posed regarding the act of mapping as itself constituting an act of appropriation. Thus, Professor Willie Smyth, for example, contends that: 'Ireland's long-standing status as a colony has, therefore, meant that the cold, clinical eye of the colonial cartographer has long gazed upon and defined the island'.[33]

Or, again, writing of the Civil and Down Surveys of the mid 17th century, Smyth has this comment:

> … basically a collection of Cromwellian ledger-books and maps list the names of the former occupiers, classify them according to their religious *cum* ethnic status, and detail the size and quality of their properties, before transferring these properties to the new conquering elites. These maps and documents are triumphant symbols of the power of the colonial government to penetrate and appropriate every corner, every place-name and every person in the land. These materials also show the newly-centralising English state bureaucracy shaping the worlds it encountered to better fit its image of what a 'proper' language, economy and society should sound, work and behave like.[34]

In the same way, the issue of place-names – how devised or decided, when and under what circumstances adopted, altered, abandoned, replaced, displaced, substituted – has prompted questions that go beyond the strictly academic study of the place-names themselves and their origin, to touch on more contentious issues of cultural conflict. Thus, for example, the corpus of writing known as the *Dinnseanchas* echoed down through the Gaelic tradition, as a celebratory literature of place. As Estyn Evans remarked:

> ... the personification of the country has been a consistent theme, and it has taken the form of female figures who were originally deities, wishful symbols of the fertility of the land and the people ... there was, too, a sense of geographical personality in the older Irish literature, a sense of the harmony and mystery of man's place in nature. The gods dwelt among the hills, and the living spirits of the land were ever present. One genre of Gaelic writing concerned itself with the preservation of a great store of oral traditions relating to places, and especially to hills. The collected stories, the Dindshencas, has been called an Irish Dictionary of National Topography.[35]

But the fitness of name to place takes on added dimensions of significance in Ireland, in the light of the historical experience of disruption, uprooting and eviction, dispossession and displacement, of plantation and appropriation by new settlers, and of the transformation of the land and of the socio-economic and cultural relationships centred on it. Rival or competing signatures on the Irish landscape give a particular resonance to the literature of place and belonging in both vernaculars in Ireland. In one sense, it is as though this obsession with a sense of place is somehow embedded in a version of a natural order of 'original settlement', a kind of pre-conquest or pre-lapsarian Celtic settlement whose signature marked the landscape (notably in place-names and in folklore and legend) since time immemorial, until rudely ruptured by the conquest and colonisation of the early modern period. This, of course, is a simplistic and, to a degree, unhistorical view, eliding as it does much of the fluidity, turbulence and mobility that marked changes in settlement patterns in Ireland throughout the centuries of Gaelic domination. But the continuing 'authority' or *geis* of the attachment to place, and the imaginative resources instinct in an intense sense of place, can be seen in the poetry of some of the most accomplished Gaelic poets down through the centuries, including the distinguished contemporary poet, Nuala Ní Dhomhnaill, in such poems as *Baile an tSléibhe*.[36]

The strong hold that the sense of place has on the literary imagination of Irish writers writing in English is so well attested by critics and anthologists as to be virtually a cliché: from the routinely celebratory songs and verses[37] to the more complex historical and associational treatment of place that we find, for example, in John Hewitt or in John Montague or Seamus Deane or even Seamus Heaney.[38] And then there are the works that address directly the problems of displacement, dispossession and appropriation: for example, Brian Friel's moving and complex handling of the naming of places in his play, *Translations*, or the menacingly obsessive version of 'possession' of land that is the core of John B Keane's play, *The Field*. And the grim attrition of the human spirit which can be the price paid for staying on the inhospitable land is harrowingly illustrated by the pathetic, aging and sexually-frustrated Paddy Maguire in Patrick Kavanagh's aptly-titled poem, *The Great Hunger*.[39] Furthermore, apart from the familiar field of imaginative literature, the cultural and ideological assumptions regarding land and society that inform or sustain different forms or modes of artistic representation of Irish land and landscape – from paintings, to postcards to films – are likewise coming under increasing scholarly scrutiny from cultural theorists and commentators during the past decade or so.[40]

There is one further dimension to the Irish land question that cannot go unnoticed. This is the version of the land as an idealised, a morally superior, site of living. While never the only or even the dominant strain in Irish nationalist rhetoric, there is a strong tradition in Irish nationalism of the 19th and early 20th centuries which did indeed idealise the 'authentic' and uncorrupted character of life on the land (close to nature, in a natural 'bonded' community), compared with the uprooted and 'fallen' world of the city, especially the large teeming cities of the developed world (eg London or New York).[41] The early Sinn Féin propaganda, though it advocated strongly the development of manufacturing in Ireland, seemed at times to wish for industrialisation without urbanisation, and certainly some of the leading cultural revivalists of the turn of the century (some Gaelic Leaguers, including Pearse, and some of the more ardent rural romantics of Yeats's Celtic literary circle) were very much prone to investing life on the land with a privileged spiritual value. This strain endured. Fianna Fáil from its foundation was committed to 'the distribution of the land of Ireland so as to get the greatest number possible of Irish families rooted in the soil of Ireland'.[42] When they were deemed not to be succeeding in this task, the Clann na Talmhan party was formed in the west of Ireland. Catholic bishops and clergy, for a variety of reasons, were prominent among those extolling the virtues of rural living, as were numerous social action organisations, such as Muintir na Tíre. Not all of these could be described as fundamentally anti-urban, though some of their rhetoric could sound like that on occasion. But they all represented, in different ways, that strain of thought or belief which idealised the land, and living on the land, in terms which were often as much moral as social in tone.[43]

Let these examples suffice. We have come a long way from the land question of the Devon Commission, or indeed even from the econometric gymnastics of recent quantitative studies. And yet we have not come near to exhausting the full complexity, the protean character, of the Irish land question as a field of study. Indeed, in recent years the debate at the

European level on the future of rural society has given yet another dimension to the question. As food production within Europe comes under close review (in terms of labour needs, and the price, range, quality and safety of products), there is a growing awareness of ecological issues, and of the global nature of the dangers and the responsibilities with regard to an increasingly vulnerable eco-system. A new custodial role has been proposed for those living on (but not necessarily *off*) the land: a role based on responsible management (rather than maximum exploitation) of the precious resource of the land itself. This debate seems likely to generate a challenging agenda of new questions relating to land occupancy and land use into the next millennium.[44]

The historian, perhaps, ought not to be too surprised at this expansive canvas of questions and contexts issuing from a consideration of the Irish land question in historical perspective. After all, was it not JC Beckett, in his inaugural address as Professor of Irish History at the Queen's University of Belfast, who proposed that:

> The history of Ireland, like the history of any other country, must be based on a study of the relationship between the land and the people – the people, that is, not just as exploiters of the natural resources, but the people considered politically, using that word in its widest sense. But at no time between the twelfth century and the twentieth can we speak of the people of Ireland as a single political community – at one time or another, groups of different cultural traditions have exercised varying degrees of control over the whole or part of the island, in more or less direct subordination to the external power of England. We have, therefore, an element of stability – the land, and an element of instability – the people. It is to the stable element that we must look for continuity ... the historian of Ireland must write, specifically, 'The history of Ireland': for it is in Ireland itself, the physical conditions imposed by life in this country, and their effect on those who have lived here, that he will find the distinct and continuing character of Irish history.[45]

Beckett's identification of the land as the central theme in Irish history was echoed by Estyn Evans in his plea for interdisciplinarity in the study of the matrix of habitat, heritage and history that constitutes the personality of a place and a people. I would only wish, by way of conclusion, to offer an endorsement, in slightly more pointed terms, of Evans's plea.

Thus, in considering this brief examination of some of the many dimensions of the Irish land question, as it has been debated in the past century and a half, we are, I believe, justified in describing the Irish land question as a series of interrelated issues deeply embedded in the fabric of human settlement and in the historically (as well as geographically) informed consciousness and imagination of large numbers of Irish people. We may wish to insist, therefore, that there are in fact many different 'Irish land questions', demanding investigation from a variety of academic pespectives. Or, as I would personally prefer, we may choose to describe the Irish land question as a critical junction or intersection, where matters of legal rights, economic forces, physical conditions, settlement, ethnic and communal identity, power and the imagination come together to provide one of the key narratives in the Irish historical experience. These junctions invite, indeed require, the collaboration of scholars of various disciplines (and also of witnesses bound by no academic discipline – writers, artists, naturalists) if the full complexity of the questions are to be explored in any satisfactory way.[46] One would like to think that this sense of the multifaceted and multilayered nature of the Irish land question (its extraordinary matrix of issues and insights) informs and is reflected in courses in rural development and land studies in our colleges and universities. As I say, one would like to think that this is the case. But one is not so sure that it is so. One may well ask, therefore, if not, why not?

Notes

1. Of the many recent studies of the Famine, the following suggest the range of current concerns: ME Daly, *The Famine in Ireland* (Dublin, 1986); Cormac Ó Gráda, *The Great Irish Famine* (Dublin,1989); Christine Kinealy, *This great calamity* (Dublin,1994); Cathal Póirtéir (ed) *The Great Irish Famine* (Cork and Dublin, 1995); Peter Gray, *The Irish Famine* (London, 1995). See, also, the relevant chapters in WE Vaughan (ed) *A new history of Ireland*, vol v (Oxford, 1989).
2. For a classic version, see JL Hammond, *Gladstone and the Irish nation* (London, 1938).
3. Disraeli, *Hansard*, lxxii, p 1016, 16 February 1844.
4. See, for example, the range of themes in LM Cullen and F Furet (eds) *Ireland and France, 17th-20th centuries: towards a comparative study of rural history* (Paris, 1980); PJ Drudy (ed) *Ireland: land, politics and people* (Cambridge, 1982); Samuel Clark and JS Donnelly, Jr (eds) *Irish peasants: violence and political unrest 1780–1914* (Dublin, 1983).
5. For Peel's initiative see DA Kerr, *Peel, priests and politics: Sir Robert Peel's administration and the Roman Catholic church in Ireland, 1841–46* (Oxford, 1982).
6. TA Boylan and TP Foley, *Political economy and colonial Ireland* (London and New York, 1992); RDC Collison Black, *Economic thought and the Irish question, 1817–1870* (Cambridge, 1960); David Steele, *Irish land and British politics: tenant right and nationality 1865–1870* (Cambridge, 1974); Clive Dewey, 'Celtic agrarian legislation and the Celtic revival: historicist implications of Gladstone's Irish and Scottish land acts 1870–1886', in *Past and Present*, vol 64 (1974) pp 30–70.
7. Dewey, 'Celtic agrarian legislation and the Celtic revival'.
8. Interpretative studies of Anglo-Irish relations include, Nicholas Mansergh, *The Irish question 1840–1921* (London, 1965); Patrick O'Farrell, *England and Ireland since 1800* (Oxford, 1975); Oliver MacDonagh, *States of mind* (London, 1983).
9. Oliver MacDonagh, *O'Connell: the life of Daniel O'Connell 1775–1847* (London, 1991).

10. See Samuel Clark, *Social origins of the Irish land war* (Princeton, NJ, 1979) pp 65–104.
11. DN Buckley, *James Fintan Lalor: radical* (Cork, 1990); also, Tomás Ó Néill, *Fiontán Ó Leathlobhair* (Baile Átha Cliath, 1962).
12. JH Whyte, *The tenant-league and Irish Politics in the eighteen-fifties* (Dundalk, 1966).
13. Paul Bew, *Land and the national question in Ireland, 1858–82* (Dublin, 1978).
14. FSL Lyons, *John Dillon: a biography* (London, 1968); Paul Bew, *Conflict and conciliation in Ireland 1890–1910* (Oxford, 1987); Philip Bull, *Land, politics and nationalism* (Dublin, 1996).
15. Paul Bew, *C.S. Parnell* (Dublin, 1980); Liam Kennedy, 'The economic thought of the nation's lost leader: Charles Stewart Parnell', in Liam Kennedy, *Colonialism, religion and nationalism in Ireland* (Belfast, 1996) pp 75–102.
16. In addition to the works cited in note 6, see also, AE Murphy (ed) *Economists and the Irish economy* (Dublin, 1984).
17. Their views are discussed in Black, *Economic thought and the Irish question*, and in George O'Brien, *The economic history of Ireland from the Union to the Famine* (London, 1921).
18. For Newenham, see HD Gribben, 'Thomas Newenham, 1762–1831', in JM Goldstrom and LA Clarkson (eds) *Irish population, economy, and society* (Oxford, 1981) pp 231–47. For pre-Famine 'investigations' of Ireland, see William Nolan, *Tracing the past* (Dublin, 1982). A recent work which applies new scholarship to traditional questions is WE Vaughan, *Landlords and tenants in mid-Victorian Ireland* (Oxford, 1994).
19. RDC Black, *The statistical and social inquiry society of Ireland: centenary volume 1847–1947* (Dublin,1947), and ME Daly, *The spirit of earnest enquiry* (Dublin, 1997). See also, Central Statistics Office, *Farming since the Famine: Irish farm statistics 1847–1996* (Dublin, 1997).
20. Horace Plunkett, *Ireland in the new century* (Dublin, 1982); Cyril Ehrlich, 'Sir Horace Plunkett and agricultural reform', in JM Goldstrom and LA Clarkson (eds) *Irish population, economy, and society* (Oxford, 1981) pp 271–85.
21. H Staehle, 'Statistical notes on the economic history of Irish agriculture, 1847–1913', in *Journal of the Statistical and Social Inquiry Society of Ireland*, xvii (1951); TW Freeman, *Ireland* (London, 1950) and *Pre-famine Ireland: a study in historical geography* (Manchester, 1957); D McCourt, 'Infield and outfield in Ireland', in *Economic History Review*, ser 2, vii, 3 (1955); SE Cousens, 'The regional pattern of emigration during the Great Famine, 1846–51', in *Transactions and Papers of the Institute of British Geographers*, vol 28 (1960); 'Regional death rates in Ireland during the Great Famine, from 1846 to 1851', in *Population Studies*, vol xiv, no 1 (1960); 'Emigration and demographic change in Ireland, 1851–61', in *Economic History Review*, ser 2, xiv, 2 (1961); 'The regional variations in population changes in Ireland, 1861–81', in *Economic History Review*, ser 2 , xvii, 2 (1964); for Austin Bourke's seminal contributions to historical agricultural statistics, see Austin Bourke, *'The visitation of God'? The potato and the Great Irish Famine* (eds) Cormac Ó Gráda and Jacqueline Hill (Dublin, 1993).
22. ERR Green, *The Lagan Valley, 1800–50: a local history of the industrial revolution* (London, 1949); KH Connell, *The population of Ireland, 1750–1845* (Oxford, 1950); JH Johnson's articles on aspects of agriculture and landed society in Co

Derry, in *Economic History Review*, ser 2, x, 2 (1957), *Journal of the Statistical and Social Inquiry Society of Ireland*, xx, pt i (1958), *Studia Hibernica*, vol 4 (1964); LM Cullen, *An economic history of Ireland since 1660* (London, 1972).

23. RD Crotty, *Irish agricultural production: its volume and structure* (Cork, 1966). See, also Joseph Lee, 'Irish agriculture', in *Agricultural History Review*, vol xvii, (1969).
24. These themes are discussed in JJ Lee, *Ireland, 1912–1985: politics and society* (Cambridge, 1989); and in MAG Ó Tuathaigh, 'The land question, politics and Irish society, 1922–1960', in PJ Drudy (ed) *Ireland: land, politics and people* (Cambridge, 1982) pp 167–89; see also, Tony Varley, 'Farmers against Nationalists: the rise and fall of Clann na Talmhan in Galway', in Gerard Moran and Raymond Gillespie (eds) *Galway: history & society* (Dublin, 1996) pp 589–622; and BS Murphy, 'The stone of destiny: Father John Fahy (1894–1969), Lia Fáil and smallholder radicalism in modern Irish society', in Gerard Moran (ed) *Radical Irish priests 1660–1970* (Dublin, 1998).
25. JS Donnelly, Jr, *The land and people of nineteenth-century Cork* (London and Boston, 1975). The influence of the writings and research direction of such leading practitioners of economic history as A Gerschenkron and David S Landes is apparent in some of the best of the American work on Irish economic history since the 1960s.
26. The writings, and bibliography, of Professor Cormac Ó Gráda are a good advertisement for the rich scholarship of recent writings: eg Cormac Ó Gráda, *Ireland before and after the Famine: explorations in economic history, 1800–1925* (Manchester, 1988); *Ireland: a new economic history 1780–1939* (Oxford, 1994).
27. In addition to the works cited above in note 26, see, in particular, Joel Mokyr, *Why Ireland starved* (London, 1983). More recent assessments of economic performance include Kieran Kennedy, Thomas Giblin and Deirdre McHugh, *The economic development of Ireland in the twentieth century* (London and New York, 1988). JJ Lee, *Ireland 1912–85: politics and society* (Cambridge, 1989); Cormac Ó Gráda, *A rocky road: the Irish economy since the 1920s* (Manchester, 1997).
28. Eg Kevin O'Rourke, 'Did the Great Famine matter?', in *Journal of Economic History*, vol 51 (1991) pp 1–22.
29. See, for example, JH Andrews, *A paper landscape: the Ordnance Survey in nineteenth century Ireland* (Oxford, 1975); Séamas Ó Catháin and P Ó Flanagáin, *The living landscape: Kilgalligan, Erris, Co. Mayo* (Dublin, 1975); Joseph Lee (ed) *Ireland: towards a sense of place* (Cork, 1985); William Nolan (ed) *The shaping of Ireland: the geographical perspective* (Cork and Dublin, 1986); Patrick O'Flanagan, Paul Ferguson and Kevin Whelan (eds) *Rural Ireland: modernisation and change 1600–1900* (Cork, 1987); Timothy Collins (ed) *Decoding the landscape* (Galway, 1994).
30. For T Jones Hughes and his influence, see WJ Smyth and Kevin Whelan (eds) *Common ground: essays on the historical geography of Ireland* (Cork, 1988); GF Mitchell, *The Irish landscape* (London, 1976); FHA Aalen, *Man and the landscape in Ireland* (London, 1978); JH Andrews, *Irish maps* (Dublin, 1978); GL Herries Davies (ed) *Irish geography: the geographical society of Ireland golden jubilee 1934–1984* (Dublin, 1984) provides a good survey. One might also mention the multidisciplinary County History series published by Geography Publications (Dublin), which began in 1985 with a volume on Co Tipperary, and of which nine volumes have now been published.

31. A good example is William Nolan, *Fassadinin: land, settlement and society in southeast Ireland 1600–1850* (Dublin, 1979); see also the economic historian, Kevin O'Neill's *Family and farm in pre-Famine Ireland: the parish of Killashandra* (Wisconsin, 1984).
32. FHA Aalen, Kevin Whelan and Matthew Stout (eds) *Atlas of the Irish rural landscape* (Cork, 1997).
33. WJ Smyth, 'Explorations of place', in Joseph Lee (ed) *Ireland: towards a sense of place* (Cork, 1985) p 3.
34. Ibid, p 3.
35. EE Evans, *The personality of Ireland: habitat, heritage & history* (Cambridge, 1973) p 66.
36. Nuala Ní Dhomhnaill, *An Dealg Droighin* (Baile Átha Cliath, 1981); for earlier examples, see Seán Ó Tuama and Tom Kinsella (eds) *An Duanaire: poems of the dispossessed, 1600–1900* (Dublin, 1981), and Mícheál Ó Braonáin, *Príomhshruth Éireann* (reprint, Limerick 1994).
37. Eg Seamus Heaney, 'The sense of place', in *Preoccupations: selected prose, 1968–1978* (London, 1980). At the level of popular culture, a vast repertoire of country and western contemporary Irish songs are so concerned with the invocation of place that they sometimes seem no more than a road-map sung in three-four time.
38. See, for example, Gerald Dawe and John Wilson Foster (eds) *The poet's place: Ulster literature and society* (Belfast, 1991), and John Wilson Foster, *Colonial consequences* (Dublin, 1991); David Lloyd, *Anomalous states: Irish writing and the post-colonial moment* (Dublin, 1993).
39. Patrick Kavanagh, *Collected poems* (London, 1972) pp 34–55.
40. AM Dalsimer (ed) *Visualising Ireland* (Boston and London, 1993); Raymond Gillespie and Brian Kennedy (eds) *Ireland: art into history* (Dublin, 1994); AM Dalsimer and Vera Kreilkamp (eds) *America's eye: Irish paintings from the collection of Brian P. Burns* (Boston College Museum of Art, 1996); Luke Gibbons, *Transformations in Irish culture* (Cork, 1996).
41. These themes are discussed in Gibbons, *Transformations in Irish culture*; see also Gearóid Ó Crualaoich, 'The primacy of form: a "folk ideology" in de Valera's politics', in JP O'Carroll and JA Murphy (eds) *De Valera and his times* (Cork, 1983).
42. Maurice Moynihan (ed) *Speeches and statements by Eamon De Valera 1917–1973* (Dublin and New York, 1980) p 131.
43. It is arguable that this idealisation of rural living was given further authority by the pioneering athropological studies of Arensberg and Kimball; see, Conrad Arensberg, *The Irish countryman* (New York, 1937), and Conrad Arensberg and ST Kimball, *Family and community in Ireland* (Cambridge, Mass, 1940).
44. See for example, *New approaches to rural development*, National Economic & Social Council, NESC Report no 97 (Dublin, 1994).
45. JC Beckett, *Confrontations: studies in Irish history* (London, 1972) p 23.
46. For a highly individualistic and sensitive perspective, see Tim Robinson, *Stones of Aran, part 1: pilgrimage* (Mullingar and Dublin, 1986) *Stones of Aran, part 2: labyrinth* (Dublin, 1995); *Connemara: part 1: introduction and gazetteer; Part 2: a one-inch map* (Roundstone, 1990); *Setting foot on the shores of Connemara and other writings* (Dublin,1996).

Chapter 3

The Modernisation of the Irish Diet, 1740–1920[1]

Leslie Clarkson

This chapter begins with a brief survey of diets before the mid 18th century. Since the start of sustained British settlement in the 16th century there have been three major periods of change in the composition of Irish diets. The first was the 'civilisation' of the diets of the upper echelons of society from the late 16th to the early 18th century, as the dietary patterns of the Old English, the Gaelic-Irish, and the new settlers gradually merged. The second affected the poorer stratum of society during the century and a half before the Great Famine when potatoes dominated diets. And the third saw the changes in the dietary habits of the lower orders in post-Famine Ireland.

At the turn of the 16th and 17th centuries English visitors were frequently horrified by the prodigious quantities of meat and milk consumed and the slovenly and disgusting manner in which they were prepared and eaten. For example, in 1581 John Derricke published, *The Image of Ireland* ..., a blatantly anti-Irish piece of war-time propaganda consisting of woodcuts accompanied by a text written in doggerel verse. Its most famous illustration is that of the Irish chieftain's feast where the assembled company squat at a legless table devouring newly slaughtered meat and offal cooked over open fires nearby. The guests, including a discomforted Sir Philip Sydney, are entertained by a poet and a harper, while members of the chieftain's court warm bare bottoms by the fire and dogs gnaw at bones discarded by the cooks.[2]

A detailed account of diets was provided by Fynes Moryson, secretary to Lord Deputy Mountjoy between 1600 and 1604, who drew important social distinctions:

> Touching the Irish diet, some lords and knights, and gentlemen of the English-Irish, and all the English there abiding … use the English diet, but some more, some less cleanly, few or none curiously, and no doubt they have as great, and for their part greater, plenty than the English, of flesh, fowl, fish, and all things for food, if they will use like art for cookery. Always I except the fruits, venison, and some dainties proper to England, and rare in Ireland. And we must conceive that venison and fowl seem to be more plentiful in Ireland, because they neither so generally affect dainty food, nor so diligently search it as the English do. Many of the English-Irish have little by little been affected with the Irish filthiness … The English-Irish after our manner serve to the table joints of flesh cut after our fashion, with geese, pullets, pigs, and like roasted meats, but their ordinary food for the common sort is of white meats, and they eat cakes of oats for bread, and drink not English beer made of malt and hops, but ale. In cities they have bread such as ours, but of a sharp savour, and some mingled with anice-seeds and baked like cakes.

Moryson turned from the semi-debased habits of the Anglo-Irish to the totally depraved behaviour of the wild, or mere, Irish:

> [They] are barbarous and most filthy in their diet. They scum the seething pot with a handful of straw, and strain their milk taken from the cow through a like handful of straw, none of the cleanest, and so to cleanse, or rather more defile, the pot and milk. They devour great morsels of beef unsalted, and they eat commonly swine's flesh, seldom mutton; and all these pieces of flesh, as also the entrails of beasts unwashed, they seethe in a hollow tree lapped in a raw cow's hide and so set over the fire, and therewith swallow whole lumps of filthy butter. Yea (which is more contrary to nature), they will feed on horses dying of themselves, not only upon small want of flesh, but even for pleasure …

As for their drinking habits, not only did the wild Irish drink unhopped ale instead of beer, but 'milk like nectar, warmed with a stone first cast into the fire, or else beef-broth mingled with milk'. When they visited market towns to sell a cow or a horse, 'they never return home till they have drunk the price in Spanish wine … or in Irish usquebagh, and till they have outslept two or three days' drunkenness'.

Apart from dead horses:

> … many of these wild Irish eat no flesh, but that which dies of disease or otherwise of itself, neither can it scape them for stinking. They desire no broth, nor have any use of a spoon … They feed most on white meats, and esteem for a great dainty sour curds, vulgarly called by them Bonaclabbe. And for this cause they watchfully keep their cows, and fight for them as for their religion and life; and when they are almost starved, yet they will not kill a cow, except it be old and yield no milk. Yet will they upon hunger in time of war open a vein of a cow and drink the blood, but in no case kill or much weaken it … The wild Irish (as I said) seldom kill a cow

> to eat, and if perhaps they kill one for that purpose, they distribute it all to be devoured at one time; for they approve not the orderly eating at meals, but so they may eat enough when they are hungry they care not to fast long …[3]

There is plenty more in this vein. Nevertheless, during the course of the 17th and 18th centuries, middling and upper levels of society in Ireland diets came to look rather like those in England (see Table 3.1).

Table 3.1 Percentage expenditure on food and drink, England and Ireland

Category	England 1688	Ireland 1674–1828
Meat	15	31
Fish, poultry, eggs	10	14
Milk, butter, cheese	13	7
Fruit, vegetables	9	4
Salt, oil, spices, groceries	6	10
Beer, ale	16	3
Wines, spirits	9	6
Bread, cakes, grain	23	25

The English figures are derived from the calculations of Gregory King in 1688. The poorest 40 per cent of society in late 17th-century England spent 69 per cent of their income on food and drink whereas the richest 5 per cent spent less than one-third. Richer people spent proportionately less on grain-based foods but more on meat, groceries and wines.[4] The Irish figures come from a detailed analysis of household account books from estates in various parts of Ireland.[5]

The second major dietary change occurred among the lower stratum of society and was most marked from the mid 18th century to the mid 19th century. At the beginning of this period lower class diets were composed principally of milk, butter, offal, meat and oats. From the mid century dietary patterns among the Irish poor – comprising up to 40 per cent of the population – became progressively simpler, very different from those of the more prosperous members of society, and markedly different from the diets of the labouring classes in England. Diets came to consist of potatoes and very little else. The potato period lasted for little more than a century but it has generated intense discussion among both contemporary writers and modern historians. The key issues are the date at which potatoes became the staple diet of the poor, the quantity of potatoes consumed, the reasons for their dominance, and the nutritional adequacy of a potato diet.

The earliest references to potato cultivation in Ireland come from the early 17th century, and by the mid century they were quite commonly grown in gardens by English and Scottish settlers. Later in the century they were being used by all sections of the population. Sir William Petty, writing in 1672, however, was quite explicit that potatoes were a seasonal addition to diets among the poor. 'The diet of these people is milk, sweet and sower, thick and thin, which also is their drink in summertime, in winter small-beer or water'. Potatoes were eaten only 'from August to May'. There was considerable variety, with mussels, oysters, cockles, eggs, butter, rabbits, poultry, 'bread in cakes', but rarely beef, 'unless it be one of the smaller animals'.[6]

During the course of the 18th century potatoes spread from gardens to fields where they were an excellent clearing crop on newly tilled land and a valuable rotational crop in the production of cereals. As the demands for Irish wheat, barley and oats increased from home and abroad, the cultivation of potatoes spread.[7] So too did their consumption. Even so, they still did not dominate diets at the mid century. The severe famine of 1740–41, for example, was the result of a failure of the grain harvest. At its height Philip Skelton published an ideal yearly diet for a farmer and his family, comprising six people, four of whom were working.

Table 3.2 Diet for a farming family of six, 1741[8]

		%
40 bushels grain making 60 lbs bread per bushel	£6 0 0	51.0
52 bushels of potatoes	£2 12 0	13.6
6 qts of buttermilk or skim milk a day	£1 10 5	12.9
1 hundred of skim milk cheese	8s 4	3.5
1 hundred of butter & do of salt	£1 4 8	10.4
An ordinary carcase of beef	£1 0 0	8.5

Skelton remarked that 'people in high life may think [it] too poor or scanty', a judgement that is confirmed by nutritional analysis. Half the expense went on grain, 35 per cent on animal products and the rest on potatoes. In terms of weight potatoes predominated. Assuming that a bushel contained 70 pounds[9] and that potatoes were eaten for nine months in the year (270 days), per capita consumption, was two and a quarter pounds a day, well below the six to eight pounds that became common by the 1830s.

Gradually, though, the potato dislodged oatmeal and other foods from their major role in the diets of the cottier. In 1780, according to Arthur Young, 'his life was determined by it'. In County Kildare, reported Young, a barrel of potatoes would last a man, his wife and four children for a week. This example implies a daily consumption of more than seven pounds per person.[10] It is clear from Young, though, that even in the 1770s, although potatoes provided a 'fair bellyful', there was much else besides, particularly oats, milk and 'vile potations of whisky'.[11]

A very similar picture emerges from the county Statistical Surveys published by the Dublin Society in the early years of the 19th century. According to Hely Hutton, writing of County Clare in 1808, a family of six consumed 22 stone of potatoes per week (ie more than seven pounds per person), grown on less than one acre.[12] In Kilkenny the daily consumption for a family of five was three stones of potatoes (8.4 pounds) plus six quarts of sour milk.[13] In County Kildare, potatoes were '... the almost constant food of the Irish peasant, [which] induce[s] both sexes early to become the heads of families ...'[14]

On the eve of the Great Famine, potatoes were king. The Poor Inquiry conducted in 1836 throughout the 2500 parishes of Ireland as a prelude to introducing a national poor law, reported the consumption of potatoes from every parish, milk from three-quarters of parishes, and oatmeal and herrings from about a quarter of parishes; other foods were insignificant.[15] More than 40 years ago, Professor KH Connell reckoned that adult males were eating 10 pounds of potatoes a day in the decades before the Famine.[16] A survey conducted by the Poor Law Commissioners in 1839 of diets of labourers living in 13 poor law unions in the south west and containing 14 per cent of the population, suggests an even higher figure. Table 3.3 presents the findings for six of the 13 unions; the remaining seven were very similar. When cottiers ate twice a day adult men consumed between six and 11 pounds of potatoes daily. When they fed three times a day they ate on average almost 14 pounds. Most labourers had a little milk or buttermilk, but oatmeal, butter, herrings and eggs were eaten only occasionally.

The most important question relating to the potato period in Ireland is why potatoes became so vital for more than a third of the population. The spread of cultivation as an adjunct of grain production is an important part of the explanation. Potatoes in Ireland performed a similar role to that of turnips in England – that of preparing tillage land for planting with grain crops – but they had the added advantage that they were highly palatable to man and beast alike and they were also highly nutritious. This is not quite the whole story. From the end of the 17th century Irish meat and dairy products poured in increasing quantities into the stream of British and Atlantic commerce; and after 1750 wheat, barley, oats, flour and meal also entered the flow of trade.[17] The staple components of traditional diets were becoming commercialised, leaving the poor in Ireland to depend on the less tradable potatoes that were the by-products of commercial agriculture. At the beginning of this process Ireland was a country with a surfeit of land and a shortage of labour. Agricultural prices were falling, landlords lacked good tenants and they

Table 3.3 Food consumed daily by the labouring poor in six poor law unions, 1839[18]

	Breakfast	Dinner	Supper
Limerick			
Men	4 $^1/_2$lbs potatoes, 1 pint skimmed milk.	The same, and in winter herrings and water instead of milk.	This meal is occasionally omitted in the city of Limerick particularly during the short days.
Women	The same.	The same.	
Rathkeale			
Men	5lbs potatoes, $1^1/_2$ pints milk in summer.	The same. When milk is scarce herrings are used.	This meal is not taken at periods of the year when potatoes get scarce, and work is not to be obtained.
Women	1 pint milk in winter. 4lbs potatoes, $1^1/_4$ pint milk in summer.	The same.	
Newcastle			
Men	$5^1/_2$ lbs potatoes, 1 quart skimmed milk.	The same; herrings, lard, and oatmeal porridge are used when milk is scarce.	This meal is not always taken.
Women	4lbs potatoes and nearly the same quantity of milk.	The same.	
Kilmallock			
Men	$4^1/_2$ lbs potatoes, 1 quart skimmed milk.	The same, with herrings and dripping when milk is scarce.	This meal is not always taken.
Women	$3^1/_2$ lbs potatoes; from $2^1/_2$ pints to a quart of milk.	The same.	The same.
Tipperary			
Men	$4^1/_2$ lbs potatoes, 2 pints of milk.	The same.	Supper is not always taken.
Women	$3^1/_2$ lbs potatoes, $1^1/_2$ pints of milk.	The same.	The same.
Cashel			
Men	$4^1/_2$ lbs potatoes, milk only used in harvest time.	The same and herrings occasionally.	Supper is not always eaten; when it is, the same quantity and quality of food is used as at other meals.

were in a weak bargaining position. Leases were therefore generous and lax, and few landlords were able to prevent tenant farmers from dividing their farms and renting out portions to sub-tenants, either family members or landless labourers. As the population grew during the 18th century, the land-labour ratio changed: land became the scarce factor of production and labour abundant. Agricultural output switched to more labour-intensive forms such as tillage. But farmers continued to let out small parcels of land to cottiers, for they needed their labour. Cottiers in their turn, were willing to rent plots on which to grow potatoes. An acre of land would yield seven tons of potatoes a year in a normal season, enough to feed a family of six together with their pigs and poultry.[19]

There remains the question of taste. Did people like potatoes so much that they ate them in preference to other foods? In the 1690s, John Dunton referred to the 'dearly beloved potatoes' of the peasantry.[20] Nearly a century later Arthur Young reported from Athy that potatoes 'are liked better' by the peasantry because an acre yielded 80 barrels of potatoes; they were available all year and were cheaper than oats.[21] Such observations, admittedly, were those of observers who were not themselves obliged to eat potatoes with thrice-daily monotony. Still, the virtues of potatoes were not lost on better-off consumers. Henry Townsend, writing from County Cork in 1810, noted that potatoes were the principal food, 'not those of the lowest order alone, but even farmers worth from fifty to one hundred pounds per annum'. Similarly, Henry Dutton in 1824, observed that in County Galway a 'partiality [for potatoes] is entertained by every intermediate rank to the palace, no table being without them'.[22]

Finally, potatoes were both healthy and nutritious, although these were qualities probably appreciated intuitively by consumers rather than consciously. Arthur Young had rarely seen a population so 'athletic in their form, as robust, and as capable of enduring labour as any on earth', as he saw in Ireland.[23] In 1812, an observer in County Antrim remarked on how much healthier children were compared with 'thirty or forty years ago when a bit of oaten bread was put into their hands in place of a potato and salt'.[24] These optimistic assessments of the healthfulness of potato-based diets are supported by work of modern scholarship, in particular by the findings that pre-Famine diets were high in calories, protein and vitamins, and that Irishmen were generally taller than their counterparts in England.[25]

The Great Famine ushered in a third phase of dietary history: a fundamental change in the eating habits of the poorer sections of society. In simple terms, there was a retreat from the potato, an increase in the range of foods eaten, a greater reliance on markets, dealers and shops, and increasing tendency to be fed via the ports rather than the farm gate. Collectively, these developments were symptoms of rising economic welfare; nutritionally they were manifestations of deterioration. The trigger to these changes was the failure of the potato crop in 1845, 1846 and 1848.

Yields were down by 33, 75 and 37 per cent; in 1847 the harvest was good, but little had been sown the previous year because of the shortage of seed potatoes. The scale and frequency of the shortfalls in 1846–8 far exceeded any previous experience of crop failure in Europe; and neither were they predictable from the limited regional potato failures that had occurred in Ireland during the early decades of the 19th century.[26] In a few short years a fungal disease changed the potato from an abundant and reliable, if monotonous, form of food into a fickle and fatal support for the poor.

The potato never recaptured its predominant position after the Famine, although it made a partial comeback in the west of the country where its unreliability threatened starvation in 1879–80 and again during the 1890s.[27] The acreage under potatoes peaked in 1845 at around 2.2 million acres. By 1850 it had fallen to 875,000 acres. There was a recovery to just over 1 million acres during the 1860s, but thereafter there was a sustained decline to under 600,000 acres by 1910. Furthermore, yields failed to recover fully and stabilised at no more than about two-thirds of their pre-Famine levels, perhaps because the labour required for heavy manuring was no longer available.[28] A combination of reduced acreage and lower yields resulted in a fall in output from around 15 million tons annually immediately before the Famine to 3 million tons on the eve of the First World War. In per capita terms output was then less than 40 per cent of pre-Famine levels.[29]

The decline in potato cultivation was matched by a contraction in arable farming more generally. The acreage under cereals fell from 3.2 million to 1.3 million between 1850 and 1910 and the value of crop production (including potatoes) halved. On the other hand, cattle and sheep numbers increased and the value of livestock output doubled.[30] These shifts were in part responses to changes in the pattern of demand for Irish agricultural produce within Ireland and the rest of the United Kingdom.

There were also important shifts in land/labour ratios that made pastoral farming more attractive. In the second half of the 19th century the population of Ireland fell by almost 50 per cent and those remaining became increasingly urbanised; 23 per cent of the population in 1901 lived in towns of 10,000 or more people, compared with only 8 per cent in 1841.[31] In 1841, 72 per cent of the male workforce was engaged in farming; in 1911 the proportion was 55 per cent. More importantly, in 1841 there were 271 farm workers for every 100 farmers; in 1911 there were only 131.[32]

An important consequence of the fall in the population was a growth in per capita incomes. Nominal wages among farm labourers doubled and wages of industrial workers also increased substantially. Even allowing for the fact that farm workers after the Famine were more likely to buy food in the market than their pre-Famine forbears and that the cost of living was higher in the town than in the countryside, there remained a significant increase in real incomes.[33] These changes in economic and social conditions after the Famine fed through into diets. The simplest way of illustrating the trends is to analyse the findings of dietary surveys conducted among the rural and urban population in 1839, 1859, and 1902–4. The first we have already seen. It covered a large swathe of the population in the south of the country. These people were not paupers, but they were very poor. The second was a survey, again conducted by the poor law authorities, of 162 families containing 1021 people living in different parts of the country. The individual dietaries were accompanied by comments describing the general dietary conditions in the region. In 1902–3 Dr J Lumsden, medical officer to the Guinness Brewery, investigated the eating patterns of the families of 20 employees or former employees of the firm. A year later two officials of the Local Government Board surveyed the diets of 21 families (containing 51 people) drawn from Dublin's urban poor. In the same year the Board of Trade investigated 123 households in Dublin, Belfast, Cork, Limerick, Waterford and Derry, and 27 families from rural parts of Ireland.[34] The results of these investigations are summarised in Table 3.4.

Table 3.4 Average daily food consumption in ounces by adult labouring males, 1839–1904[35]

Food	1839	1859	1902/4 rural	1902/4 urban
Potatoes	184	61	38	17
Milk	61	28	14	10
Indian meal	0	18	*	0
Oatmeal	?	11	15*	1.5
Flour	0	12	*	23**
Bread	0	11	5.0	**
Meat	0	0.05	0.3	1.12
Bacon	0	0.04	1.7	1.16
Fish	?	0.30	0.1	?
Eggs	0	0.02	0.6	0.6
Butter	0	0.50	0.7	2.0
Tea	0	0.03	0.3	0.4
Sugar	0	0.30	3.0	3.0

* Indian meal, oatmeal and flour grouped together.
** Flour and bread grouped together.

The most striking feature of this table was the decline in potato consumption from over 10 pounds a day in the pre-Famine countryside to one pound among the urban poor. The process was a gradual one. Dr Edward Smith who conducted his own dietary investigations in 1863 observed that, 'there can be no doubt, from the universal testimony of all classes, that potatoes are a most highly prized food amongst the labouring population of Ireland, and one in which they indulge as largely as the supply and the enlarged capacity of their stomachs will admit'.[36] Consumption of potatoes remained high in the west and a description of conditions in the Kerry mountains in 1886–7 is reminiscent of the pre-Famine times:

> They live on potatoes and porridge; seldom eat bread, meat never; wine, beer, tea, coffee are to them unknown luxuries ... Viewing things in the most optimistic light, supposing the year to have been an exceptionally good one, the potato crop to have been plentiful, the cow to have been out in the hillside, the necessary grass for the making of a little butter all that will be sufficient perhaps to prevent starvation.[37]

The consumption of milk also declined in the later 19th century, although this was offset by a rise in tea drinking which increased 10–fold. In the early 19th century tea had been commonplace among the upper and middling classes and even among strong farmers and urban workers. Sally, the old servant in the least bad hotel in Dunmore, County Galway in Trollope's *The Kellys and the O'Kellys*, presided over a large brown teapot and in times of stress filled a slop bowl and, to take 'a long pull': threw back her head till the top of her mop cap was flattened against the side of the wide fireplace, and the bowl was turned upward, so that the half-melted brown sugar might trickle into her mouth.[38]

A taste for strong sweet tea spread rapidly in rural areas as incomes rose. The Base Line Reports prepared by the Congested Districts Board in 1892 show how widespread tea-drinking had become. It was 'the principal drink' near Letterkenny, County Donegal. In Glencolumbkille it was drunk, 'in excess three times a day by most, and by all once or twice'. In County Mayo tea was sometimes drunk without milk but with 'a greater quantity of sugar'.[39]

Table 3.4 obscures the trends in cereal consumption. Before the Famine, oatmeal, in the form of porridge, stirabout, or griddle cakes was eaten widely if intermittently, especially in Ulster. Oatmeal remained important in country diets, but it had competition from Indian meal and bakers' bread. Indian meal had been imported occasionally in the early 19th century when locally-produced food was scarce, and it was imported on a large scale during and after the Famine. Imports continued throughout the rest of the century, and although much was used as cattle feed, 'yellow meal' became a regular part of rural diets.[40] It was frequently mentioned in the Base Line Reports, although its consumption was reported to be in decline as, 'it is everywhere admitted that the standard of living is increasing'.[41]

Bakers became the normal source of bread in the later 19th century. Alexander Irvine remembered that as a child in Antrim town in the 1870s, 'when hunger got ahead of wages, the family bread was bought at Sam Johnston's bakery'. The order was 'usually a sixpenny loaf, three ha'pence worth of tea and sugar, and half an ounce of tobacco'. It was only 'when work and wages got a little ahead of hunger' that his mother baked soda bread, oatmeal bread or 'fadge'.[42] County Antrim was one of the more prosperous parts of Ireland, but bakers' bread was consumed also in most of the districts surveyed in the Base Line Reports.

By definition, the reports covered the poorest and remotest parts of Ireland and are an official testimony to a slow but irreversible trend to modern patterns of eating. The inspectors noted 15 items of food consumed by the poor. Besides the still ubiquitous potato, the list included bread (78 districts), tea (70), milk or buttermilk (62), Indian meal (58), fish (58), eggs (35), oatmeal (25), bacon (23), butter (15), sugar (12), cabbage (10), meat (5) and coffee (1). Bacon was eaten mainly by 'those in better circumstances', although the very poor would fry potatoes and cabbage in 'the grease of a small quantity of fat American bacon'.[43]

The modernisation of the diet had various consequences. One was the evolution of a system of wholesale and retail trade, which is a subject for separate investigation. Of more immediate relevance were the effects on nutritional standards and the health of the population. Table 3.5 presents an analysis of the nutritional content of labourers' diets in 1839, 1859, and 1902–4.

Table 3.5 Daily nutritional content of labourers' diets[44]

	1839	**1859**	**1902–4**
Protein (g)	135	110	82
Fat (g)	4	40	87
Carbohydrate (g)	1099	760	590
Energy (kcal)	4720	1348	650
Calcium (mg)	2398	1348	650
Iron (mg)	25	23	20

The nutritional standard of pre-Famine diets were superior in all respects except fat. The reason was the predominance of the potato. The 1839 diet also scored highly on vitamin C of which potatoes are a rich source, although it was somewhat deficient in vitamins A and D. The retreat from the potato was not immediately good for health. In the last quarter of the 19th century the incidence of tuberculosis increased in Ireland while it was declining in other parts of the United Kingdom. The crude death rate remained stubbornly high even though it was falling in England and Wales. Infant mortality, that had been below levels prevailing in England and Scotland in the 1880s, similarly remained stuck, or even rose a little as mortality declined in other parts of the United Kingdom.[45] Looking into the 20th century, the perils of modern eating –

tooth decay, obesity, gall stones, diseases of the gut – all increased. But by then Irishmen and women were living longer, the better to enjoy the consequences of affluence and to suffer the afflictions.

NOTES

1. This paper is based on LA Clarkson and EM Crawford, *Food in Ireland 1500–1920: a social history* (forthcoming). The 19th century sections, in particular, rely heavily on Dr Crawford's work.
2. John Derricke, *The image of Ireland with a discoverie of the wood kerne* (London, 1581, new edition, Edinburgh, 1883).
3. Fynes Moryson, 'The itinerary of Fynes Moryson', in CL Falkiner, *Illustrations of Irish history and topography, mainly of the seventeenth century* (London, 1904) pp 225–30.
4. Richard Stone, 'Some seventeenth century econometrics: consumers' behaviour', *Revue Europeene des Sciences Sociales*, vol 81 (1988) pp 40–41.
5. From Clarkson and Crawford, *Food in Ireland*, chapter 2.
6. W Petty, *The political anatomy of Ireland*, (1st ed, London, 1691, facsimile edn, Shannon, 1970) p 81.
7. Raymond Crotty, *Irish agricultural production: its volume and structure* (Cork, 1966) p 28.
8. Triptolemus (pseud. Philip Skelton), *The necessity of tillage and granaries in a letter to a member of parliament* (Dublin, 1741) pp 9–10.
9. Arthur Young, *A tour in Ireland ...* (London, 1780) vol ii, p 120.
10. Ibid, vol i, p 64.
11. Ibid, vol ii, pp 117, 118.
12. Hely Hutton, *Statistical survey of County Clare* (Dublin, 1808) pp 178–9.
13. William Tighe, *Statistical survey of County Kilkenny* (Dublin, 1800–1) p 474.
14. TJ Rawson, *Statistical survey of County Kildare* (Dublin, 1807) p 23.
15. LA Clarkson and EM Crawford, 'Dietary directions: a topographical survey of Irish diet, 1836', in Rosalind Mitchison and Peter Roebuck (eds) *Economy and society in Scotland and Ireland 1500–1939* (Edinburgh, 1988) p 174.
16. KH Connell, *The population of Ireland*, 1745–1850 (Oxford, 1950) p 149.
17. Crotty, *Irish agricultural production*, pp 276–7.
18. *Sixth Annual Report of the Poor Law Commissioners*, BPP 1840, vol XVII, appendix (D), 2, p 244.
19. Austin Bourke, *'The visitation of God?': The potato and the Great Irish Famine*, (eds) Jacqueline Hill and Cormac Ó Gráda (Dublin, 1993) pp 114–25.
20. Quoted Bourke, *'The visitation of God?'*, pp 16–20.
21. Young, *Tour in Ireland*, i, p 68.
22. Henry Townsend, *Statistical survey of County Cork* (Dublin 1810) p 415; Henry Dutton, *Statistical survey of County Galway* (Dublin, 1824) p 350.
23. Young, *Tour in Ireland*, ii, p116.
24. WS Mason, *A statistical account or parochial survey of Ireland*, 3 vols (Dublin, 1814, 1816, 1819), vol 1, p 257.
25. Cormac Ó Gráda, 'The heights of Clonmel prisoners 1845–9: some dietary implications', in *Irish Economic and Social History*, vol XVIII (1991) pp 23–33;

Cormac Ó Gráda, *Ireland: a new economic history 1780–1939* (Oxford, 1994) pp 91, 105–10.
26. Cormac Ó Gráda, *The Great Irish Famine* (London, 1989) pp 19–22; Peter Solar, 'The Great Famine was no ordinary subsistence crisis', in EM Crawford (ed) *Famine: the Irish experience, 900–1900* (Edinburgh, 1989) pp 112–18.
27. TP O'Neil, 'The food crisis of the 1890s', in Crawford (ed) *Famine: the Irish experience*, pp 176–97.
28. Joel Mokyr, 'Irish history with the potato', in *Irish Economic and Social History*, vol VIII, (1981) p 20; Liam Kennedy, 'Regional specialization, railway development and Irish agriculture in the nineteenth century', in JM Goldstrom and LA Clarkson (eds) *Irish population, economy, and society* (Oxford, 1981) p 183.
29. Bourke, *'The visitation of God'?*, p 55.
30. Kennedy, 'Regional specialization', pp 182, 185; Michael Turner, 'Output and productivity from the Famine to the Great War', in *Irish Economic and Social History*, vol XVII (1990) pp 65–6.
31. LA Clarkson and Liam Kennedy, 'Birth, death and exile: Irish population history 1700–1921', in BJ Graham and LJ Proudfoot (eds) *An historical geography of Ireland* (London, 1993) p 161.
32. David Fitzpatrick, 'The disappearance of the Irish agricultural labourer, 1841–1912', *Irish Economic and Social History*, vol VII (1980) pp 87–8.
33. Ó Gráda, *Ireland: a new economic history*, pp 236–9.
34. *Sixth Annual Report of the Poor Law Commissioners*, 1840 p 244; *Thirteenth Annual Report of the Poor Law Commissioners*, BPP, 1860, vol XXXVIII, pp 40–81; J Lumsden, *An investigation into the income and expenditure of seventeen brewery families and a study of their diets, being a report made to the directors of A. Guinness Son & Co. Ltd* (Edinburgh, 1905); *Royal Commission on the Poor Laws and the relief of Distress*, BPP, 1910, Appendix, vol X, appendix no II (D), pp 339–87; *Consumption and cost of food in workmen's families in urban districts of the United Kingdom*, BPP, 1905, vol LXXXIV, pp 19–44; *Second report by Mr Wilson Fox on the wages, earnings and conditions of agricultural labourers in the United Kingdom*, BPP, 1905, vol XCVII, pp 247–608.
35. The methodology used to generate the amounts is set out in EM Crawford, 'Aspects of Irish diet, 1839–1904', University of London, PhD thesis, 1985.
36. *Sixth Report of the Medical Officer of the Committee of the Privy Council*, No 6, Report by Dr Edward Smith, 'Food of lowest fed classes', BPP, 1864 [3416], vol XXVIII, p 286.
37. P Daryl, *Ireland's disease* (London, 1888) pp 147, 149.
38. Anthony Trollope, *The Kellys and the O'Kellys* (1848), chapter XXIV.
39. Base Line Reports of the Congested Districts' Board for Ireland, 1892–8 (Trinity College, Dublin) pp 87, 177, 346.
40. EM Crawford, 'Indian meal and pellagra in nineteenth-century Ireland', in Goldstrom and Clarkson (eds) *Irish population, economy, and society*, pp 113–24.
41. Base Line Reports, pp 442, 458.
42. Alexander Irvine, *My lady of the chimney corner* (1913, republished Belfast, 1980), pp 43–5.
43. Base Line Reports, pp 72, 259.
44. Crawford, 'Aspects of Irish diet'.
45. Clarkson and Kennedy, 'Birth, death and exile', pp 170–2.

Chapter 4

Co-operation and Rural Development: Plunkett's Approach

Carla King

Horace Curzon Plunkett (1854–1932) is generally remembered in Ireland as the founder of the Irish co-operative movement and of the Department of Agriculture and Technical Instruction (DATI), the forerunner of today's Departments of Agriculture (Republic of Ireland and Northern Ireland). In addition, he was active in a range of other organisations, both in Ireland and elsewhere, broadly concerned with fostering rural reform. However, apart from his considerable organisational contributions, his significance as a pioneer of the idea of systematic rural development on these islands is sometimes overlooked. The originality of his approach was well understood by his contemporaries, however, and his ideas were influential not only in Ireland and Great Britain, but also in the United States, among European reformers, and as far afield as South Africa[1] and India.[2] In his day, Plunkett House in Merrion Square, the headquarters of the co-operative movement, became a destination for foreign visitors and commentators on Ireland.[3] *Contemporary Ireland* (1906) by the French writer, Louis Paul-Dubois, and *Modern Ireland and her agrarian problem* (1906) by the German economist, Moritz Bonn, for example, both show the influence of Plunkett's ideas.[4]

Agricultural co-operation was introduced in Ireland, as in other countries, as a form of economic self-defence and adaptation on the part of farmers whose livelihoods were threatened by the difficult conditions associated with the agricultural depression of the late 19th century. Thus creamery co-operation was established to enable Irish dairy farmers to invest jointly in modern equipment which would allow them to compete in the international market for butter. Agricultural societies jointly purchased agricultural necessities, such as seed, fertiliser and tools, and engaged in some joint marketing of produce. Co-operative banks made small loans available at low interest to enable farmers in the west and elsewhere with very little capital to invest in their holdings. Therefore, the economic importance of co-operation was to make changes and adaptations to new, more market-oriented conditions possible for groups of farmers, which might have been beyond the reach of individuals. As such, it had a considerable impact on Irish farming during a time of transition.[5]

Plunkett and his followers saw co-operation as much more than an economic tool, however. It was to provide a means of introducing the spirit of self-help and progress, so beloved of 19th-century reformers, to Irish farmers. Furthermore, in co-operation and joint enterprise, rural society, suffering severely from emigration and social decline, and resulting loss of morale, would be enabled to rebuild a sense of cohesion and hope. Rural-based industries would be established on a co-operative basis to provide employment for non-farming members of the rural community and supplementary income for farming families. Evening schools and advisory services would be made available to farmers to acquaint them with up-to-date methods. Village halls and local libraries would be built to provide facilities for local meetings, reading, music-making and other social activities which would serve to make rural life more stimulating and stem the flow of younger people to the cities.[6] Thus Plunkett's vision encompassed the need to build up what he called a 'rural civilisation'. It was a concept he developed in collaboration with George Russell, (Æ), writer, poet and painter, who was also the editor of the co-operative movement's weekly newspaper, the *Irish Homestead*.[7]

This idea of a method – co-operation – applied to both economic and social development of the countryside and the conviction that the two must come together, summarised in his slogan: 'Better farming, better business, better living', was an important innovation in the English-speaking world. In addition, it was a secular and a non-party-political programme, characteristics which made it frequently an object of mistrust in Ireland.

In the years between 1889, when he returned from 10 years spent as a cattle rancher in Wyoming, and 1923, when he left Ireland following the destruction of his home during the civil war, Plunkett was the driving force behind the co-operative movement, and the most prominent publicist and activist in the cause of rural reform in Ireland. His career has been examined by several authors and it is not proposed to recount it here.[8] Rather, the aim of this chapter is limited to an examination of three aspects of the outlook and policies of the co-operative movement that are attributable primarily to Plunkett's leadership. These are: the approach of the movement to social class; the role of women in the process of rural reform; and the relation of the co-operative movement to the state.

THE CO-OPERATIVE MOVEMENT AND SOCIAL CLASS

In 1889, when Plunkett began his efforts to found a co-operative movement, the Irish countryside was in deep conflict. The Land War, which had continued intermittently over the previous 10 years, was in its second phase, the Plan of Campaign.[9] Some 203 estates, or around 1 per cent of Irish landed properties, were directly affected by the land agitation, thousands of tenants were evicted and their leaders imprisoned, and feelings were running high.

As a son of Lord Dunsany, Plunkett came from a wealthy landlord background and many of his friends were landlords. His method of procedure in the first stage of the movement was to travel around the countryside, staying in friends' houses and addressing meetings of farmers, frequently organised by the landlord or his agent, attempting to persuade his audience to form co-operatives. Some landlords, among them Edward O'Brien and Lord Monteagle in Limerick and Sir Josslyn Gore-Booth in Sligo, played an important part in founding and running local co-operatives, as well as participating in the national movement. Between 1894 and 1915 at least 21 different landlords served on the committee of the Irish Agricultural Organisation Society, the central body of the co-operative movement.[10] Indeed, Plunkett saw them as fulfilling important leadership functions in the early phase of the movement.[11] This was not unusual in European terms; in parts of France landlords took a prominent role in founding agricultural co-operatives.[12] However, given the extent of polarisation between landlords and tenant farmers that existed in Ireland, it laid the movement open to suspicions of being part of a political agenda on the part of landlords to wean tenants away from support for the land struggle and home rule. Plunkett always denied this and, although he was a Conservative MP for South Dublin from 1892 to 1900, he emphasised continually that the movement was non-political. He was fond of pointing out that even if peasant proprietorship and home rule were granted the next day, the problems of rural underdevelopment that he was striving to overcome would still have to be faced: 'Alike in its material and in its moral achievements this [co-operative] movement has provided an effective means whereby the peasant proprietary about to be created will be able to face and solve the vital problems before it, problems for which no improvement in land tenure, no rent reductions actual or prospective, could otherwise provide an adequate solution'.[13]

Nationalist leaders had also recognised the need for economic reforms to accompany political change. Parnell was interested in the reclamation of waste land in order to expand non-viable small farms and in migration of farmers onto less settled grazing land. He too was anxious to see an expansion of tillage.[14] He might well have understood and sympathised with Plunkett's aims but a proposed meeting between the two in 1890 failed to take place when Parnell was unable to attend.[15] Others, such as John Dillon, were suspicious of rural reform as potentially divisive of the national struggle, claiming of the co-operative movement that: 'I know from my own knowledge that it is from top to bottom a machine to burst up and destroy the national movement'.[16]

Moreover, in the context of a bitterly divided party, following the Parnell split, much attention tended to be focused on mutual recrimination. A number of nationalist politicians on the Parnellite side, among them TP Gill, W Field and John Redmond, were prepared to work with Plunkett, but once the party reunited in 1900, nationalists tended to distance themselves from the co-operative movement and the DATI under Plunkett's management.

Historical writing over recent decades has moved away from viewing Irish rural society in the late 19th century purely in terms of conflict between landlords and tenants. In fact, the situation was a great deal more complex, with additional class cleavages between smaller farmers and graziers; between farmers and labourers; and in some areas, between farmers and shopkeepers.[17] Plunkett's rural development policy had to take account of these.

Plunkett seems to have come across the idea of co-operation during his college days at Oxford in the 1870s and he had even set up a co-operative store on the family's estate at Dunsany, County Meath in 1878. On his return from Wyoming he commenced his co-operative campaign by trying to promote co-operative retail stores, launching one, at Doneraile, County Cork in 1889. However, opposition on the part of local shopkeepers, who portrayed retail co-operation as a landlord plot to distract tenants from the land struggle, hampered his efforts. Becoming acquainted with the difficulties facing Munster farmers in their butter exports at the time, Plunkett shifted his attention to the promotion of creamery co-operation, which proved successful. However, the move from consumer to producer co-operation was probably more significant than Plunkett realised at the time. It was soon to put the fledgling Irish movement at odds with its overwhelmingly consumer-oriented parent body, the Co-operative Union, leading to a break between the two. Moreover, it led Plunkett to look beyond the British example to Continental models, not only for co-operation but for other aspects of rural development as well, such as systems of agricultural instruction and evening schools in farming methods and rural handicrafts.

The one area in which the Irish movement continued to engage in consumer co-operation was in agricultural societies, strongest in the south-east of the country where tillage was most important. These provided for the joint purchase of agricultural necessities, such as seeds, fertilisers and tools, enabling farmers to deal directly with wholesalers, thereby lowering prices and ensuring the quality of the product. The societies were bitterly attacked by retailers, who also resented the establishment of co-operative banks in the west. The banks were aimed at combatting rural debt, common among small farmers, whose creditors were most often shopkeepers. Propaganda on the part of the co-operative movement characterised these creditors as 'gombeen men', sucking the life blood from the rural community.[18] Therefore, it is possible to argue that if the Irish co-operative movement sought to smooth over class differences between landlords and tenants, it emphasised those between farmers and shopkeepers.[19]

Despite social differences within the movement, it spread rapidly. By 1903 there were over 800 societies in the country,[20] though the number stabilised thereafter and had not risen significantly by 1914.[21] The further spread of co-operation was limited by the fact that it was not applied to the cattle industry, which was the most rapidly growing sector in Irish agriculture at the time.

For 10 years Plunkett had lived as a cattle rancher in Wyoming and had crossed the vast agricultural regions of the United States many times by train. As a result he was acutely aware of the great disparities in scale between what he had seen in the New World and the small-scale farming practised by Irish farmers, both beef husbandry and arable. He was well aware that no British government, with its large and growing industrial population, anxious to buy food at the lowest price, would introduce tariffs to protect Irish farmers. The solution he sought instead was a concentration on more intensive farming, dairying and the production of more valuable crops such as fresh vegetables and soft fruits, which, with a high labour input and the opportunities they provided for food-processing industries could offer more jobs to the farming population, thereby helping to stem emigration. During his years as vice-president (acting head) of the DATI, he put a great deal of effort into investigating the potential for such intensive farming.

By the end of the 19th century there was growing concern about the condition of agricultural labourers in Ireland. As a class they had suffered most during the Famine and from post-Famine emigration. With cattle grazing on the increase, their employment opportunities continued to decline. They had gained nothing by the expansion in farm ownership and their wage levels and living conditions remained woefully bad. Plunkett's policy had little in the way of immediate gains to offer them. The kind of agricultural revolution he envisaged, with increased tillage and ancillary industries, would have provided greatly increased employment opportunities but it did not take place. Although by no means all labourers had access to land on their own account, following the Labourers' Act of 1883 the Boards of Guardians provided a half-acre plot of land with their labourers' cottages, increased after 1892 to one acre. The co-operative movement's publications urged that they be encouraged to make the most beneficial use of this and urged farmers to admit them to local co-operative societies, pointing out that they could be provided with loans from the co-operative banks to enable them keep pigs, poultry and bees, in order 'to add to the somewhat precarious income derived from working for large farmers'.[22] However, there seems to have been strong social prejudice against them on the part of farmers who were unwilling to admit labourers and cottiers to membership of the societies. This attitude led to the formation of a separate farm labourers' co-operative bank, at Lattin, County Tipperary in 1902.

WOMEN AND RURAL DEVELOPMENT

The issue of the place of women in rural development had been intrinsic to the work of the co-operative movement almost from the beginning. Plunkett's slogan: 'Better farming, better business, better living', assumed a role for women in the last part, in improving the quality of life in the rural community. From its inception, the *Irish Homestead*, the weekly newspaper of the co-operative movement, was aimed at a female as well as a male readership.[23] Home industries societies were set up from 1896 and poultry societies from 1897, with a predominantly female membership in mind.[24]

Plunkett had long been interested in improving the lot of women. In 1890 he published an article on 'The working of women suffrage in Wyoming'.[25] He remained a supporter of women's suffrage, visiting Constance Lytton in February 1910, on her release from imprisonment as a suffragette. He wrote in his diary: 'Saw Lady Constance Lytton in bed recovering from her gaol experiences as a suffragette. She told me a most thrilling tale of prison life. She is, I think, a little exaltée. But she is a noble woman with the real martyr's spirit'.[26]

Constance Georgina Lytton (1869–1923), a supporter of Emmeline Pankhurst in the Women's Social and Political Union, the more militant wing of suffragism, was imprisoned several times but always released on health grounds when on hunger strike, probably in consideration of her aristocratic background. In 1911 she disguised herself as a working woman and on her imprisonment and hunger strike in Liverpool, after being passed as fit and forcibly fed, she suffered a stroke, and remained partially paralysed. Plunkett offered to join the committee of the women's suffrage movement in 1910,[27] though it is unlikely that he did so, as the topic was not mentioned again in his diary.

In 1891 Plunkett investigated, on behalf of the Congested Districts Board, the possibility of providing assistance to young Irish women emigrating to the United States and Canada. By this time, however, public opinion had turned so strongly against emigration that the idea had to be dropped when it was attacked in the press.[28]

The problem of how to improve the lives of rural women was among those addressed by President Theodore Roosevelt's Country Life

Commission in the United States, which Plunkett was instrumental in initiating in 1906.[29] The writer and social thinker, Henry George had brought the issue of the harsh lives of rural women to public attention in the United States in the 1890s. Plunkett's involvement on the Country Life Commission undoubtedly influenced him to turn his attention to the question of Irish women's lives and role in the countryside.

Plunkett had discussed the need to set up an organisation for women within the co-operative movement with the wives, daughters and sisters of prominent co-operators and with women in bodies such as the Women's National Health Association, the Irish Industries League and the Royal Irish Industries Association. In the end, it was a group of women who took the initiative, inspired by a speech by George Russell to the Annual General Meeting of the IAOS in 1909, on 'The building up of a rural civilisation'.[30] The United Irishwomen was launched in Plunkett House on 30 September 1910. To judge by Plunkett's diary, he did not have a strong organising influence on the movement, although he did try to protect it against the wrath of Lady Aberdeen, who saw it as a competitor to her Women's National Health Association.[31] He also helped the new committee apply to the Pembroke Charities fund for assistance.[32]

By April 1912 the new organisation was seriously divided on the suffrage question, and Plunkett wrote anxiously for advice to his friend, Lady Betty Balfour, wife of the former Chief Secretary, Gerald Balfour and a supporter of women's suffrage. There had been several resignations over the matter. Plunkett's own view was: 'that there is no more reason why the U.I. should adopt the principles of the W.S. movement than that the latter should adopt the principles of the former'.[33]

The United Irishwomen was established at a time of transition for rural women in this country. They had lost much of their traditional role in the peasant economy and were in the process of searching for another. Despite a generally buoyant economy, women were being forced back into the home by a relative decline in the position of women's labour within the paid labour market. They were losing an economic role as producers and being urged to become full-time housewives.[34] Indeed, in replacing home-churning of butter with creamery manufacture, the co-operative movement had contributed to this process. The United Irishwomen aimed largely to bolster women's position in the home by teaching cooking and domestic economy, organising charities, and running local social events. In her outline introducing the organisation, its first president, Ellice Pilkington, suggested that each branch should choose according to the needs and possibilities of the area, definite objects, citing as examples: 'cottage gardening, bee-keeping, poultry, sewing, embroidery, knitting, cheap meals for fair days, and a district nurse'.[35]

Plunkett's own approach was slightly different. In the first few lines of his chapter introducing the United Irishwomen he makes an argument for a greater role of women in *public* life, but hastens to qualify this by asserting that he writes 'of women's work, not women's votes' and expands this into a role of social service to their community.[36] Joanna Bourke, in *Husbandry to housewifery* writes that: 'commentators represented the typical United Irishwoman as triumphantly extending "her interests beyond the home" in reformatory zeal, but failed to note that this extension occurred only in areas uncontentiously regarded as women's proper sphere in the first place'.[37]

And yet, in his outline of possible issues the United Irishwomen might address, Plunkett suggested a wider view, including 'sanitation under the Local Government Board, the manifold activities of the Department of Agriculture and Technical Instruction, and the County Committees of Agriculture and Technical Instruction which work with it', involvement in the rural schools and increased representation on local representative bodies,[38] as well as increased participation in the co-operative movement: 'They ought to be the predominant element in poultry and egg and bee-keeping societies, and to be represented on the committees of co-operative creameries'.[39]

Had the aims Plunkett outlined been realised there would have been a much greater input into public life, in terms of women's outlook and demands.

However, given the prevailing atmosphere of the time, perhaps unwilling to arouse the considerable resistance there would have been to women taking on these roles, the organisation, as it evolved, carved out a more limited sphere for itself. In effect, there were wider and narrower programmes open to it, Plunkett suggesting a wider one, but that which emerged representing a more restricted one. Plunkett, quite correctly, did not attempt to impose his view on the organisation and in the event, the United Irishwomen was swept aside within a few years.[40]

What really might have kept women in the countryside and stemmed the flow of emigration that aroused such concern was greater employment opportunities. The example of the woollen industry at Foxford might have been followed, or food processing industries could perhaps have been established, but the opportunity for such industries was limited. On the other hand, as Bourke points out, the home industries encouraged by various organisations, including the co-operative movement, could not offer women a real livelihood – they were inefficient in comparison with mechanised production.[41]

The Co-operative Movement and the State

One issue still faced today by those engaged in rural development is the relationship between the state and the voluntary sector. In his work, given the mood that prevailed in the country, Plunkett had to tread a difficult path between the great possibilities opened up by state aid on the one hand, and the need to foster self-reliance on the other. Co-operation was based on the principle of self-help, not of the individual but of the group, which the pioneers of the movement often counterposed to what they saw as a tradition of looking to state action alone for solutions. On the other hand, some rural problems that they encountered in their work were clearly too great to be resolved by a voluntary body alone. Moreover, there were examples of co-operative movements in other parts of Europe which worked closely and in apparent harmony with the state. Unfortunately, in the Irish case there was a government still committed (if less so than before) to a policy of *laissez-faire*, coupled with a nationalist public opinion to which, given the experiences of the previous decades, any government policies would be automatically suspect.

One area of Plunkett's involvement in rural development was his service on the Congested Districts Board, a state-funded development board charged with economic and social improvement in the west of Ireland. Although often deeply critical of what he saw as excessive paternalism on the part of the board, he also appreciated the value of much of its work, continuing to participate on it, as its longest-serving member, until his retirement in 1919.[42]

The structure of the Congested Districts Board had been laid down by statute of 1891, mainly drafted by Arthur Balfour, the Chief Secretary.[43] Plunkett had more scope to mould the co-operative organisation according to his own views. He and his colleagues established the Irish Agricultural Organisation Society (IAOS) in 1894, as the co-ordinating centre of the co-operative movement. He envisaged it as developing into a democratic structure with links, through district conferences, back to the village community level. But in parallel with this he sought a state body that would offer assistance and co-operation with the IAOS, while refraining from interference in its working.

It was with such a division of functions between the state and voluntary sectors in mind that Plunkett set up the Recess Committee in 1895, in order to press for the establishment of a department of agriculture and industries.[44] His proposal was based on an examination of continental models, in some of which, notably Denmark and France, close co-ordination did exist between state and voluntary organisations.[45] In Plunkett's view this was indispensable to rural development because, while the state could provide services and a legal framework to which the voluntary organisations could not aspire, the organisations would offer a structure aimed to utilise to the full the services the state could deliver: 'without organisation for economic purposes amongst the agricultural classes, state aid to agriculture must be largely ineffectual, and even mischievous'.[46] The co-operative societies around the country would provide a supportive milieu for instruction and experimental projects carried out by the department.[47] The projected department was aimed, therefore, both in structure and concept, to represent a radical innovation into the Irish system.

Eventually the Recess Committee's efforts met with success and a Department of Agriculture and Technical Instruction (DATI) was set up in 1900, with Plunkett as its first vice-president and acting head. As such, he played an innovative role and the department in its early years carried out pioneering work.

Relations between the IAOS and the new department, however, were to prove anything but smooth. Plunkett seems to have been the only one among his co-operative colleagues who favoured a close relationship between them. Following two years of fairly harmonious coexistence, problems began to emerge between the two organisations. The source of these may be traced to their different aims and natures. The IAOS was a voluntary body with a relatively small paid staff, which relied largely on the efforts of the local farmers' societies, with all the delays and inefficiencies that entailed. The DATI was a government department, with a much larger budget and a trained staff, which saw its aims as improving the agricultural production and technical education of the country. As a democratic organisation, the IAOS deeply resented what it saw as dictation by a bureaucratic body which, moreover, it saw as largely its own creation. Plunkett, as head of the DATI, was accused of showing favouritism to the co-operative movement. Now that the IAOS had a subsidy from the department, farmers' subscriptions dropped off which made the co-operative movement dependent on government support, with a resulting loss of its autonomy. By 1906 the co-operative organisation was in debt and facing bankruptcy. Nevertheless, Plunkett resisted a suggestion that the DATI simply take over the IAOS, holding to the belief that co-operation was best run through voluntary organisations. This was a view he maintained all his life, criticising the Indian co-operative movement in 1928, on the basis that it was state-run.[48]

Thus there was an almost audible sigh of relief from the co-operative leadership when Plunkett was forced to resign as vice-president of the DATI in 1907. His successor, TW Russell, was hostile to the IAOS and cut the grant to it when the matter came up for review and the movement staggered on, supported by private donations, until some further support was provided in 1913. Nevertheless, although the two organisations failed to work in harmony, the fact that they both existed and made important contributions to Irish rural development, is largely due to Plunkett's efforts.

Conclusion

Plunkett's rural ideas are important because he was not only able to provide a clear-headed analysis of the economic and social ills of rural

Ireland in the late 19th century but also to offer realistic remedies for them. More broadly, his efforts can also be seen as part of a turning back of public attention in Western Europe and the United States from industrial life, which had dominated it for much of the 19th century, to rural issues, which had been relatively neglected.

Plunkett provided a vision of future development for rural society. Against the fact that he did not live to see all of it accomplished, one has to answer that very few social reformers ever do. Yet he had a profound effect, not only on Ireland but on the social thinking of his day. His greatest obstacle was his failure to win over Irish nationalist opinion, suspicious of his motivation. This was understandably increased by his political affiliation to Unionism. However, it is evident from what he wrote on the subject that rather than his social reform efforts being aimed to serve a political purpose, that of winning Irish farmers away from the home rule struggle, he in fact compartmentalised political and economic aims to a degree unusual both then and now.

Some of the points that Plunkett made, such as the insights that in traditional societies innovation is more effectively carried out on a group basis than on an individual one, and undertaken voluntarily by the target group; and that the comfort of their surroundings affects not only how people feel about themselves but also their effectiveness at work, so that social and economic reform should encompass both aspects simultaneously, remain important principles to this day.

Notes

1. Margaret Digby, *Horace Plunkett: an Anglo-American Irishman* (Oxford, 1949) pp 267–8.
2. He was influential among policy-makers in India, writing a report on co-operative agriculture for the Royal Commission on Agriculture in India, 1928. Ibid, pp 279–80.
3. In *Ireland in the new century* (Dublin, 1904) Plunkett refers to enquirers from Germany, France, Canada, the United States, India, South Africa, Cyprus and the West Indies 'in the last two years' (p 205).
4. Louis Paul-Dubois, *Contemporary Ireland* (1906); Moritz Bonn, *Modern Ireland and her agrarian problem* (Dublin, 1906).
5. It is impossible to quantify this impact because much of it was indirect, in assisting structural change, making farming more efficient and improving the marketing of products. A limiting factor was that market conditions, coupled with the economic effects of the land tenure reforms in the late 19th century, strongly favoured beef farming rather than those areas in which the co-operative movement was most closely involved. JP Huttman, 'The impact of land reform on agricultural production in Ireland,' in *Agricultural History*, xlvi, 3, July 1972, pp 353–68.
6. This vision is also worked out in George Russell's *Co-operation and nationality: a guide from this to the next generation* (Dublin, 1912); reprinted Irish

Academic Press, 1982; but it was one that Plunkett shared. See, for example, *Ireland in the new century*, ch vii; Horace Plunkett, *The rural life problem of the United States: notes of an Irish observer* (New York, 1910).

7. Plunkett, *Ireland in the new century*, pp 148–60.
8. However, see Digby, *Horace Plunkett* and Trevor West, *Co-operation and politics: an Irish biography* (Gerrard's Cross and Washington, DC, 1986) for excellent biographies of Plunkett. For a wide-ranging and most informative source on the co-operative movement, see Patrick Bolger, *The Irish Co-operative Movement: its history and development* (Dublin, 1977).
9. Philip Bull, *Politics and nationalism: a study of the Irish land question* (Dublin, 1996) pp 95–6.
10. Carla King, 'The early development of agricultural co-operation: some French and Irish comparisons' in *Proceedings of the Royal Irish Academy*, vol 96, no 3 (1996) pp 3–86.
11. Horace Plunkett, *Noblesse oblige: an Irish rendering* (Dublin, 1908).
12. Suzanne Berger, *Peasants against politics: rural organization in Brittany, 1911–1967* (Cambridge, Mass, 1972); Augé-Laribé, *L'Évolution de la France agricole* (Paris, 1912); King, 'The early development of agricultural co-operation'.
13. Plunkett, *Ireland in the new century*, p 207.
14. Liam Kennedy, 'The economic thought of the nation's lost leader,' in DG Boyce and Alan O'Day (eds) *Parnell in perspective* (London, 1991) pp 171–200.
15. *IAOS annual report, 1907*, Appendix D, minutes of annual general meeting, 20 December 1907; West, *Horace Plunkett: co-operation and politics, an Irish biography*, pp 36–7; Liam Kennedy, 'The economic thought of the nation's lost leader,' in DG Boyce and Alan O'Day (eds) *Parnell in perspective*, pp 171–200.
16. *Freeman's Journal*, 12 November 1906.
17. Samuel Clark, *Social origins of the Irish land war* (Princeton, 1979); DS Jones, *Graziers, land reform, and political conflict in Ireland* (Washington, 1995).
18. Fr TA Finlay, 'The usurer in Ireland', in *New Ireland Review*, vol i, pp 304–16, March-August 1894; and 'The progress of co-operation', in *Journal of the Statistical and Social Inquiry Society of Ireland*, vol x, September 1897, pp 229–37.
19. Liam Kennedy, 'Traders in the Irish rural economy, 1880–1914', in *Economic History Review*, 2nd ser, vol xxxii, 2 (May 1979) pp 201–10; Liam Kennedy, 'Farmers, traders and agricultural politics in pre-independence Ireland' in Samuel Clark and JS Donnelly, Jr (eds) *Irish peasants: violence and political unrest, 1780–1914* (Manchester, 1983) pp 339–73.
20. Plunkett, *Ireland in the new century*, p 192.
21. *IAOS annual report, 1915*, Appendix XIX.
22. *IAOS annual report, 1902*, p 10.
23. The *Irish Homestead* had a woman assistant editor, the poet, Susan Mitchell.
24. *IAOS annual reports*; Bolger, *The Irish co-operative movement: its history and development*.
25. Horace Plunkett, 'The working of women suffrage in Wyoming', in *Fortnightly Review*, new ser. v. 47 (1890) pp 656–69.
26. Horace Plunkett Diaries, Plunkett Foundation, Oxford, 8 February 1910.
27. Plunkett Diaries, 23 February 1910.

28. Mary Bolger, 'The Congested Districts Board and the assisted emigration question', unpublished MA thesis, St Patrick's College, Maynooth, 1995.
29. MR Swanson, 'The American Country Life Movement, 1900–1940,' unpublished DPhil dissertation, University of Oklahoma, 1972; C Keating, 'Sir Horace Plunkett and rural reform, 1889–1914', unpublished PhD dissertation, NUI, 1984.
30. Bolger, *The Irish Co-operative Movement*, p 105; Ellice Pilkington, 'The United Irishwomen and their work', in *The United Irishwomen, their place, work and ideals* (Dublin, 1911); reprinted in Patrick Bolger (ed) *And see her beauty shining there* (Dublin, 1986) p 30.
31. Plunkett Diaries, 28 October 1910; 29 March 1911.
32. Plunkett Diaries, 22 March 1911.
33. Horace Plunkett Papers, Plunkett Foundation, Oxford, BAL/84, Plunkett to Lady Betty Balfour, 13 April 1912.
34. The topic is treated very fully in Joanna Bourke, *Husbandry to housewifery: women, economic change, and housework in Ireland, 1890–1914* (Oxford, 1993).
35. Pilkington, 'The United Irishwomen and their work', pp 59–60.
36. Plunkett, 'Their place', in *The United Irishwomen*, p 15.
37. Bourke, *Husbandry to housewifery*, p 240.
38. Plunkett, 'Their place', pp 25–6.
39. Ibid, p 27.
40. Although it was later to be revived in the form of the successful and enduring Irish Countrywomen's Association, founded in 1935.
41. Bourke, *Husbandry to housewifery*, pp 120–41.
42. Keating, 'Sir Horace Plunkett and rural reform, 1889–1914'.
43. However, Balfour did consult Plunkett, among others, in drafting the bill. Plunkett Diaries, 26 May, 30 May, 1 June, 1891.
44. West, *Horace Plunkett, co-operation and politics*, pp 41–54; Keating, 'Sir Horace Plunkett and rural reform, 1889–1914'.
45. *Report of the Recess Committee* (Dublin, 1896).
46. Plunkett, *Ireland in the new century*, p 241.
47. Ibid, p 241.
48. *Report of the Royal Commission on Agriculture in India*, [Cd. 3132] H.C. (1928) viii, 9, memorandum by Horace Plunkett.

Chapter 5

Defending Rural Interests Against Nationalists in 20th-Century Ireland: A Tale of Three Movements

Tony Varley and Chris Curtin

Introduction

By early in the 20th century, in what was to become the Irish Free State in 1922–23, the representation of rural interests, at least in the sphere of electoral politics, was largely under the control of anti-colonial nationalists. This is not to suggest that Irish nationalists had by then settled all their internal differences. A re-united Irish Party that formally put the Parnell split behind it may have come into being by 1900, but the presence of opposing tendencies within nationalism, and the emergence of new rival groups, were not destined to disappear. Anti-colonial nationalists were divided as to the aims they pursued (devolved home rule versus outright political separation) and in what they took to be legitimate tactics (physical force versus constitutionalism).[1] The politics of the second decade of the new century were to be dominated by competition between the Irish Parliamentary Party and Sinn Féin. Ultimately that struggle was to end in victory for a restructured Sinn Féin movement and in the demise of the Irish Party. In the aftermath of the Anglo-Irish Treaty of 1921, however, Sinn Féin was itself to split into pro- and anti-Treaty factions which very soon would confront each other in dark and bitter civil war.

Nationalists may have dominated the party political sphere in the south by the late 19th century, but they had not succeeded in monopolising the representation of rural interests across the board. A co-operative movement, formed in 1894, had made some inroads, particularly among Munster's dairy farmers.[2] With the formation in 1910 of the United Irishwomen (later to become the Irish Countrywomen's Association), we have the beginnings of what was to become a national movement of non-political rural women.[3] Under the stimulus of wartime conditions – especially the compulsory tillage regime introduced in 1917 – farmers were to organise in their own right, first *via* the Irish Farmers' Union as an interest group and then *via* the Farmers' Party as a political party.

The wartime period was also to provide farm labourers with opportunities for collective action. Pushed on by wage pressure that was accentuated by the introduction of compulsory tillage in 1917, and the rapid spread of syndicalist-style trade unionism that favoured worker-controlled co-operatives, they threatened for a spell to become a powerful force.[4] What brought the farm labourers' advance to a halt was the downward wage pressure exerted by the post-war slump. This put them on the defensive and the balance of power shifted decisively in favour of farmers when, with the critical backing of the new state's coercive apparatus, they succeeded in dealing rural labour a comprehensive defeat in the Waterford strike of 1923.[5] Not till the formation of the Federation of Rural Workers in 1944 was the prospect rekindled for renewed collective action aimed at defending the interests of farm labourers.[6] By then, of course, just around the corner were rural electrification and the post-war wave of oil-driven farm mechanisation, which would complete the shift from wage to family labour in Irish agriculture.[7]

A leading argument of late 19th-century Irish nationalism was that Ireland had done poorly in economic terms under the Act of Union of 1800, and that she would continue to occupy an underdog position within the United Kingdom as long as the existing constitutional arrangements remained intact.[8] The proposal of one of the more notable early 20th-century exponents of this position, Arthur Griffith, was that the advent of political independence should be used to stimulate manufacturing industry behind tariff walls. By such means, and principally with the help of invited Irish-American capital, were the foundations of an industrial society in southern Ireland to be laid.[9]

A nationalist argument against the large-scale grazing system, which had become an intrinsic element of the increasingly cattle-based 19th century agrarian economy, was that it enriched the few and impoverished the many, thereby precipitating flight from the land and the decline of rural communities. Local nationalist support for a series of land agitations helped keep the issue of redistributive land reform alive in the early decades of the 20th century, at least in certain parts of Ireland.[10]

Cultural regeneration was another facet of Irish anti-colonial nationalism. The idea behind the movements to revive the Irish language and Gaelic games as well as the Irish-Ireland project was in part to define and cultivate a distinctive sense of Irish identity.[11] Some elements of the nationalist project of cultural regeneration, in particular the use of the Irish language in state education and civil service recruitment, were to be vigorously promoted by the new state during the early decades of native rule.[12] In contrast, decisions were taken by the pro-Treaty Cumann na nGaedheal ruling party that seemed to reject the arguments of the economic nationalists. We find the cattle economy remaining intact in the 1920s, the dropping of wartime compulsory tillage and an official reluctance to favour spatially dispersed import-substituting industrialisation over free trade and the maintenance of the *status quo*.[13] A process of rationalising local government and subjecting it to tighter central control got under way.[14]

With the appearance of the anti-Treaty Fianna Fáil party in 1926, and its meteoric rise to become the dominant force in Irish politics, public policy seemed set to change fundamentally.[15] The early Fianna Fáil was to adopt much of Griffith's economic programme. In opposition after 1927, the party pledged itself to introducing pro-smallholder land reform, lessening the pastoral character of Irish agriculture and promoting a form of spatially dispersed import-substituting industrialisation.[16] After the electoral victory that brought Fianna Fáil (with Labour Party support) to power in 1932, some strides were made with land reform and with stimulating a native-owned, protected form of industrialisation. Yet, the rhetoric and campaign pledges were not matched by performance sufficient to constitute a decisive breakthrough, at least in the eyes of the government's critics. In particular, by the closing years of the 1930s, the Fianna Fáil government's record in dividing land and in dispersing manufacturing industry had become the source of considerable disappointment in the west of Ireland.[17]

It is this disenchantment that provides us with our point of departure in this chapter. We propose to consider three movements that appeared in the post-independence period and that took as their common theme the notion that the dominant nationalist political establishment was not serving rural interests well, if at all. The three movements in question are: Muintir na Tíre [People of the Land] and Clann na Talmhan [Family of the Land], each of which appeared on the scene in the 1930s, and the popularly named 'Save the West' campaign which came to life in the 1960s. Our intention, in examining how these three movements grappled with the problems of 'representation' and 'state policy', will be to look at the circumstances of their origins, their aims and ideology, their organisation and appeal, the tactics they came to use and how they actually fared in trying to reach the goals they set for themselves.

Muintir na Tíre

Since the 1930s one tradition of organising communities for their own development and of representing local interests has been linked to Muintir na Tíre (Muintir), a rural renewal movement inspired initially by perceived societal breakdown at home and by the examples of the

Belgian Boerenbond and the Catholic Social Movement abroad.[18] The new movement associated itself very much with the constructive heritage of Irish nationalism, as this was taken to be embedded in the experiences of the Land League and the pre-split Sinn Féin movement.[19] A cause of major concern to Muintir's founder, Fr John Hayes of Tipperary, was the bitter and community-destroying factionalisation of the nationalist movement that had followed the break-up of Sinn Féin and the post-Treaty descent into civil war. Fr Hayes's basic idea was to try to create a sphere in civil society where the destructive factionalisation associated with post-Treaty nationalist politics would find no home. His basic suggestion was that, for this to happen, patriotism in Ireland would have to be re-thought as a phenomenon that was rooted in identification with the local community. No longer, as Fr Hayes frequently put it, were Irish people being called upon to lay down their lives for their country; the challenge now was to *live* for Ireland, by building a tradition of practical patriotism and Christianity at the level of the local community.[20]

Economic and cultural difficulties were also at the heart of Fr Hayes's conception of rural crisis in the 1930s. Powerful evidence for the view that rural Ireland was firmly set on a downward journey of decline was provided by the economic difficulties of the post-war period, especially the privations of the economic war (1932–38) that accompanied the sharp drop in farming incomes. Other developments which Fr Hayes found disturbing were the blight of emigration, and the intrusion into the countryside of what were taken to be the morally destructive influences of urban materialism.

When Muintir appeared first in 1931 (as Muintir na Tíre Ltd) it was as an attempt to create an alliance of producers' co-operatives, modelled on the Belgian Boerenbond. Before long, a number of experiences were to convince Muintir's founder of the need to re-organise his movement along radically different lines. Conflicts surfaced between different groups of farm producers in the alliance of producers' co-operatives,[21] and difficulties were experienced in persuading farm labourers to participate.[22] Above all, it seems that new papal teaching on the voluntary sector and on state-civil society relationships came to have a profound effect on Fr Hayes's thinking about how rural interests might best be organised.

The papal encyclical *Quadragessimo Anno* had in fact appeared but one week following Muintir na Tíre Ltd's launch in 1931. As well as re-emphasising the ideal of building alliances between classes as an organising principle in society and as an alternative to class warfare, *Quadragessimo Anno* advocated a subsidiary role for the state in public life, and emphasised the right of voluntary, 'intermediate' groups to exist between the citizen and the state.[23] Suspiciousness of the overly interventionist state lay at the heart of the principle of subsidiarity and was to supply one strand of the new Muintir's case for a representation of interests that was strictly independent of the state and party politics. Presenting itself as a parish-based rural renewal movement, this new Muintir na Tíre formally appeared in 1937.[24]

The new Muintir of 1937 aspired to become a national organisation of parish councils/guilds, dedicated to the advancement of the common good. For a genuine national network to emerge, each Catholic parish in the country would ideally have to organise its own council capable of deciding on a programme of self-help activities in response to perceived local needs. By such means were Muintir's 'economic, cultural and recreational' aims to be realised.[25] Regular gatherings at rural weekends and weeks were viewed as supplying a national dimension to what easily could become little more than a collection of spatially separated and largely unconnected parish councils.[26] More formally, a set of organisational layers provided for county and provincial federations as well as for a national executive and central council.

It was not only popular participation that Fr Hayes wanted in the new Muintir but active involvement as well. As he put it in 1941, the well-established pattern before the appearance of Muintir was that '... where the people selected a committee they usually left everything to that committee. Their interest expired after the effort of election. It was the only method they knew. We wanted something that would give us a good representative parish council and yet keep alive parochial interest among the people'.[27]

So as to achieve 'a living enthusiastic body behind the council', Fr Hayes urged that a parochial 'guild' be created alongside the council in each parish. These guilds would 'consist of all the people of the parish who [were] willing to take an interest in the parochial community'.[28] Two forms of participation thus feature in the thinking of Fr Hayes, the narrower one being restricted to the membership of the parish council and the broader one spread across the membership of the parish guild. Fr Hayes expressed a preference for consensual decision making within the parish councils. 'I would like to add', he wrote optimistically in 1941, 'that never once was a vote necessary at our council meetings, and I believe this to be true of every Muintir na Tíre Council in Ireland'.[29]

The parish guilds were to be composed of different sections, each of which would select its own representatives to sit on the parish council. It was left to each parish to decide its own number of sections. The very first parish council, established in Tipperary town in 1935, recognised farmers, rural labourers, tradesmen, business and professionals and the unemployed as distinct sections. The resulting council of 25 members was later supplemented by some co-options.[30] On occasion women and youths might be admitted as distinct sections in their own right in the way the guilds/parish councils were constituted.[31]

If the ultimate aim was to cover the country with a network of parish council/guilds, what actual progress was made? Stimulated by the post-war rural electrification drive, Muintir's period of greatest expansion occurred between 1945 and 1950 when affiliated parish council/guild numbers increased by 188 per cent (from 106 to 305).[32] Slightly more than 50 per cent of these council/guilds, however, were clustered in the counties of Limerick, Tipperary and Cork. The number of affiliated council/guilds appears to have peaked at 417 in 1955.[33] Muintir's activity at parish level was organised voluntarily and, unsurprisingly in view of where its strength lay, those few non-clerical organisers that took to the roads trying to stimulate interest in the early decades were based in Munster.[34]

What did the Muintir parish councils/guilds actually do? In the early years, parish councils/guilds tended to centre their activities heavily on the construction of local halls and on organising leisure activities. Direct involvement in economic activity was exceptional.[35] Notwithstanding the early suspiciousness of the interventionist state, the work of the early parish guilds came quickly to reflect what the state officially defined as national priorities. We therefore find parish councils organising potato growing and turf harvesting to meet wartime shortages,[36] and lending assistance to private afforestation, group water schemes and the rural electrification drive of the early post-war years.[37] Most of Muintir's activity may have been reactive but, in the late 1940s, a modified version of the national organisation's 'parish plan' for agricultural modernisation via reform of the advisory system was accepted by James Dillon, who held the agriculture portfolios in the 1948–51 and 1954–57 inter-party governments.[38]

How did the Muintir parish councils actually operate? Representativeness, in the sense of structuring the local organisation in such a way as to entitle it to speak for the local community, along with effectiveness, have always been the twin sources of Muintir's claim to popular legitimacy. Both representativeness and effectiveness, it quickly became apparent, could be influenced by a range of contingencies. Some parish councils had to contend with domination by cliques or even by single individuals (frequently priests), disruptive internal conflicts,[39] and apathy (so severe on occasion as to cause parish councils to expire). Frequently, continued existence depended on small numbers of dedicated activists.[40] There is a variety of ethnographic evidence – derived from McNabb's account of east Limerick in the 1950s,[41] Bax's late 1960s study of the Munster village of 'Patricksville',[42] Harris's portrayal of a north Mayo village in the late 1970s[43] and Eipper's study of the town of Bantry in the 1980s[44] – to suggest that control over parish councils tended to be assumed by local propertied and professional classes.

Fr Hayes's preference was that his new community movement should be broadly Christian rather than narrowly Catholic; Protestants were therefore not to be denied membership.[45] Yet, however much Fr Hayes might have wished to present Muintir as Christian and non-denominational rather than exclusively Catholic,[46] it was difficult for an organisation founded by a Catholic priest, organised around the Catholic parish and which relied heavily for its activists on priests to disguise its heavily clericalist and Catholic character. What is more, Fr Hayes seems to have seen his movement as exclusively Catholic at the outset. In the early 1930s, he apparently looked upon Muintir na Tíre Ltd as 'a Catholic platform to unite the people on the principles of Catholicism'.[47]

The founder's later preference that Muintir project itself as non-sectarian and Christian rather than exclusively Catholic in who it was prepared to admit to membership was to provoke the ire of some of his own followers.[48] Nor was such criticism confined to the ranks of Muintir activists; the opposition of some senior ecclesiastics, most notably Archbishop John Charles McQuaid of Dublin and Bishop Michael Fogarty of Killaloe,[49] was to retard Muintir's spread in some parts of Ireland. Local parish councils, to their cost, could also incur the hostility of unsympathetic parish clergy.[50] On the other hand, clerical involvement was often critical to the survival of Muintir at local level; sometimes parish guilds collapsed when an energetic priest was moved on and his replacement showed no enthusiasm for the parish council and its activities.[51]

It was no surprise, in view of the way the lines were drawn between Treatyites and anti-Treatyites in the post-civil war period, that Muintir should profess itself to be non-political and that politicians *qua* politicians should be denied parish council membership.[52] Did the movement succeed in remaining free of party politics in practice? Given the intensely politicised character of local and national life, it was no easy task to exclude party politics and politicians. Evidently in the very early days, Muintir na Tíre Ltd's committee of management had become so divided that the annual general meeting of 1934 broke up after 'rabid supporters of the rival political parties came into open conflict'.[53] In the aftermath of this incident, Fr Hayes secured the power to hand-pick his own management committee.[54] Equally, at local level, a number of parish guilds were later on to break up because of political differences among the members.[55] Yet, based on the reasoning that some benefits could accrue from their inclusion, an accommodative approach of admitting party politicians to membership of the parish councils seems to have swiftly established itself.[56]

It was the principle of subsidiarity, which asserts the right of voluntary or 'intermediate' groups to exist between the citizen and the state, that became the basis of Muintir's preference for a mode of representing interests that was separate from the state and party politics. Muintir's acceptance of the principle of subsidiarity had as a corollary a suspiciousness of the interventionist state. Dependence on the state, it was believed, would prevent the movement from projecting an autonomous identity and from speaking its mind freely. Although the Fianna Fáil government was keen to recruit Muintir's support for its 'approved local councils', introduced under the 1941 Local Government Act, it did not necessarily seek to present what it had in mind as a take-over of voluntary groups by the state. Éamon de Valera (the Taoiseach and leader of the Fianna Fáil party) at least, in a speech delivered at a wartime rural week-end held in 1941, sought to make it clear that:

> The whole idea would be destroyed if the state came in and made the local groups part of the general state organisation. It is precisely because it is a voluntary coming together, with full independence of action, that this movement promises so well. I would deem it a great misfortune if there should be any attempt to deprive it of that character. I believe that if such an attempt is made, it will not be by the government, but by the local groups, which would be too ready to look to the government for aid and protection. We may in a general way give a certain amount of aid and protection, but that should be as little as possible, even in a general way.[57]

Unless it remained formally independent of the state and bureaucratic control, the new movement was seen by Fr Hayes as having little chance of building an autonomous identity and of advancing its own aims. It was for this reason that it was decided to reject the offer of state assistance for 'approved local councils' as an attempt at incorporation which threatened to rob the Muintir parish councils of their independence.[58] Many of the Muintir parish councils, however, quickly settled down to establishing good working relationships with officialdom. Some of them were to become adept at playing the role of broker in representing local communities before a variety of state agencies.[59]

By the late 1950s Muintir's national leadership had come to the view that 'community development' (a term imported into Ireland in the late 1950s) worthy of the name was possible only on the basis of close and formalised co-operation between voluntary groups and various arms of the state. Indeed, after Fr Hayes's death in 1957, Muintir became an early advocate of what nowadays has come to enjoy a vogue as the 'partnership-based' approach to community development. For all that, the life-threatening crisis conditions that Muintir has had to contend with in recent years can be linked to the movement's relationship with the state in no small part. When, for instance, its annual state grant-in-aid was cut in half (from £30,000 to £15,000) as part of the MacSharry public spending retrenchment of 1987, practically the entire paid organising staff had to be let go or placed in part-time work, thus bringing the administrative and field operations of the national organisation close to total collapse.[60]

Clann na Talmhan

The attempt to organise Irish farmers in the late 1930s that gave rise to the agrarian party known as Clann na Talmhan (Clann). It is mainly identified with the west. Clann was to win a number of Dáil seats in the 1940s and 1950s before fading out in the 1960s. Its strength in the west can be attributed to a delayed reaction to the economic war of the 1930s and, more especially, to the severe damage this had inflicted upon store cattle producers.[61] As strong as it undoubtedly was in parts of the west, Clann's founders dreamed of creating a genuinely national body and it looked, for a time in the 1940s, as if this goal might not be entirely beyond their reach.

A leading contention of the farmer activists who came to organise Clann was that those in control of the state were either directly or indirectly responsible for rural decline. The central charge levelled against the nationalist political establishment was that politicians were more interested in factional struggles than in pursuing the prosperity of agriculture and the well-being of rural inhabitants. Evidence to support these contentions was found in the effects of the protracted post-war slump, the economic war of the 1930s and in the rising costs that reflected the increasingly heavy burden of the property rates and the excessive and often wasteful public spending that was pushing up this form of taxation. The pay increase politicians had received in 1938 was to reinforce the view that their whole approach to public life was self-serving rather than nationally-minded. These professional politicians were dismissed by Michael Donnellan, Clann's first leader, as 'pocket' nationalists.[62] 'The only ploughman the politicians are interested in', he caustically suggested, was 'the ploughman on the pound note'.[63]

An assortment of mainly Fianna Fáil-inspired state interventions in the agrarian economy made for other sources of farmer discontent. Here the regulation of the bacon curing industry was seen to have had the effect of enriching the processor at the farmer's expense.[64] For the westerners, who grew little wheat and sugar beet, the subsidised tillage programme of the 1930s could be faulted as being of little use to them.[65] The dearer consumer goods associated with the new manufacturing industries provided farmer activists with another grievance. In light of the fact that Irish farmers were largely dependent on the vagaries of export agriculture, the protection offered to the new industries caused considerable resentment.[66]

Those who organised the new farmers' movement of 1938–39 saw it as critical that an alliance be built up that was capable of uniting all Irish farmers. The challenge, at a practical level, was to bring farmers of different regions, sizes and agricultural specialisms together as a single, powerful collective force. To get anywhere, farmers would have to recognise their own distinctive class identity and strategic national importance as producers, upon whose labour the entire country depended. This line of argument allowed the farmer's cause to be equated with the national interest. A particular feature of the occupational identity which farmers were urged to cultivate was that they had to see themselves in opposition to professional politicians and other establishment figures. Here the tendency was to set the downtrodden countryside against the privileges enjoyed by remote and uncaring urban-based political, administrative, business and other élites. A flavour of the contempt in which politicians and other establishment figures were held, as well as the populist conception of productive labour as the only genuinely creative force in society, is well conveyed in Donnellan's suggestion of 1942 that: 'You could take all the TDs, all the Senators, all the Ministers and members of the judiciary and all the other nice fellows and dump them off Clare Island into the broad Atlantic. Still, Ireland would succeed. But without the workers and producers the country would starve in 24 hours'.[67]

Farmers may have had reasons aplenty to be drawn to defensive collective action in the late 1930s, but the large number of groups claiming to represent agricultural interests in Ireland in the 1930s did not augur well for the attainment of overall farmer unity. In the event two rival groups – one in the east and another in the west – were to appear in pursuit of the aim of achieving a national organisation of Irish farmers. Conceived as an umbrella group for county-based farmer associations and for those organisations (such as milk suppliers and sugar-beet growers) established to represent specialised farming interests, the mainly Leinster-based Irish Farmers' Federation (IFF) had appeared in 1937.[68] The group that ultimately was to take shape as Clann grew out of a county-based farmers' association that had been organised in Galway in 1938–39.

It quickly became clear that the ideal of an all-farmer alliance would be hard, if not impossible, to achieve in practice. For one thing, the IFF's appeal was mainly confined to the Leinster counties, and even there its local organisation was never to achieve the same density and strength attained in the west by the early wartime Clann. The refusal of the very powerful Irish Sugar Beet Growers' Association to affiliate with it did nothing for the IFF's claim to be a genuinely national representative body.[69] Unity negotiations between the westerners and the IFF were to break down on the issue of the derating of agricultural land. While the IFF would not budge from its demand for full derating,[70] the westerners, mindful of the predominance of smallholders in the countryside they wished to represent and believing that both justice and equity required it, stuck doggedly to the principle of having a tiered system of derating that favoured smallholders. It was at this point (in 1939) that the westerners, despairing of ever forming an alliance with the IFF element, determined to launch a specifically western attempt at building a national organisation of Irish farmers.[71]

In view of the fate of previous farmers' parties, it was hardly surprising that both the IFF and those elements that rallied as Clann in 1939 should at first opt to steer clear of direct participation in party politics. The idea instead was to organise along 'trade union' lines.[72] The imminence of a by-election in Galway West in 1939–40, however, caused Clann to enter the contest. A later justification presented for this U-turn by Michael Donnellan was that unless the election was contested, there would be no hope of keeping together those recently united within the movement.[73] Clann may have entered the realm of party politics (although it was to taste defeat at the polls in the 1940 by-election), but it continued to profess itself to be a 'non-political' vocational party and, when compared to the mainstream nationalist parties, as the only movement that had a genuine conception of the national interest. Casting itself in this role, it saw itself standing above the sterile competition that marked relations between the mutually hostile nationalist factions that had come to dominate the domain of party politics to the detriment of rural Ireland.

A farm commodity strike organised in Leinster in late 1939 was to end in defeat for the IFF after the state had taken a firm stand against the strikers. This setback, in the eyes of some at least, showed up the limitations of exclusive reliance on the trade union approach to representing farming interests. With a general election drawing nearer, some leading IFF activists (including the independent farmer TD, Patrick Cogan) were to establish the National Agricultural Party in 1942.[74] When the leading lights of this new movement showed themselves to be willing to concede on the derating question, a merger between the westerners and the easterners that gave birth to Clann na Talmhan – the National Agricultural Party – was completed in January 1943. It looked at this point as if the ambition of achieving a large-scale farmers' political alliance was in the offing. Ten seats were won by the new Clann in the 1943 election and the farmers found themselves holding the balance of power in the new Dáil. The preference of the farmers' party was for a national government, but Fianna Fáil blankly refused to countenance any talk of a grand coalition. Apparently swayed by the need to preserve stability in wartime, the farmers did not in the end block Fianna Fáil's attempt to form a single-party government.

Although the winning of 10 seats on their first outing might seem to have been a promising start, it clearly did not signify that Irish farmers were about to desert the mainstream nationalist parties *en masse*.[75] Before long the attempt to constitute Irish farmers as a political class, and the united front that had been forged for electoral purposes in 1943, began to crumble. As some county executives of the farmers' party insisted on controlling the actions of their public representatives, the danger of the movement fragmenting along county lines had always existed. Tensions and divisions between the interests of big and small farmers, and between those practising different types of farming, began to surface and were to contribute to a change in the leadership in 1944.[76] Whereas the IFF-National Agricultural Party element was wedded to fixity of land tenure, a number of Clann's Mayo TDs insisted on pursuing the question of redistributive land reform in a way their parliamentary party colleagues perceived to be threatening. Eventually matters were to come to a head when Patrick Cogan, the leading IFF figure behind the initial emergence of the National Agricultural Party, resigned from the Clann parliamentary party in 1946, in protest at the part played by two of his colleagues in an agitation over the sale of a Mayo farm.

It was against this background of internal party discord that the party found it impossible to build on earlier gains. The party's vote was to drop by 50 per cent in 1948 and to halve again in 1951.[77] The decision to participate in the two inter-party governments was to leave many of the originally pro-Fianna Fáil supporters that had found a home in Clann deeply alienated. The party's professedly non-political stance of maintaining independence of each of the main nationalist political groupings, one of its earliest and strongest attractions, was further compromised as it allowed itself to become progressively more identified with a reviving Fine Gael party in the 1950s. As if this was not bad enough, participation in government hastened the process whereby the party became little more than the constituency machines of what had, for all intents and purposes, become a dwindling band of independent TDs.

Saving the West

By the early 1960s Clann was as good as gone and Muintir, though having pushed forward in some of the western counties in the 1950s, was entering a phase in which its identity and organisational forms would become the subject of intense internal debate. The 1960s in the west were to witness the birth of a number of new rural defence mobilisations – principally the 'Charlestown Committee' (which after some years evolved into the 'Defence of the West' movement, less formally known as the 'Save the West' (STW) campaign)[78] and Gluaiseacht Chearta Sibhialta na Gaeltachta (the Gaeltacht Civil Rights Movement). Gluaiseacht's appearance was prompted by the dissatisfaction of a rising group of well-educated and politicised Gaeltacht men and women, at a time when civil rights campaigning elsewhere was giving encouragement to others, with the state's continuing inability to check the progressive economic and social decline of the remaining Gaeltacht areas (mainly along Ireland's western seaboard) where Irish continued to be the vernacular.[79] In comparison to Gluaiseacht it was the ongoing and accelerating destruction of the western smallholder class, and with it the main plank of the region's rural economy, that would become the prime focus of the STW campaign.

The campaign's central message was that only immediate and appropriate action would now stave off the terminal decline of the west of Ireland's smallholder population.

The STW campaign, as it developed, was built heavily around the leadership of the energetic Donegal priest, Fr McDyer, whose ability to speak with authority on the issue of western decline was based on his efforts to transform the economy of his own parish of Glencolumbkille. The Glencolumbkille experience, where the Errigal Co-operative Society had added to a series of earlier McDyer-instigated developments by entering into a joint venture with the Irish Sugar Company to grow and process local vegetables, was seen to provide the basis of a blueprint that other similarly situated western communities could reasonably hope to emulate.

The lesson Fr McDyer drew from what was unfolding in Glencolumbkille was that the fundamental solution to problems of western decline was to be found in local initiatives. 'People', in the Donegal priest's words, 'must not wait on governments or strangers to come and improve their lot. They must do it the hard way and that was to unite into community co-operatives and embark on a job creation spree'.[80] Henceforth communities would have to be mobilised around a development strategy which emphasised 'the right of local community groups to choose and implement their own development plans'.[81] The struggle to be waged both inside and outside Glencolumbkille was represented as 'a rebellion against paternalism and an assertion of the rights of communities to forge their own destinies'.[82]

To go by his own retrospective account, the issues of identity and culture were critical to the prospects for local collective action. 'Every nation', Fr McDyer was to write, 'should have the chance to strive to preserve its own identity and its own culture', and if efforts at preservation were to succeed then the 'ordinary people' would have to recognise their 'collective strength'.[83] The further one went from the locality, the more remote the prospects for true patriotism became. Unless the power of local communities was somehow strengthened, policy-making in Ireland would always remain insulated from popular democratic pressure.

It was also realised by Fr McDyer that places like Glencolumbkille, for all their individual vitality and promise, were always likely to be weak and vulnerable as long as they faced the mostly hostile political and economic forces of the outside world on their own. Reflecting on his Donegal experience, he suggested that 'we were so isolated that we could not be taken seriously'.[84] Only by creating alliances with the other Glencolumbkilles of the rural west could the whole approach he advocated hope to have a real impact.

At the public meeting where Fr McDyer spoke in Mayo in the first half of 1963, blame for the accelerating pattern of western economic and social decline was attributed in large part to decades of neglect by the independent state.[85] By no means, however, was it solely a question of official neglect. The inability of the smallholders to resist their own economic marginalisation at farm level, and the failure of western interests to build their own autonomous defensive organisations, had also to be given their due weight. Collective self-help initiatives may have held much of the answer to the west's rural problems, but the many obstacles that lay in the way of effective local initiatives were not ignored. Among the difficulties that would have to be tackled were those created by the authoritarian educational system, the tendency for emigration to result in the weaker elements being left behind and the dependency and apathy that were part and parcel of the 'dole' mentality.[86]

Even if numerous Glencolumbkilles could spring to life in the west this might not be enough to save the entire region from decline. Sometimes giving in to pessimism, Fr McDyer was ready to concede that the decline had perhaps gone too far to be reversed in some places. A state, in the best of all possible worlds, might be expected to put the common good first and so be prepared to turn with enthusiasm to the project of saving the west. But in the real world the official resolve to act, with such notable exceptions as that provided by the Sugar Company under General Costello's enlightened leadership, seemed to be fast disappearing and about to be replaced by a policy of betting on the strongest and allowing the smallholder communities of western Ireland to fade into oblivion. The new development strategy, associated with the moves towards trade liberalisation and the gradual acceptance of a policy of growth centres,[87] was read as bad news indeed for the remoter rural places. In this context, Fr McDyer made specific reference to 'the climate of opinion fostered by a group of economists who now openly declare the further dispersal of small communities in the west of Ireland to be not only in the nature of things, in an expanding economy, but a condition for economic expansion'.[88]

To accept such an analysis would be to give approval to a process of accelerating rural decline in the most disadvantaged regions. It was not sufficient to voice protest; the STW movement had to be innovative and come up with a viable alternative. This, of course, was where the value of the Glencolumbkille model – which in essence was based on a partnership-type relationship with a commercial state-sponsored company – was to come into its own.

The series of public meetings that marked the beginnings of the STW campaign in Mayo in 1963 were therefore aimed at raising public awareness of the dire economic and social predicament facing the rural west while at the same time holding Glencolumbkille up as the only real glimmer of hope on the horizon. Public meetings, convened with the idea of raising consciousness, attracting publicity and keeping the issue of western decline in the public mind, were in fact to become the central means relied upon to garner popular support for the STW's campaigning programme. These public meetings stimulated considerable popular interest, particularly in Mayo, the county in which the campaign made the best strides and where crowds of 400–500 people assembled to hear the analysis of the Donegal priest and his fellow activists.[89] Delegations to the Taoiseach and his cabinet colleagues were used to bring direct pressure to bear on the executive.

The prime intention in the STW movement was not so much to build a formal organisation that would see the creation of new groups, as it was to provide a means by which existing groups could link together and so become more effective than they could hope to be individually in promoting a programme of saving the west.[90] It is notable that where attempts were made to build an STW organisation of sorts (as in Mayo), these were to focus more on the county than on the province or even the wider western region (including Donegal). The pattern in Mayo was to encourage local branches of the National Farmers' Association, the Irish Countrywomen's Association and Chambers of Commerce to send delegates to general meetings of a county organisation and to nominate persons for membership of a county committee. Parishes, whose delegates were normally selected by the local clergy, were also requested to send two representatives. The Catholic clergy of the west, in fact, proved to be a major organisational resource for the STW campaign. 'It was a wonderful thing', Fr McDyer declared in Foxford in February 1965, 'to realise that in the hour of crisis Ireland had the bishops and priests behind it. The people of Mayo should be particularly pleased to see so many priests anxious to help out in the great movement to save the west'.[91]

How receptive was the ruling Fianna Fáil party to the STW campaign? Since 1963, when a request of the Charlestown Committee had prompted the government to reconvene the interdepartmental committee to consider a proposal to extend the Glencolumbkille approach by means of a series of 'pilot areas', considerable official attention had come to focus on the issues raised by the western campaigners.[92] By 1965 the campaign to save the smallholder west from disintegration had come up with a 10–point plan that consisted largely of demands for various types of state interventions. Among the elements of the plan were calls for the provision of grants, loans and subsidies to smallholders prepared to follow a farm plan; the empowering of the Irish Land Commission to sub-divide commonage; a programme of local drainage; the completion of sub-regional resource surveys; the teaching of rural science in schools; and the establishment of co-operatives in each parish.[93]

In the early months of 1965, with the prospect of a general election in the air, some politicians of the ruling Fianna Fáil party were apprehensive about the force of the anti-government protest which they associated with the STW campaign. The Minister for Agriculture, Charles J Haughey, on a visit to the west in January 1965, declared himself '... anxious to see officials and farmers and learn at first hand the background to the problems which face the western community'.[94] Back in the west again in April, Haughey outlined a programme for economic revival. At Belmullet he concluded his speech by pointing out that 'We [the Fianna Fáil government] regard this western revival as a national not a local problem and I give you a solemn assurance that no other matter will receive more unremitting and determined attention from the new Fianna Fáil government than the economic revival of the west'.[95]

County Mayo's Dáil Éireann candidates were asked to indicate their views on the movement's 10–point plan to save the west during the course of the election campaign.[96] To press home their perceived advantage, some of Fr McDyer's supporters wished to challenge the politicians directly at the polls. Fr McDyer, though successfully resisting attempts to politicise the campaign in this way,[97] was later to regret vetoing a suggestion to stage a mass protest meeting in Dublin so as to highlight official inaction on the question of western development.[98]

What did the STW campaign achieve? All in all, the commitments obtained from both the Taoiseach and the minister for agriculture were never, in the view of the movement's leadership, anywhere near adequate to meeting the scale of the western problem. Most importantly, the request that the state give the go-ahead for a scheme of Glencolumbkille-type ventures in the west was turned down. The pilot areas scheme that was offered was directed at individual farmers in the first instance, though the collective dimension to the challenge of smallholder survival was given considerable emphasis. As a demonstration exercise in indicating how income levels on small farms might be increased, the pilot areas scheme was judged to be largely a success.[99] Fr McDyer himself, however, considered the pilot area scheme to have failed because the individual pilot areas were scattered across too wide a territory to be effective.[100] At any rate the approach associated with the pilot area scheme never went beyond the pilot phase, and the whole pro-smallholder position that Fr McDyer and his followers stood for was to be swept from the policy agenda once Ireland joined the Common Market and the Common Agricultural Policy displaced national structural policies.

Reflecting on the events of the 1960s after the elapse of more than a decade, Fr McDyer conceded rather pessimistically that his movement was always 'too dissipated to be a success'.[101] As there was 'no chance to return to any location and consolidate', the level of local organisation achieved by the movement could never be anything but meagre.[102] The threat the campaign posed to the political establishment was to be relatively short-lived. Three reasons above all can be suggested for why this was so: the failure to win an early policy success with the pilot areas proposal of 1963 and so sustain the momentum built up on the strength of Glencolumbkille; the excessive dependence on Fr McDyer whose credibility rested on the continued success of the Glencolumbkille experiment;[103] and the inability to transform the consciousness that had been raised around the issue of western decline into a more challenging (as against largely defensive) force. Once Fr McDyer disengaged in 1968 the movement quickly disintegrated.[104]

Conclusion

Each of the three movements we have been considering was born out of crisis conditions that had come to be regarded as life-threatening in their implications for rural communities (in Muintir's assessment), for farmers as a class (in the Clann analysis) and for western smallholders (as was the contention of the STW campaign). In thinking about how these various crises had come about, the same analysis came to be shared in a number of respects. We find it being suggested, more explicitly in some cases than in others, that nationalist politicians were failing to provide the people of rural Ireland with adequate representation. The genesis of the various crises conditions to which these rural movements directed their attention was relatedly seen to be rooted largely in what state policy had done or failed to do.

Essentially each of the three cases presents a populist-type analysis which was critical of the way large-scale political forces were operating. The people, it was agreed, would have to be empowered at the expense of politicians and the state if the forces that were marginalising local communities, farmers as a class and the entire west of Ireland were to be effectively combated. The inclination in each case was to look to collective action as the means of bringing threatening large-scale forces under popular control and of returning power to the people. Building a capacity for collective action among those victimised by the *status quo* was therefore taken to be the *sine qua non* of progressive social, economic and political change. In the context of this capacity-building process, another notable feature of these movements was that their leaderships saw what they were doing as fitting within a rural tradition of popular resistance that had its most spectacular flowering in the Land League of the late 19th century.[105]

Where, on the other hand, the ideologues of our three movements parted company was in the way they conceived of the people, in the approaches they adopted to collective action and in the solutions they brought forward to deal with the various crises of the Irish countryside. From one perspective, what we have in our three movements are different attempts to imagine the people as comprising a class (farmers/smallholders in Clann's case), as local communities (Muintir) and as the west of Ireland as a distinct region (the STW campaign). Clann began as a popular anti-government mobilisation which aspired to become a farmers' trade union. Gradually it was to evolve into a political party, albeit a professedly 'non-political' one. Muintir commenced its career as an alliance of producers' co-operatives only to quickly transform itself into a federation of local, parish-based community groups. The loosely-structured and short-lived regional protest STW campaign had its real origins in the idea that the sort of innovations being pioneered in Glencolumbkille could somehow be generalised into a programme capable of revitalising the western region as a whole. The STW campaign might have grown into a political party of sorts but, under the leadership of Fr McDyer, this was not to be.

How well did the three movements succeed in mobilising the people for collective action? These movements may have claimed to speak for the people, but the actual support they could command was, in certain respects, quite limited. Nor did their claims to represent the people go uncontested.[106] When compared with the two main nationalist political parties, that of Fianna Fáil especially, none of these movements managed to achieve a genuinely nationwide appeal or coverage. Clann's aspiration was to transform Irish farmers into a powerful political class. Yet, its results at the polls in 1943 and 1944, while not without promise, did not amount to a mould-shattering breakthrough. Eventually the party ended up holding a handful of 'safe' Dáil seats, but found it impossible to put down serious roots outside the western counties of Galway, Mayo and Roscommon. Muintir's core strength remained stubbornly tied to a number of the Munster counties, though the 1950s did see it breaking into new territory in the west. It is hard to be definite about the size of the support commanded by the STW campaign, but there is no mistaking how heavily this popular mobilisation was concentrated in Mayo and Galway. Even there, little formal organisation to speak of was put in place and, compared with Muintir or Clann, its appearance on the public stage was to be a very fleeting one.

Our three movements may have aspired to return power to the people, but did they attempt to be 'participative' in the way they organised themselves? Is there a sense in which these movements, by virtue of depending so critically on a coterie of committed and relatively well-educated leading activists, cannot qualify as popular at all? Those who spoke on behalf of these movements, though few in number, did of course claim to be of 'the people' and to be capable of giving public voice to the people's concerns. There can be no doubt but that each of them managed to attract a following, though without the leadership supplied by priests (in the cases of Muintir and the STW campaign) it is hard to imagine them ever getting off the ground. In addition, the manner in which the leadership provided by Catholic priests was to supply Muintir and the STW campaign with their distinctive organisational forms is unmistakable. Fr Hayes's approach, in putting together the second version of Muintir (based on the parish councils/guilds), was not only to consult widely but to look beyond 'the people' by soliciting the views of 'some of the best brains in the country'.[107]

The second version of Muintir may have insisted on the necessity of reserving a place for the rural labouring interest in the parish councils, but it was founded on an acceptance of the prevailing class and 'sectional' structures of Irish society. The rural middle class (including many parish clergy) tended to hold the local level leadership positions both in Muintir and in the STW campaign. Muintir's early anti-urban ideology contrasts strikingly with the reality of urban and town domination at the higher reaches of the movement's organisation.[108] It is quite impossible to imagine the STW campaign in the absence of Fr McDyer's contribution.[109] Fr McDyer, for his part, recognised the importance of working with local professionals, such as teachers and agricultural advisers.[110] Several commentators have drawn attention to the Donegal priest's excessively authoritarian style of leadership.[111] No less than much of the local leadership, the top leadership of Clann was firmly in the hands of more substantial farmers.[112]

How anti-establishment were these movements in practice? Leaving aside the often stridently anti-establishment tone of the early Clann's rhetoric, the party, in its attempts to steer state policy in a certain direction, quickly settled into the established patterns of party politics and government in Ireland. At one level, Fr Hayes was keen to place a distance between his movement and the state. We have only to look, however, at Muintir's involvement with the parish plan and the post-war rural electrification campaign to see how quickly the state bulked large in its analysis of what needed to be done. However insistent Fr McDyer may have been that all the advances made in Glencolumbkille were 'achieved not by politicians or bureaucrats but by local people',[113] he and his followers clearly saw the survival of his Donegal parish, and all the other Glencolumbkilles of the western periphery (observe the STW's 10–point plan of 1965, for instance), as critically dependent on the right type of state assistance.

Try as they might, of course, none of these movements succeeded in their attempts to pressure the state into taking action sufficient to halt the atrophy of rural communities, the progressive disappearance of smallholders as a class and the process of regional decline, especially in the remoter pockets of the west. This failure can largely be read as evidence of how much the power of large-scale centralising economic and political forces lay beyond the efforts of what were at most unevenly (if not always weakly) organised collective actors to control.

NOTES

1. See Tom Garvin, *The evolution of Irish nationalist politics* (Dublin, 1981) pp 106–118.
2. See Patrick Bolger, *The Irish Co-operative Movement* (Dublin, 1977). As it turned out, the dairy co-operatives were to be one strand of the movement whereby 'women were driven out of the industry' (Joanna Bourke, *Husbandry to housewifery: women, economic change and housework in Ireland* (Oxford, 1993) p 81. For a variety of reasons Irish nationalists tended to be '... generally hostile to the economic reforms embodied in the cooperative programme' (see Liam Kennedy, *Colonialism, religion and nationalism in Ireland* (Belfast, 1996) p 145).
3. See Liam O'Dowd, 'Church, state and women: the aftermath of partition' in Chris Curtin *et al* (eds) *Gender in Irish society* (Galway, 1987) p 11.
4. Emmet O'Connor, *Syndicalism in Ireland* (Cork, 1988) pp 74–6, 33–53.
5. Ibid, pp 114–127, 157–64.
6. Daniel Bradley, *Farm labourers: Irish struggle 1900–1976* (Belfast, 1988) p 74.
7. See RE Kennedy, *The Irish, emigration, marriage and fertility* (Los Angeles, 1973) pp 95–109.
8. See LM Cullen, 'Irish economic history: fact and myth' in LM Cullen (ed) *The formation of the Irish economy* (Cork, 1969) pp 120–2; Liam Kennedy and DS Johnson, 'The Union of Ireland and Britain, 1801–1921' in DG Boyce and Alan O'Day, *The making of modern Irish history: revisionism and the revisionist controversy* (London, 1996) pp 49–59.
9. Griffith did not find it far-fetched to suggest that, were it not for the Act of Union, an economy capable of supporting a population of 20 millions would have existed in Ireland by 1911 (RP Davis, *Arthur Griffith and non-violent Sinn Féin* (Dublin, 1974) p 130).
10. See Paul Bew, *Conflict and conciliation in Ireland 1890–1910: Parnellites and radical agrarians* (Oxford, 1987); Philip Bull, *Land, politics and nationalism: a study of the Irish land question* (Dublin, 1996); Paul Bew, 'Sinn Féin, agrarian radicalism and the war of independence, 1919–1921' in DG Boyce (ed) *The revolution in Ireland 1879–1923* (Dublin, 1988) pp 217–234; DS Jones, *Graziers, land reform, and political conflict in Ireland* (Washington, DC, 1995); Tony Varley, 'Agrarian crime and social control: Sinn Féin and the land question in the west of Ireland in 1920' in Mike Tomlinson *et al* (eds) *Whose law and order? Aspects of crime and social control in Ireland* (Belfast, 1988) pp 54–75.
11. See KT Hoppen, *Ireland since 1800: conflict & conformity* (London, 1989) p 133; Terence Brown, *Ireland: a social and cultural history 1922–1981* (London, 1981) pp 56–7; Patrick Maume, *DP Moran* (Dublin, 1995); Marcus de Búrca, *The GAA: a history* (Dublin, 1980) pp 27, 90–1.
12. One consequence of this, as Whitaker points out, was that rural science which had been a compulsory national school subject until 1934 'was dropped to permit of increased attention to Irish', *Economic Development* (Dublin, 1958) p 238.
13. See TK Daniel, 'Griffith on his noble head: the determinants of Cumann na nGaedheal economic policy, 1922–32', in *Irish Economic and Social History*, vol 3, (1976) pp 55–65.
14. See Joseph Lee, 'Centralisation and community', in Joseph Lee (ed) *Ireland:*

towards a sense of place (Dublin, 1985) p 84; Liam O'Dowd, 'Town and country in Irish ideology', *Canadian Journal of Irish Studies*, vol 2, no 2 (1987) p 48.

15. The formation of Fianna Fáil, as a political party representing the defeated side in the civil war, and the peaceful transfer of power to the anti-Treatyites after the general election of 1932, were to mark critical junctures in the history of the constitutional tendency in Irish politics.
16. See ME Daly, *Industrial development and Irish national identity, 1922–1939* (Dublin, 1992).
17. See Peter Moser, Staatliche und Bäuerliche Vorstellunger einer Landreform: Die Auseinandersetzungen um die Landnutzung im Westen Irlands, *Schweizerische Zeitschrift für Geschichte*, vol 40 (1990) pp 30–54; ME Daly, *Industrial development and Irish national identity, 1922–1939* (Dublin, 1992) p 181; JJ Smyth and TA Boylan, 'Industrialisation and the contribution of multinational companies to economic development in County Mayo, in T Varley et al (eds) *Rural crisis: perspectives on Irish rural development*, (Galway, 1991) p 158; J Anthony Gaughan, (ed) *Memoirs of Senator Joseph Connolly (1885–1961)* (Dublin, 1996) pp 379–80; MAG Ó Tuathaigh, 'The land question, politics and Irish society, 1922–1960', in PJ Drudy (ed) *Ireland: land, politics and people* (Cambridge, 1982) p 185.
18. Jerome Toner, *Rural Ireland* (Dublin, 1955) p 51.
19. Stephen Rynne, *Father John Hayes* (Dublin, 1960) p 103.
20. Interview, Tom Fitzgerald, Tipperary, 20 August 1998. Tom Fitzgerald, who has now been employed by Muintir for almost 50 years, accompanied the founder up and down the country to Muintir meetings in the 1950s.
21. The interests of grain farmers who wanted to sell dear and pig farmers who wanted to buy cheap feed, for instance, were always inclined to move in different directions (Rynne, *Father John Hayes*, p 107).
22. The prospects for Muintir na Tíre Ltd appear to have been badly 'hampered by the often bitter conflict between farmers and their labourers'. In fact, many of those who subscribed to Muintir na Tíre Ltd appear to have been 'urban based professionals such as solicitors and doctors' (Eoin Devereux, 'Saving rural Ireland – Muintir na Tíre and its anti-urbanism, 1931–1958', in *Canadian Journal of Irish Studies*, vol 17, no 2 (December 1991) pp 25, 26).
23. JH Whyte, *Church and state in Modern Ireland, 1923–1979* (Dublin, 1980) p 67.
24. Apparently it was at the Fermoy rural weekend in 1935 that the decision was taken to build a movement based on 'parish guilds' (Rynne, *Father John Hayes*, p 137).
25. Rynne, *Father John Hayes*, p 103.
26. The recollection of Stephen Rynne, a prominent Muintir enthusiast, was that the 'rural week-ends' attracted the participation of 'a mixture of serious experts, idealists, cranks and crack-pots' (Rynne, *Father John Hayes*, p 137).
27. Fr Hayes, 'The beginning', *Muintir na Tíre Official Handbook 1941*, p 45.
28. Ibid, p 46.
29. Ibid, p 46.
30. Ibid, p 46.
31. Jeremiah Newman, 'The "specific situation" of Ireland in relation to community development', in Jeremiah Newman (ed) *Organising the community* (Tipperary, 1963) pp 20–4. About the involvement of women Fr Hayes wrote: 'Muintir na Tíre has a place for the women of the parish also. It has

never forgotten their importance. In some Guilds and Councils they have their own sections and in others they take their place representing the sections of their calling' (Fr Hayes, 'The beginning', *Muintir na Tíre Official Handbook 1941*, p 47).

32. Eoin Devereux, 'Muintir na Tíre: the theory and practice of community development, 1931–1988', unpublished MA thesis, University College Galway, 1988, p 92.
33. Ibid, p 92.
34. Eoin Devereux, 'The lonely furrow: Muintir na Tíre and Irish community development, 1931–1991', in *Community Development Journal*, vol 28, no 1 (1993) p 49.
35. Ibid, p 51.
36. See the Muintir publication, *Rural Week Record* (Tipperary, 1942) pp 28, 39, 101–6.
37. Jerome Toner, *Rural Ireland* (Dublin, 1955) pp 35–9; Rynne, *Father John Hayes*, pp 242–3; Michael Shiel, *The quiet revolution: the electrification of rural Ireland* (Dublin, 1984) pp 180–2. The organisational growth of the late 1940s and early 1950s, in fact, has been very much linked to the eagerness with which parish councils threw themselves behind the rural electrification campaign and competed with one another to be first to get the power (Michael Mernagh, 'The relationship between Muintir na Tíre and the government in Ireland', unpublished Diploma in Community Development dissertation, Department of Adult Education, University of Manchester, 1970, pp 43–5; JDR O'Connor, 'The origins, ethos and geographical expansion of Muintir na Tíre 1931–1970', unpublished MA thesis, University College Cork, 1988, pp 138–9, 149).
38. In seeking to represent the interests of Irish farmers, Muintir found that its credentials were questioned by specialised agricultural interest groups such as the young farmers' movement, Macra na Feirme (formed in 1944), and the National Farmers' Association (formed in 1955) (Rynne, *Father John Hayes*, pp 261–2). According to Devereux, 'the leadership of the three organisations openly clashed on the question as to which organisation was more entitled to represent the inhabitants of rural Ireland' (Devereux, 'Muintir na Tíre: the theory and practice of community development, 1931–1988', p 16).
39. Conflict between 'urban' and 'rural' sections, it seems, led to the collapse of one County Cork guild (Devereux, 'The lonely furrow', p 51).
40. Ibid, p 50.
41. Patrick McNabb, 'Social structure', in Jeremiah Newman (ed) *The Limerick rural survey* (Tipperary, 1964) p 208.
42. Mart Bax, *Harpstrings and confessions: machine-style politics in the Irish Republic* (Assen/Amsterdam, 1976) pp 94, 152.
43. Lorelei Harris, 'Class, community and sexual divisions in north Mayo', in Chris Curtin *et al* (eds) *Culture and ideology in Ireland* (Galway, 1984) pp 163–4.
44. Chris Eipper, *The ruling trinity: a community study of church, state and business in Ireland* (Aldershot, 1986) pp 56–7.
45. Rynne, *Father John Hayes*, p 113.
46. Ibid, p 113.
47. Ibid, p 119.

48. Ibid, p 136.
49. Ibid, pp 170–1. See JDR O'Connor, 'The origins, ethos and geographical Expansion of Muintir na Tíre 1931–1970' pp 112–3; 153.
50. Devereux, 'The lonely furrow', p 50.
51. Devereux, 'Muintir na Tíre: the theory and practice of community development, 1931–1988', pp 93–4.
52. Mernagh, 'The relationship between Muintir na Tíre and the government in Ireland', p 32.
53. Rynne, *Father John Hayes*, p 118.
54. Ibid, pp 118–9.
55. Devereux, 'The lonely furrow', pp 50–1.
56. See, for instance, the movement's own journal, *Landmark* (vol 7, no 6 (1950) p 8; vol 19, no 8 (1962) p 12; vol 24, no 3 (1967) p 18).
57. Jerome Toner, *Rural Ireland* (Dublin, 1955) p 54. See Mernagh, 'The relationship between Muintir na Tíre and the government in Ireland', pp 33–8.
58. Mernagh, 'The relationship between Muintir na Tíre and the government in Ireland', pp 33–8.
59. Devereux, 'The lonely furrow', p 51.
60. See Diarmuid Ó Cearbhaill and Tony Varley, 'An Irish community development movement's experience of crisis conditions: Muintir na Tíre's struggle for survival', *Journal of the Community Development Society*, vol 27, no 1 (1996) pp 1–16.
61. The chances, in the view expressed by the movement's first leader, Michael Donnellan, were that Clann na Talmhan would never have seen the light of day were it not for the actions of the Fianna Fáil Minister for Agriculture, Dr James Ryan (*Parliamentary Debates Dáil Éireann*, vol 91, col 64, 1 July 1943).
62. *Connacht Tribune*, 25 February 1939.
63. *Irish Press*, 4 June 1943.
64. *Connacht Tribune*, 25 February 1939; *Irish Farmers' Paper*, vol 1, no 9, April 1942.
65. *Connacht Tribune*, 29 July 1939; M Donnellan, Commission on Vocational Organisation. Minutes of Evidence, National Library of Ireland, MS 931, 18 April 1941, p 3186.
66. *Connacht Tribune*, 25 May 1940; 30 March 1940; *Irish Independent*, 9 April 1943; *Irish Farmers' Paper*, vol 2, no 9 (June 1943).
67. *Irish Farmers' Paper*, vol 2, no 1 (July 1942).
68. This group had its origins in the United Farmers' Protection Association, which had been active in the no rent/rates campaign waged in the mid 1930s against the Fianna Fáil-controlled state (EF Bobbett, Commission on Vocational Organisation. Minutes of Evidence, National Library of Ireland, MS 929, 24 October 1940, pp 2635–6).
69. Ibid, p 2635.
70. This had been granted in England and Northern Ireland in 1929.
71. *Connacht Tribune*, 8 July 1939. For further details, see Tony Varley, 'Farmers against nationalists: the rise and fall of Clann na Talmhan in Galway', in Gerard Moran and Raymond Gillespie (eds) *Galway: history & society* (Dublin, 1996) pp 589–622.
72. The IFF had officially registered itself as a trade union in 1937 (*Farmers' Gazette*, 13 March 1937).

73. M Donnellan, Commission on Vocational Organisation. Minutes of Evidence, National Library of Ireland, MS 931, 18 April 1941, p 3191.
74. The IFF continued in existence as a farmers' trade union after the National Agricultural Party's formation.
75. Besides the ten Clann members, there were as many as six independent farmer TDs who ominously decided to keep their distance from the new party.
76. In this change, Joseph Blowick, a large Mayo farmer with a Blueshirt background, came to replace the more dynamic (albeit somewhat volatile) Donnellan.
77. Richard Sinnott, *Irish voters decide: voting behaviour in elections and referendums since 1918* (Manchester, 1995) p 62.
78. See James McDyer, *Fr McDyer of Glencolumbkille: an autobiography* (Dingle, 1982) p 84. Since the activities of the Charlestown Committee and Defence of the West revolved around Fr James McDyer and are now remembered indistinguishably as 'Save the West', our approach will be to treat them together as the 'Save the West' campaign.
79. See Michie Akutagawa, 'A linguistic minority under the protection of its own ethnic state: a case study in an Irish Gaeltacht', in Gearóid Mac Eoin, Anders Ahlqvist and Donncha Ó hAodha (eds) *Third international conference on minority languages: Celtic papers* (London, 1987); Donncha Ó hÉallaithe, 'Níl sibh ceart agus níl sibh sibhialta!', *Pléaráca '92*, (2), 1992, pp 20–4.
80. McDyer, *Fr McDyer*, p 84.
81. Vincent Tucker, 'State and community: a case study of Glencolumbkille', in Chris Curtin and Thomas Wilson (eds) *Ireland from below: social change and local communities* (Galway, 1987) p 287.
82. McDyer, *Fr McDyer*, p 109. All these assertions, of course, have to be set against the state's critical involvement in the Glencolumbkille experiment – the Irish Sugar Company was a commercial state-sponsored company and the vegetable processing factory had been grant assisted by the state.
83. Ibid, p 16.
84. Ibid, p 79.
85. Dismay at the high level of out-migration, the closure of branch railway lines, and the growing burden of the property rates figured prominently as recurring themes in Fr McDyer's speeches (*Western People*, 18 March 1963; 15 June 1963).
86. See McDyer, *Fr McDyer*, pp 27, 50, 56.
87. It was ultimately to be the Buchanan report, which opted for a policy of focusing development in a handful of regional growth centres, that came to be popularly seen as summing up the official intention for the remoter rural areas (see Liam O'Dowd, 'Town and country in Irish ideology', in *Canadian Journal of Irish Studies*, vol 12, no 2 (1987) pp 49–50).
88. Inter-Departmental Committee on the Problems of Small Western Farms, *Report on pilot area development* (Dublin, 1965) p 19. TK Whitaker's famous report, *Economic development*, contains the following passage: 'In our present circumstances, with virtually the whole country undeveloped, it seems wasteful to subsidise remote areas especially by providing more extensive grants. Special subsidisation of this kind entails additional burdens on the community as a whole and retards progress in the more suitable areas where

concentrated effort could give better results', *Economic development* (Dublin, 1958) p 160.

89. Apparently, crowds of 300 to 400 persons, with public officials also attending, were drawn to County Galway meetings (*Connacht Tribune*, 11 November 1966, p 1).
90. 'To the ICA [Irish Countrywomen's Association], all Development Associations, Chambers of Commerce, Tourist Bodies, Fishing Groups and all farming groups', Fr McDyer announced, 'we extend a gesture of co-operation to work together and submerge individual and sectional interests' (*Connacht Tribune*, 6 August 1966, p 1).
91. *Western People*, 6 February 1965, p 3.
92. As well as vegetable processing factories, the Charlestown Committee envisaged that pig fattening stations be placed in these proposed pilot areas (See Inter-Departmental Committee on the Problems of Small Western Farms, *Report on pilot area development*, pp 7–8, 3).
93. *Western People*, 23 January 1965, p 1.
94. *Western People*, 9 January 1965, p 1.
95. *Western People*, 3 April 1965, p 1.
96. *Western People*, 3 April 1965, p 9.
97. In his autobiography, Fr McDyer writes that he opposed the suggestion for the reason that a priest could play no part in 'divisive' party politics (McDyer, *Fr McDyer*, p 85).
98. Ibid, p 85.
99. For a discussion of the scheme and the nature of the work undertaken in the 12 pilot areas between 1964/65 and 1969/70, see John J Scully, *Agriculture in the west of Ireland: a study of the low farm income problem* (Dublin, 1971).
100. McDyer, *Fr McDyer*, p 86.
101. Ibid, pp 84–5. The campaign against Irish membership of the Common Market in which he actively participated also failed, in his opinion, because it was 'too geographically dispersed', p 87.
102. Ibid, p 85.
103. Before long the whole co-operative-based approach in Glencolumbkille began to run into very serious trouble, with the Errigal Co-operative showing an accumulated loss of £37,000 by 1965 (see Vincent Tucker, 'Community development through co-operatives: a case study of Glencolumbkille in the northwest of Ireland', unpublished PhD dissertation, Washington University, 1984, p 248; McDyer, *Fr McDyer*, pp 79–80).
104. Apparently he was obliged to do this for health reasons and out of a desire to pay closer attention to the spiritual and material affairs of Glencolumbkille. On his own admission, Fr McDyer had always been reluctant to over-involve himself in the wider movement if this meant spreading himself too thinly and if it involved neglecting his clerical duties in Glencolumbkille (*Fr McDyer*, p 84).
105. Some continuities of personnel are observable as well. We find, for instance, some Clann activists and some units of Muintir becoming active in the STW campaign in Mayo (see *Western People*, 9 November 1963; 2 January 1965).
106. In the case of the so-called parish plan, we have seen how Muintir's claims to represent the farming community was challenged by more specialised farming interests. In the recent period, the claim of Muintir-affiliated local

community councils to be the democratically constituted mouthpiece for local interests has regularly been contested by other community groups as well as by local politicians. See Diarmuid Ó Cearbhaill and Tony Varley, 'Community group/state relationships: the case of west of Ireland community councils', in Reginald Byron (ed) *Public policy and the periphery: problems and prospects in marginal regions* (Belfast, 1988) p 289.

107. Fr Hayes, 'The beginning', *Muintir na Tíre Official Handbook 1941*, 1941, p 45.
108. Eoin Devereux, 'Saving rural Ireland: Muintir na Tíre and its anti-urbanism, 1931–1958', in *Canadian Journal of Irish Studies*, vol 17, no 2 (December 1991) p 25.
109. The Taoiseach, Seán Lemass, speaking at the formal launch of the Errigal co-operative in 1962, went so far as to say: 'If there was a Father McDyer in every area, the whole situation would soon be greatly improved' (see National Archives, Department of the Taoiseach, 'Gaeltacht and congested areas: permanent organisation for economic and social development', S15054 D/62).
110. McDyer, *Fr McDyer*, pp 58–60.
111. See Colm Regan and Proinnsias Breathnach, *State and community: rural development strategies in the Slieve League peninsula, Co. Donegal* (Maynooth 1981) pp 52–4; Tucker, 'Community development through co-operatives', pp 290–4; LJ Taylor, *Occasions of faith: an anthropology of Irish Catholics* (Philadelphia, 1995) pp 142–3.
112. The IFF's dynamic secretary, Elizabeth F Bobbett, stands out as the only woman active in the leadership ranks of the farming groups we have been discussing.
113. McDyer, *Fr McDyer*, p 108.

Chapter 6

Images of Development and Underdevelopment in Glencolumbkille, County Donegal, 1830–1970

Vincent Tucker

The standard image of underdevelopment is one of regions and peoples removed from the centres of government, remote from the hub of enterprise and innovation, stagnant and lacking in dynamism, indeed resistant to change. They are viewed as lacking in resources and living lives which are flawed and unsatisfying. They are described as 'backward', 'peripheral', 'traditional' or 'underdeveloped', all of these descriptions indicating that the societies in question are deficient and on the margins when compared to the more 'advanced', 'modern' or 'developed' societies. They are portrayed as being left behind by the great universal historical processes which constitute progress and development. Development is represented as the process whereby these 'marginal' peoples or regions are integrated into the more dynamic sectors of society through mechanisms of planning, restructuring and social engineering. Perceived in this way, development and underdevelopment are unproblematic notions and can be regarded as self evident. The agreed objective standards of development are comparative ones based on economic or productivist criteria, but also on notions of governance and law. Seen in this way, the goals of development and the direction in which societies must move are taken as given. To use Marx's phrase, the more developed societies show the underdeveloped societies the face of their future.

Much development thinking is subject to what one African scholar has called an 'evolutionary hallucination'[1] whereby places which are more remote from the designated centres of development are imagined as being further back in time. Armed with this pervasive social imagery,

Conrad sailing up the Congo river and more recently anthropologists visiting rain forest villages could imagine themselves as travelling back in time. Likewise, government agents and travellers following the coast road from Donegal town to Glencolumbkille imagined themselves travelling back to another era in history, to places which had somehow been left behind by time and its sister progress in their universal march onwards. Viewed in this way the societies in question were regarded as representatives of an earlier form of life, of the way in which our remote ancestors lived. They were without history, and were denied contemporaneity. That they would inevitably change or disappear was, in accordance with the Enlightenment vision of progress, inevitable. But notions of *progress*, *modernisation* and *development* implied more than a way of seeing peoples as *underdeveloped*: they also implied a moral imperative to transform them; to extend the benefits of *civilisation* and *development* to all, even to the most remote corners of the world. The road to development was through integration into the larger society. These notions implied a project which was at once an economic and a moral enterprise. What was referred to as the 'white man's burden' in Africa was the task of the improving landlords in Ireland. The natives were to be improved, regulated and, to use Foucault's term, disciplined.

Some 20 years ago when I began research in Glencolumbkille, County Donegal, my approach to the area was strongly influenced by the writings of dependency and world systems theorists who challenged the notion that underdevelopment was some primal condition, or a way of describing the economic status of a 'traditional' society. From a dependency perspective underdevelopment was not a state but a process. It was part of the same process that produced development, thus the phrase 'the development of underdevelopment'. According to dependency theorists, societies were underdeveloped not simply because of indigenous factors, nor because they had not yet been integrated into the developed economy and society, but precisely because of the way in which they had been integrated into the larger systems. Samir Amin made the point succinctly: '... the essential fact is left out, namely: that the underdeveloped countries form part of a world system; that the history of their integration into the system forged their special structure – which thenceforth has nothing in common with what prevailed before their integration into the modern world'.[2]

I wanted to see the relevance of such global theoretical perspectives for a microcosm on the periphery of the periphery. I wanted to examine the way in which south-west Donegal, and in particular Glencolumbkille, had been integrated into the wider world and to analyse the impact of this on the local society.

Coming from an anthropological perspective I was also aware that much development theorising did not pay sufficient attention to the specificity of different localities and tended to treat local societies as pawns in the great historical processes which swept over them, whether these were conceived of as development or underdevelopment. But while they were subjected to processes of domination and exploitation they did not submit passively. A more adequate account would need to take into consideration the varying ways in which they adapted, accommodated, manipulated or resisted the transformations to which they were subjected. In the process, they also shaped and transformed the larger social systems and produced their own discourses. Such an account would also need to consider the fact that small-scale societies are not homogeneous in their interests. Various local actors and sections of the community have different interests, gain and lose in different ways from the transformations, and have different relationships with the larger systems.

Recently, the subject of development studies has taken a more interpretative or reflexive turn. In the light of these new approaches, this chapter reassesses the Glencolumbkille study and complements the political economy insights of dependency theory by the addition of cultural analysis. It is now recognised that development is both an ideological and a material project. It is a moral as well as an economic enterprise which serves particular interests and not others. The taken for granted discourses of *modernisation*, *underdevelopment* and *development* are being subjected to scrutiny and their social imagery traced to the sets of interests which constructed them historically.[3] While dependency theorists helped us identify the interests served by development and modernisation they did not question the goals or meaning of development. Modernisation theorists, Marxists and neo-Marxists all shared a materialistic notion of development. The desirability and universality of the goals of this approach have now been challenged. It follows that the meaning of development can no longer be taken for granted. It too has become contested terrain and depends upon the location of the actors.

This chapter examines the development encounter as experienced in Glencolumbkille, a rural community in south-west Donegal. It explores the social ecology of this area, the interrelationship of land, social organisation, and development processes which are at once economic, military, religious, scientific and cultural.

The first part of the chapter examines the changing relationship of the population to land and sea, from the period immediately before 1845 and the Great Famine, until the 1880s, which for Glencolumbkille was the time of greatest hardship. For Glencolumbkille, the Famine was not a cataclysmic event which once and for all transformed society: this famine and subsequent famines were symptoms of a process of ecological destabilisation. It is argued that this resulted from a process of development carried out in south-west Donegal between the 1830s and the 1880s under a colonial regime.

The second part looks at the post-World War Two period, the era of modernisation. In the post-colonial period, a new development discourse, which had deliberately distanced itself from the taints of colonialism, emerged under Truman in the United States. Taken up at Bretton Woods it soon became a global discourse under the aegis of the Marshall Plan, the International Monetary Fund, the World Bank and the United Nations. This discourse promised the 'modernisation of traditional societies'. The modernising project was taken up with confidence by postcolonial regimes throughout the world. It became the flavour of the day from 1945 until the 1960s and later. It was enthusiastically adopted by the Irish Department of Finance under TK Whitaker and formed the basis for Ireland's first development plans. From the peripheralised regions things looked different and Fr McDyer of Glencolumbkille, echoing the dependency theorists, saw it as 'sounding the death knell for small farmers'. An alternative development discourse emerged challenging the vision of government planners. It echoed and indeed appropriated aspects of the oppositional discourse of the previous century, advocating a return to communal farming arrangements as the most rational solution to the development of the area and indeed of the entire west coast.

Glencolumbkille and the Wider World

The province of Ulster had long been the most impenetrable stronghold of Gaelic resistance to outside domination. With the defeat of the great Northern chieftains O'Neill and O'Donnell in Kinsale in 1601, the Gaelic overlords were swept away and James I set about colonising Ulster in the same way as he had settled the Scottish Highlands, with Scottish and English planters. In 1610, the Plantation Commission made its camp near Donegal town and published its list of divisions. South-west Donegal was declared one unit and reserved for lowland Scottish settlers. But, as reported in Poynars' survey in 1619, the plantation was not a success as it failed to attract sufficient settlers, and so the substructure of Gaelic society remained in place without any substantial change in their economy or settlement patterns.

Despite the apparent remoteness of the place, with its rugged landscape and lack of roads, Glencolumbkille had substantial links with the wider world. From 1327 until 1568, Teelin is prominently featured as an important fishery. Arthur Dobbs, writing in 1729, described the fisheries:

> ... the greatest quantity of the best cod and ling in Europe, is among the Lewes and Western Isles of Scotland, and upon the banks to the westward of them which extend to Killybegs and Sligo, in Ireland, and a great many leagues to sea westward. It was there the great fishery was, which supplied Europe before the discovery of Newfoundland. There the French and Biscayers supplied themselves, and all the southern and western coasts of Europe with cod and ling.[4]

Accounts by Arthur Young from 1776 attest to a booming herring industry with 47 boats in Teelin harbour. Nearby Killybegs was known to have several hundred sailing vessels there at one time purchasing or curing herring.[5] This international trade was further boosted by bounties on shipped herring paid by the English government. The catch was shipped to England from Teelin in 100 ton boats owned by the local landlord and other entrepreneurs. The local fishermen were at this time quite dependent on the cash economy particularly in view of the declining agricultural holdings and increasing rents.[6]

With the fall in prices at the end of the Napoleonic wars this trade ended and the merchant ships no longer called. There was also the disappearance of the herring shoals from the inshore area, the domain of the local small boats. Larger Scottish and English trawlers continued to fish the deep waters while local fishermen remained idle. However, the local fishermen were later to become involved in fishing for cod and ling, fish that the merchant fleet had never shown an interest in. Despite the fact that the international herring fishery based in Killybegs had disintegrated by 1823, local fishing continued and salted fish were a basic source of cash for the fishermen. They were traded across the bay to Connaught and were also transported overland by 'carters' who were local traders with donkeys and carts.[7]

The growth of this new middleman trader class created a double dependency on the part of the local farmers and fishermen. They were dependent on these merchants to sell their produce for them but were also dependent on them for the purchase of basic commodities and materials. Once this pattern had been established, local producers and consumers had little choice. They were at the mercy of middlemen and of market and political forces over which they had no control. As they had to wait until crops were harvested, animals fattened and sold, and fish marketed, in order to obtain cash they were forced to obtain credit from the merchants. The interest rates were high and were considered 'usurious' by the inspectors. It was this practice by the merchant money lenders which gave rise to the contemptuous title 'gombeen man'. Most of the population were in debt to these merchants and in many cases were obliged to hand over land in lieu of payment. This process created a new class of considerable wealth and resources. With the creation of the town of Carrick by Connolly, the landlord, in 1840, most of these people settled to become shopkeepers. These traders had a monopoly and were in a position to control trade in both directions. Like peripheralised areas elsewhere in the world, Glencolumbkille found itself at the end of a chain of exchanges in which it paid the highest prices for imported commodities and was paid lowest prices for what it produced.

Despite its vulnerability to outside factors, such as the colonial state and economic fallout resulting from the drop in prices at the end of the Napoleonic wars, the population managed to provide for most of its basic needs and to pay rents and tithes. They were self-sufficient in food, however basic, and in fuel. Consumer commodities from the colonies such as tea and sugar were still unknown except among the gentry. Clothing continued to be made from homespun wool and local weavers flourished in Glencolumbkille until the late 1830s before the introduction of shop cloth. In the post-war slump of 1825, British manufacturers were left with large stocks of cloth which were dumped on the Irish market at prices with which local weavers could not compete. By 1830 the production of woollens was half what it had been in 1800 and it was estimated that by this time three-quarters of the cloth worn by the peasants was imported.[8] Another domain which had hitherto been self-sufficient now became a source of dependency and a drain on meagre cash resources.

A further victim of the incursion of the colonial state was the informal economy which was based on sea trading and distilling. In the context of the colonial state, concerned as it was with the extraction of revenue, these activities came to be redefined as 'smuggling' and 'illicit distilling'. These activities constituted a major source of income until abolished in the 1830s (see Figure 6.1). The extent of the industry may be gauged from the fact that farmers in the better lands of Derry and Antrim were growing barley for distillers in Donegal. Poteen was sold throughout Ireland and its manufacture, sale and distribution were regular commercial activities at the turn of the century. This was soon to change. In 1821, Mr Dobrain, a revenue commissioner, visited the Glencolumbkille area to investigate these 'illicit' activities. It was part of his task to determine where coast-guard stations should be set up in order to end these activities. His report of 23 November 1821 to the secretary of the treasury in London gives an idea of the extent of this informal economy.

> I returned from Dublin yesterday having surveyed the coast from Sligo to Lough Swilly. Smuggling on that line of coast has been and still is carried out to an extent unequalled elsewhere. Donegal Bay is deep and dangerous and has not been hitherto frequented by smugglers at the point to the N. W. of Teelin Head where smuggling of tobacco has been carried out to an unparalleled extent. From unquestionable authority I have been informed that within these last nine months upwards of fourteen thousand bales of tobacco (about 65 pounds each) have been landed in the neighbourhood of Teelin; the duty of which would amount to £182,000; out of this immense quantity not fifty bales have been seized. In addition to the smuggling of tobacco, illicit distillation is also carried out in open day to an extent I certainly could not have credited, had I not been an eye-witness to it. In one day I saw no less than fifteen stills at work; and I did not pass a mile of road without meeting large quantities of illicit whisky conveyed by men on horseback and unarmed.[9]

Dobrain recommended that coast-guard stations be set up at Trabane (St John's Point), Teelin Harbour East and Teelin Harbour West (one on either side of the mouth of the bay), Malin Beg, Malin More, and

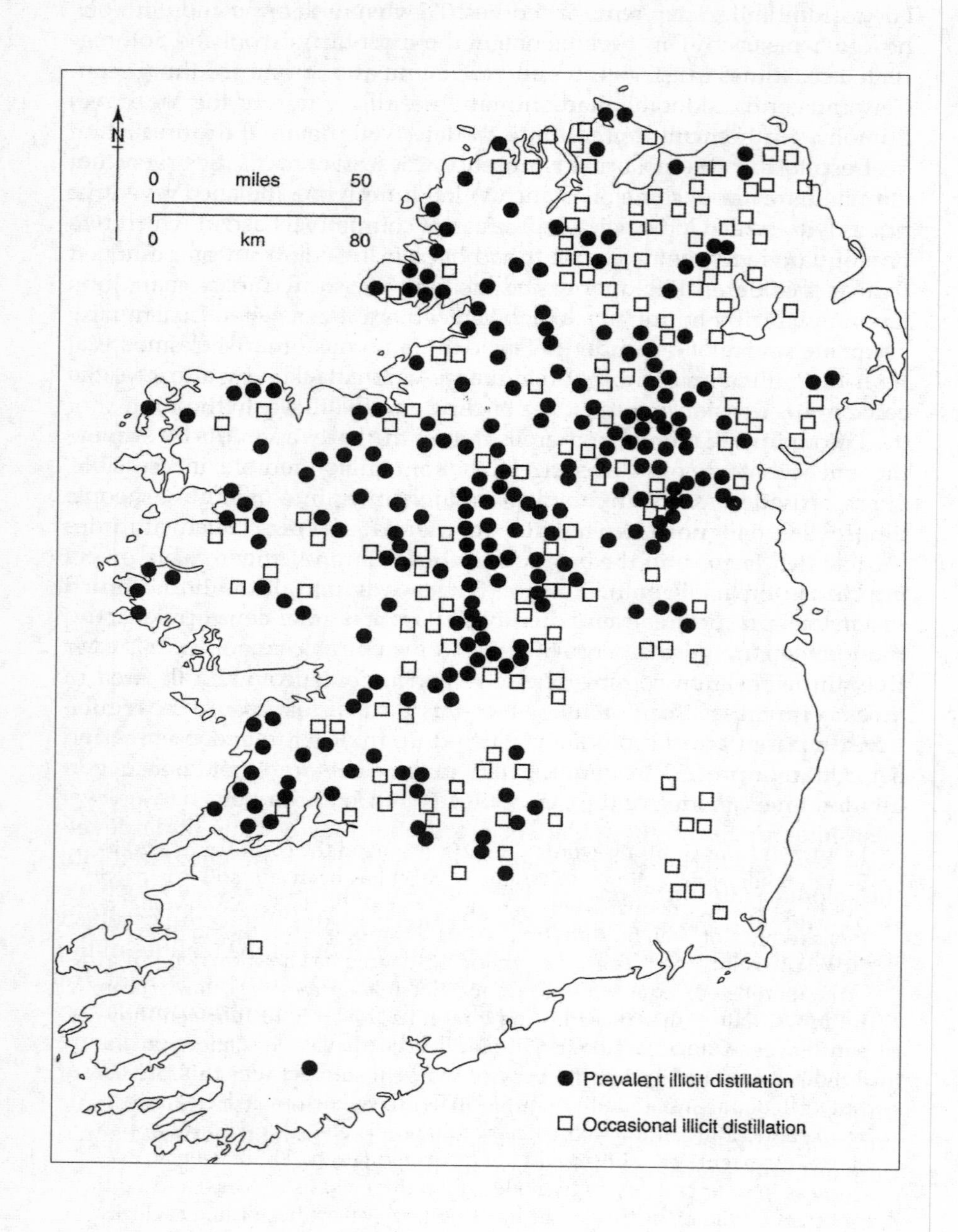

Figure 6.1 Location of illicit distillation, 1836, based on a map prepared by Dr Kevin Danagher of the Department of Irish Folklore, University College Dublin.

Glencolumbkille. Each was staffed with 12 men with arms and with one or two boats each. This became one of the most heavily policed and regulated coastlines in the country and the elimination of the informal economy caused considerable hardship and the disruption of the local cash economy further contributed to the underdevelopment of the area.

Despite the heavily armed presence, these local activities were not eliminated without some resistance. A letter from the Trabane Preventive Station, dated 25 October 1823, gives an account of a chase in which two coast-guards were injured and their boat left leaking from grapeshot. A further incident in 1832 involved the killing of a local Carrick man, John Cunningham, by John Huxtable, the chief boatman of Teelin Coastguard. There are several versions of this incident. The coast-guards claimed that he had an illicit still and that the guards were attacked by a 'mob' who came to his assistance when the police attempted to close the still.

The picture that emerges here is not, as the early accounts by surveyors and other state officials suggest, that of a region remote, inaccessible, characterised by 'social immobility' and inhabited by a 'primitive' people whose life had not changed for thousands of years. Such attitudes reflected the new notions of 'progress' and 'improvement' which were popular in the metropolitan centres in the early part of the 19th century. From this perspective, as in today's discourses on development and modernisation, those beyond the pale of the enlightenment were 'primitive' throwbacks from a bygone era of social evolution and in need of 'improvement' and discipline. In fact, it was in large measure the regulations imposed by the colonial state that destroyed local economies and set in train a process of underdevelopment. They were not, as is generally assumed, primitive and underdeveloped because they had not yet been integrated into the wider society. Rather they became underdeveloped precisely because of the manner in which they were integrated into the colonial state and economy. The images of Glencolumbkille which we find in the various accounts at the beginning of the 19th century reflect the interests and ideologies of a colonial power but not the realities of life as experienced by the local population. These discourses provided a rationale for the 'improvements' which were imposed on the population of south-west Donegal throughout the 19th century, policies of enclosure and the rationalisation of agriculture. In a real sense it was this process of imposed development which created the conditions for the endemic famine throughout the period and which set the foundations for stagnation and underdevelopment lasting to the present.

Images of underdevelopment

There were a variety of agents of civilisation who wished to transform or improve the region of Glencolumbkille and integrate it into the larger economic and political system. These agents were principally the colonial state and the church. With the aid of surveyors, coast-guards, landlords, estate agents, priests, ministers and missionaries they set about bringing the civilising process to this remote area. They would map, regulate, order and discipline this society so as to bring it into the ambit of modernity.

One of the first official accounts of the area comes from John Ewing who became Protestant Administrator of Glencolumbkille in 1824. His memo was a preliminary report for the ordnance surveyors. Donegal was the first county to be surveyed as part of a detailed ordnance survey of the colonial territories. Like most surveys of its kind it was to be used for taxation and military purposes. The account is quoted at some length as it was the first detailed written account of the area by an outsider. Ewing emphasises the remoteness and inaccessibility of the area.

> The coast is very bold, rugged and precipitous, was much frequented by smugglers but this has been greatly cramped of late by the coastguards who have 3 stations in this parish … No modern buildings, no towns, no gentlemen's seats … no inn, roads horribly bad: not a perch of good road in the parish … The food of the inhabitants chiefly potatoes and fish, not much oatmeal. Milk and butter pretty plenty, fuel invariably turf or peat … diseases are usually of the scorbutic class. Fevers not more prevalent than in other parts of Ulster. Inhabitants not remarkable for their longevity or the contrary … From what I know of them I would say that the inhabitants are quiet, peaceable and inoffensive. There is neither lawyer, attorney, magistrate or policeman in the parish … All the Protestants and some of the Roman Catholics speak the English language which is fast increasing since the establishment of the coastguards…[10]

He goes on to describe the local traditions 'which are very numerous indeed, but in general too ridiculous to mention'.

> Children are generally employed in taking care of cattle. Education here is very far back indeed. There is a local school on Robinson's [Robertson's] foundation which is very numerously attended, another where the master is paid entirely by the pupils [a hedge school]. The London Hibernian and Kildare Street Societies had a school here, but during last winter the pupils were withdrawn. [This was due to a dispute about Bible reading.] There is an old church near which a new one is shortly to be erected. No R.C. chapel nor meeting house … Tradesmen neither numerous nor good … The first steps to be taken in the improvement of this parish is to make the roads or at least a road into it. At present a wheel car with half a load could not enter the parish on any side whatever … People from the interior cannot come here for flannel, butter or fish.[11]

Despite Ewing's emphasis on the remoteness and backwardness of the area we also learn from his account that there was already a considerable 'civilising' presence in the area including several schools, a Church of

Ireland church and administrator, five coast-guard stations and their garrisons. We also learn that the population were producing a surplus of fish, butter and flannel. This was clearly not an untouched isolated area but was already integrated into the larger systems which impinged on it. John O'Donovan, who was employed by the Ordnance Survey Office, visited the area in 1835 and wrote a further account. O'Donovan's account is more a reflection of the social evolutionary thinking of the era than an accurate account of the economy of the region. He presents a notion of a people who have been long cut off from the rest of the world and who remained in this changeless state until the present.

> What their forefathers thought, said, believed and did a thousand years ago, they think, say, believe and do at present. They are primitive beings who have few points of contact with the civilised world. They hate, as indeed they should, the travelling preacher, and cling to notions of their fathers with a dignified independence. Social immobility seems to me the dominant trait in the character of these people who live in what may be called the extreme brink of the world, far from the civilisation of cities, and the lectures of philosophers.[12]

O'Donovan's way of seeing the people of Glencolumbkille reflects the discourse of 'primitiveness' and 'civilisation' which later came to characterise colonial ideology in Africa and India.

At the time when these reports were written, Glencolumbkille was already in economic decline as a result of colonial policies which restricted economic activities or eliminated sources of income. While the remoteness of the area was a recurring theme in various accounts, this represented an outsider's perspective which overlooked the fact that Glencolumbkille was and had long been connected to the wider world but in a manner different from that conceived of by the colonial regime. What they portray as a 'primitive' society, an earlier stage of evolution, stagnant and cut off from the rest of the world and in need of development was in fact a society which had extensive trade links with the European mainland. Indeed it was in an attempt to halt this trade that the coast-guard stations had been built and a permanent garrison installed in the 1820s. But the most radical transformation of the landscape and society of Glencolumbkille was yet to come. This was the process of rationalisation of land tenure in accordance with the principles of private property, increased productivity and the extraction of profits through rent.

The Agricultural Revolution in South-West Donegal

The Cromwellian revolution in England, by breaking the power of the king, removed a major barrier to the enclosing landlords and prepared England for rule by a 'committee of landlords'. By 1790, eight years before Malthus wrote his treatise on overpopulation, three quarters of the land of England was owned and controlled by landlords and there were approximately one and a quarter million paupers in the countryside. With the support of acts of parliament the country was being converted into a patchwork of private property and a pattern of land tenure and of landownership had emerged which would come to shape rural life in Britain and much of her colonies.

From the earliest days of colonisation in Ireland the indigenous systems of land use were described as 'savage' or 'primitive'. The lands were regarded as wild and empty wastes. Indigenous practices such as 'booleying' were regarded as 'barbaric and lawless'. The poet Edmund Spenser was proposing radical schemes for eliminating 'savagery' and turning the wilderness into a prosperous 'civilisation' in Ireland. Sir John Davies, who was responsible for the implementation of the plantation of Ulster, wrote as follows about the indigenous practices:

> The fast places were kept unknown by making the ways and entries hitherto impassable; there they kept their creaghts or herds of cattle, living by the milk of the cow, without husbandry or tillage; there they increased and multiplied unto infinite numbers, by promiscuous generation among themselves; there they made assemblies and conspiracies without discovery; but they discovered the weakness of the English dwelling in the open lands, and thereupon make their sallies and retreats with great advantage. Whereas, if they had driven the Irish into plains and open countries where they might have had an eye and observation upon them, the Irish had been easily kept in order, and in short time reclaimed from their wildness.[13]

Their habits were characterised either by irrationality or a lack of enterprise and motivation. A method of growing potatoes in raised beds was believed to be the result of indolence, thus the name 'lazy beds'. The practice of rundale, the indigenous land use system, was uneconomical and 'very injurious'. It was also seen as inhibiting the growth of new winter crops since there were 'insufficient ditches not of use to keep any beast which rendered a herd boy necessary at all times.'[14] In the colonies, from the mid 18th century, policies of land enclosure were regarded as 'improvements'. We see here the emergence and growth in hegemony of some of the key notions in development; the idea of advanced and backward societies, the idea of stages of development which is central to most Marxist and modernising notions of development. But the discourses on 'improvement' were also discourses on 'primitiveness' and 'backwardness'. They were moral discourses.

This was also the period of the Agricultural Revolution and of the application of science to the countryside in a fashion not unlike the 'Green Revolution' of the present century. French science was booming and the Physiocrats, drawing on Arab physics, were beginning to understand the process of the growth of plants. The publication of *Elements de L' Agriculture* in 1762 explained for the first time the laws of growth, the process of respiration, the circulation of sap and the relationship between roots and soil. Linneaus published his treatise on the nomenclature of plants and Turgot was expounding on efficient land use as well as procedures for efficient administration and standardisation. In England Jethro Tull (1647–1740) was promoting the horse drill, straight rows and the gentleman farmer Lord Townsend introduced crop rotation. New techniques such as the increased use of fertiliser, new crops, a scientifically derived system of crop rotation and the construction of lime kilns for fertiliser were introduced. In south-west Donegal, systems for crop rotation, of 'infield' and 'outfield' use, of the calculation of carrying capacity refined to half or even a quarter of a 'cow's grazing', existed in the indigenous system but were regarded as 'injurious' and lacking sophistication.

From the middle of the 18th century, landlords with holdings in Ireland, such as Lord George Hill of Gweedore, followed the lead of their peers in England and adopted these new practices on their estates. The transformations were brought about in characteristically autocratic fashion and were motivated mainly by the prospect of extracting more rent and enjoying greater security of payment. The primary purpose of land was now the production of rent for its owner. The English landlords who owned most of the land did not live in Ireland and had little identification with or feeling for the people or their ways of life. They saw themselves as part of a vast conquering empire on which the sun never set while, in their estimation, the Irish and other colonial peoples had not yet emerged from a barbarous and uncivilised condition. For this reason, 'a gentleman of fortune' could not be bothered with the drudgery of paying attention to such minutiae as the collection of rent from the poorer classes of tenants 'who lived in extreme poverty and insecurity of tenure and were not to be depended upon to have punctuality in the payment of rent'.[15] Their Irish estates were, for most landlords, simply a source of income. To avoid inconvenience but at the same time to assure their income, they let the land to 'some intermediary person of substance, at a lower rent, in order that the profit may be his inducement and reward for becoming a collector'.[16] This led to the establishment of a parasitic hierarchy of extraction.

Arthur Young, who visited Ireland and travelled the entire country between 1776 and 1778, gives us one of the most detailed and vivid accounts of the transformation of Irish rural society. Young was an apostle of the new scientific agriculture and a keen sociological observer. He was a man of his time and his ideas reflect the discourses of the Scottish Enlightenment and the French Revolution, in particular the notion that, shaped by science, human society could be perfected or improved. He gives an extensive account of land use and agricultural practices and an incisive account of the new class system superimposed on the indigenous system. He rails against a class of landlords whose behaviour would be disapproved of and regarded as unprogressive in England.

> This age has so much improved in humanity, that even the poor Irish have experienced its influence, and are every day treated better and better; but still the remnant of the old manners, the abominable distinction of religion, united with the oppressive conduct of the little country gentlemen or rather vermin of the kingdom, who were never out of it but bear very heavy upon the poor people, and subject them to situations more mortifying than anything we ever behold in England.[17]

The passage continues to speak of despots and slavery, of oppression and of ill judged laws which make the poor slaves in the bosom of liberty. Young is like the contemporary liberal agricultural development advisor reporting on the condition of agriculture and of rural life in a 'Third World' society. Young is particularly interesting in that, despite his liberal sentiments and progressive ideas, he is a staunch defender of the system of agriculture including the practice of absentee landlordism. He reminds us of the International Monetary Fund's notion of structural adjustment with a human face when he argues: 'There will arise, in spite of his tenderness a necessity of securing a regular payment of rent; I would advise him to disdain without favour or affection, at a certain period of deficiency. This will appear harsh only upon a superficial consideration. The object is to establish the system ... At all events let him persist in this firmness though it be the ruin of a few; for he must remember that if he ruins five, he assuredly saves ten'.[18]

The upward sweep of progress would lift some but others would be swept away, survival depended on the tenants' ability to pay their rent. The majority of landlords in Ireland were interested only in extracting wealth from their estates. The improving landlords combined wealth extraction with agricultural science. Indeed they saw the transformations brought about by the new agriculture primarily as a means of extracting more rent. On Tom Connolly's estate in south-west Donegal, rents increased from £8000 to £14,000 following the reorganisation of land tenure.[19]

The 18th century also saw the formation by landlords of new agricultural societies. These imported new ploughs and other implements, such as the light iron swing plough and the Scots cart; they experimented with new methods of farming, encouraged flax cultivation, spinning and weaving, fish curing, afforestation and fruit growing. The improving landlords also promoted the reclamation of mountain and boggy land, introduced new crops and new breeds of animals, planted trees and hedgerows, erected lime kilns, helped their tenants build better houses and built roads and bridges.[20] Even in the poorest areas of the country, such as Donegal, the spirit of the Agricultural Revolution was felt.

> In 1800, the 'resident gentlemen of the barony' founded the 'Tirhugh Farmer's Society' to 'encourage industry and farming among their tenants.' Every year one meeting was held in Ballyshannon and one in

> Donegal town; and according to McParlan 'a plain farmer's dinner was provided for such members as chose to remain'. There is no record of those who chose to eat the dinner, but it is evident that, at least in the early years, the proletarian farmers were not a force in the society. The society advocated enclosure, reclamation, drainage, the introduction of wheat and green crops, and the establishment of a mart in Ballyshannon.[21]

As with agricultural extension workers in developing countries today, the 'improving farmers found that it was difficult to get through the conservativeness of the people'.[22] The tenants and smallholders for their part had good reason to resist the changes which were being imposed on them. As with the modern 'Green Revolution' only the better off were in a position to gain from the 'improvements'. Because of insecurity of tenure, the tenants had no claim to any improvements they might have made and were liable to further increases in rent and a major disruption in their economy and way of life through enclosure and resettlement. For the improving landlords, a more prosperous tenantry meant a greater return on their investments.

The transformation of indigenous society

The indigenous settlement and land use system consisted of a joint farm held in 'rundale' and worked co-operatively by a group of kinsfolk. These combined in the common task of ploughing, cultivating, and fishing. The area of land was coextensive with the modern townland and the settlement consisted of a 'clachan' or cluster of four or five houses. Plots on which potatoes, barley, oats, and flax were grown were cultivated on a shifting basis on the arable land or 'infield' in the vicinity of the cabins. The land was frequently reallotted as a means of assuring equality between holders and of adjusting holdings to population growth. The laying out of lots was a complex procedure in which many factors, such as proximity to the clachan, quality of land and exposure to wind, had to be taken into account. McCourt describes the process in 'which they will take upon themselves to be judges of an extreme nicety of the quality and quantity of each rood of ground, to make sure they will bring their ropes to measure as formally as a surveyor his chains … this done, and not before, begins the bustle and wrangle, for they to whom the worst lot falls are sure to cavil at all the faults of his share, and there is no peace until all must fall anew to divide more equally again'.[23]

Likewise the use of the commonages was carefully regulated. There were restrictions on the number each could graze on the commonages. The common measure was the 'grass of a cow' which was the amount of grass needed by a full grown cow during the season. In this way the carrying capacity of the commonages was estimated. As pressure on lands increased measures such as 'half a cow's grass' and even 'quarter of a cow's grass' entered into the accounting. As the summer migrations of young people and animals to the 'booley grounds' departed, the older people watched to assure that nobody exceeded their quota. Coastal areas had their particular version of this system with regard to fishing and the collection of sea weed for fertiliser. This system, which had its origins in the pre-colonial period, showed remarkable resilience despite the intrusions of the colonial state and lasted until the late 1800s and even into the early part of the present century in Glencolumbkille.

In Glencolumbkille it was the break-up of the rundale system and not the Great Famine which brought about the greatest changes in rural life and landscape. Over time, all societies produce dynamic adaptations to a particular ecological niche. This ecological niche consists not only of the local physical environment but also of the social environment. The social environment is shaped not only by local conditions but also by national and global processes. The colonial state and its agents, the landlords, estate agents, government officials and planners, supported by coastguards and constabulary initiated a process of improvement or development, which over a period of about 100 years, severely disrupted the indigenous system, leading to ecological imbalances, of which the recurring famines were but the more severe symptoms.

Colonialism had both coercive and persuasive dimensions. It was underpinned by a new developmental ideology which allowed such transformations to be seen as progress, despite the great hardships caused to societies undergoing these changes. Sociologist Edward Spenser, writing around the time of the Great Famine, was an influential theorist and populariser of a version of social evolution which provided the ideological underpinnings for colonialism and which has become central to development thinking ever since. Practices such as enclosure, which led to the destruction of indigenous systems, were understood as part of a process of the survival of the fittest in its pre Darwinian sense. Change was inevitable and those who stood in the way must make way for the stronger.

For the landlords and their agents the system of land use and settlement patterns described above were regarded as obstacles to progress and improvement. For the landlords and their agents the rationalisation of land use through the abolition of rundale and the enclosure of openfield was a measure which 'could enable the tenantry to better pay their rents'. The system of rundale was also believed to lead to vice and laziness. On joint farms where rent was paid by townland or in companies this was believed to result in 'the wealthy being subject to constant distress for the indolent'. More important still, higher rents could be extracted from individually rented holdings.

Two methods of enclosure were used. One method called 'squaring' involved the laying out of holdings as square fields. The clachans were broken up and the new dwellings built on each of the holdings. There was considerable resistance to this method as it caused disputes over the quality of different plots and also difficulties over access to the different kinds of land, such as bog for gathering turf, mountain for grazing and suitable tillage land, all of which were assured under the rundale system. The other method created 'ladder farms' or long narrow strips running from valley bottom to hill margins and even up hillsides at right angles to the roads (see Figure 6.2). This was to ensure that each tenant got a portion of each of the different kinds of terrain, mountain, lowland, and bog. There was considerable resistance to this also as can be gleaned from the accounts of Lord George Hill's efforts to break up rundale on his estate in Gweedore.[24] In particular, many resisted the break-up of the clachans and the scattering of the dwellings. Dwellings were now scattered at intervals throughout the countryside as in the contemporary landscape which owes its formation to these changes.

The Glencolumbkille and Ardara estates were bought in 1798 by Tom Connolly, an MP for Donegal. A large part of Glencolumbkille was subleased to William Hume, an unpopular landlord who once escaped an assassination attempt only because he was wearing a coat of mail. The rent Hume paid to Connolly in 1830 was the same amount as paid by his father in 1774 but the number of tenants on his land had approximately tripled in the intervening period. When the Devon Commission toured Ireland in 1844–45 investigating relations between landlords and tenants, his tenants complained of 'extraordinary rents' and stated that because of this rack-renting only one family in 20 could afford to keep a cow.[25] One tenant declared, 'We are living on potatoes and God knows what many are living on'. In 1830, Connolly's agent, Alex Hamilton, who described himself as 'a landed proprietor, land agent, and magistrate',[26] surveyed all the property with a view to carrying out enclosure. New 'mearing lines' were mapped out and the lines were drawn as perpendicular to the road as possible. Where a village holding a farm in common prevailed, it was broken up and divided into small lots, each tenant receiving six acres thus bringing into existence the present system of fragmented and non-viable small farms. Tenants drew lots for the new holdings and suitable sites for building the new houses were chosen as central to the farm as possible, resulting in the typical ribbon patterns that now carve up the landscape. Allotments were measured in terms of units of 'cow's grass' as in the old system. Some of the strips were so narrow that the houses had to be built sideways so as to fit between the stone walls enclosing the strip of land.

Two years were allotted for the tenant to remove the old dwellings and construct new ones on the new allotments. In the first year, the tenant sowed his potato crop on the new holding but left his cereal ground to the new occupant. In the new individual holdings the potato became increasingly important as it was the only crop with a sufficient yield to support a family on such a small area. A shift also took place

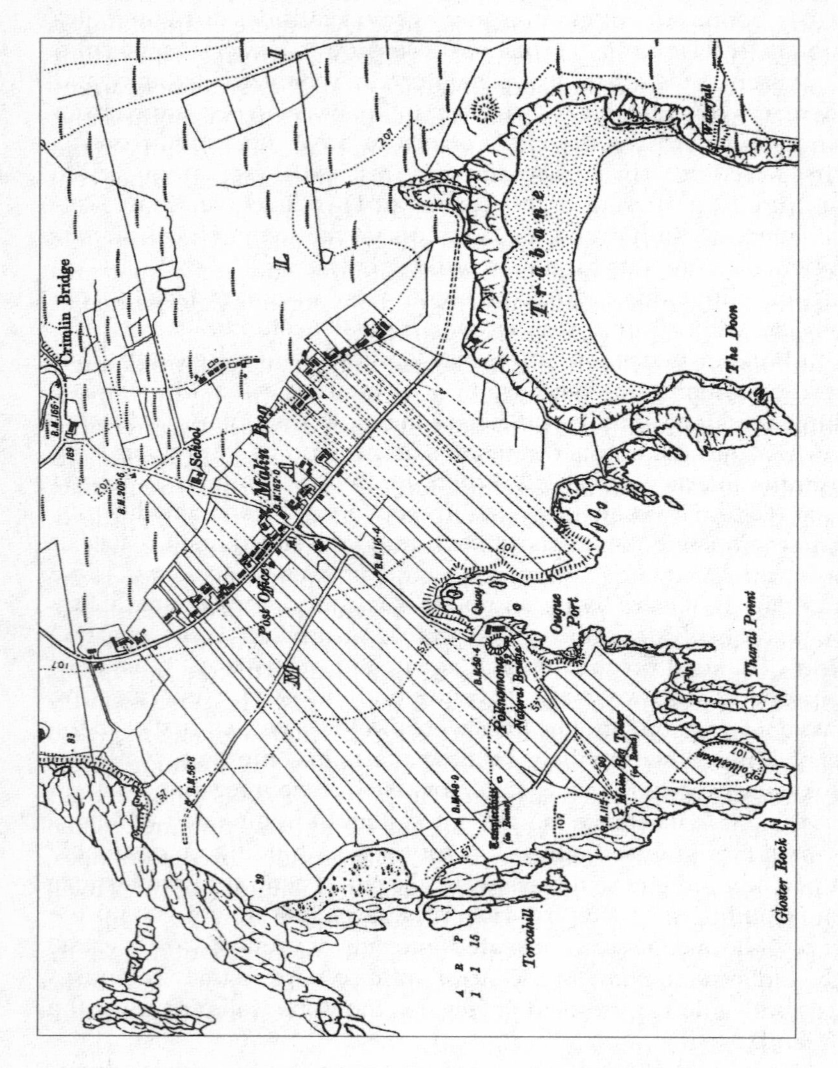

Figure 6.2 This map of Malin Beg shows the settlement after the introduction of enclosure and 'striping'. Extract from Ordnance Survey 6 inch map C (1906) Permit No MP001799.

whereby livestock became less important and the tenants relied more on tillage. The reorganisation involved considerable dislocation and some sections of the population were separated from the land. These tenants were bought out and the 'rate of purchase of goodwill' averaged £6 an acre. Other tenants and 'surplus' population from the joint farms were settled on moorland or reclaimed wasteland. These were charged only a nominal fee during the first three years of tenancy, during which time they worked to improve the land. Evidence from the Ordnance Survey maps of 1836 and 1845 and from the reports to the Devon Commission[27] show that 'very extensive improvements were made' as a result of land reclamation. Between 1831 and 1845, there was an increase of 8 per cent in improved land in Donegal.[28] New individual rents were assessed during this period and Connolly's rent almost doubled. Approximately £14,000 was extracted from tenants, an enormous sum for a poor area such as this. In the process, the security of many tenants deteriorated as longer leases were replaced by tenancy at will.

The number of families living in Glencolumbkille had approximately tripled between 1774 and 1835. Many were now attempting to cultivate unproductive land and the size of holdings had decreased appreciably. Rents, however, had doubled while wages had increased little. Tenants on Connolly's estate were now getting far less value for their rents than had their fathers. Connolly, who was considered an improving landlord, was better liked by his tenants than many other landlords because he rarely evicted his tenants and he paid some compensation towards the construction of new houses for tenants who had been displaced. Nevertheless, as in most other parts of the country, the tenantry struggled to subsist in poverty while all of their surplus was extracted to support the indolent lifestyle of the landlord and his agents. The poor tenantry survived 'by means of converting every pig, fowl and even egg into cash to make up their rent'.[29] Thomas Foster, describing the situation of the Donegal tenantry in 1846, tells us that: 'The farmer pays his rent and rates by disposing of his butter, pigs, eggs, beef, hay and oats – and milk, when he can sell it. He usually sells the whole of his produce, except potatoes, and in the dear seasons even part of his stock of potatoes, and buys meal on credit in order to pay his rent and country cess'.[30]

As the century progressed, a combination of population growth, enclosure and extraction of all surplus through rack-renting led to the creation of a precarious ecological balance between population and resources in which famine was endemic.

During this period clachans grew in size and number. While earlier the average size of a clachan was between three and five houses, by 1810 some clachans had grown to between 20 and 30 dwellings. New settlements appeared on moorlands and other wastelands reclaimed from bog. The boundaries of the townlands were also altered as is indicated by the interjection of 'upper', 'lower', 'east' and 'west' into modern townland names. Under this system the potato provided an important economy of space by providing a high yield from a small area. The potato was also an excellent means of reclaiming wet boggy land by extracting moisture from the soil. But the pressure was extreme as crops had to be grown to pay the landlord's rent as well as for food. Every inch of land was cultivated as is evidenced by the 'lazy bed' ridges that are still visible today on the steep sides of mountains and in bogs which have long since fallen into disuse. While the rundale system provided a degree of flexibility, this delicate ecological balance was decisively upset where rundale was rationalised through the imposition of enclosure.

Poverty and famine were endemic throughout most of the century with recurring periods of severe shortage. The potato failure of 1817 is remembered in Glencolumbkille as 'the Dear Summer' when many people had to resort to chicken weed to assuage their hunger. The Famine was not as severe in Glencolumbkille, however, as in other parts of the country, with little drop in population and an actual increase in some areas. In 1821, the population was 3050. In 1831, it had risen to 3752, and in 1841 to 4356. By 1851, it had fallen to 3881, probably because of emigration. There is no record of any deaths from hunger in Glencolumbkille during this period. In August 1847, 105 families were receiving relief in the adjoining parish of Kilcar, while only 31 received relief in Glencolumbkille. Parliamentary papers indicate that in 1847, 556 farms in Glencolumbkille grew 170 acres of oats, 140 of barley, 241 of potatoes, 123 of turnips and two of cabbage. The wheat and barley would have been used almost exclusively to pay the rent and tithes.

What happened in Glencolumbkille was not the cataclysmic transformation of society as a result of a single great calamity, the famine, but rather an ongoing process of destabilisation resulting from enclosure, the destruction of the existing system of adaptation and the bleeding of the area and its resources through rack rents and tithes to the Church of Ireland. It was a process through which the area was slowly underdeveloped and squeezed of all its produce and cash, except for such potatoes as were necessary to keep the tenants alive. It was this vulnerability, created and maintained by colonial interests, which led to the precarious balance between population and resources which was so readily destabilised by the potato blight. But because the process of enclosure had not proceeded as rapidly in Glencolumbkille, with most tenants still farming communally in the 1850s, the system was better able to support its growing population, albeit at a low level of subsistence. Even Young, despite his commitment to enclosure and commercial agriculture, saw advantages to the indigenous system of collective farming. Describing the situation in the late 1800s where:

> ... by means of living themselves in the very poorest manner, and converting every pig, fowl and even egg into cash, they will make up their

> rent, and get by very slow degrees into somewhat better circumstances. Where it is the custom to take in partnership the difficulties are easier got over; for one man brings a few sheep, another a cow, a third a horse, a fourth a car and some potatoes, a fifth a few barrels of corn and so on, until the farm among them is tolerably stocked, and hands upon it plenty in labour.[31]

The situation of the Glencolumbkille tenantry was also helped by the fact that Connolly, while he did squeeze his tenants, did not engage in widespread clearing of tenants from the land as was the practice in other places. There were no recorded evictions in Glencolumbkille but by the 1860s the estate was badly in debt.

The Encumbered Estates Act facilitated the sale of such estates on terms congenial to the previous owners. The act aimed at putting the estates in the hands of a new commercial breed of landlord who would manage them on strictly business lines. By 1867, the estate of 21,201 acres was sold to John and James Musgrave, a Belfast company of iron founders and engineers, for the sum of £21,750. The Musgraves were not improving landlords and were not well regarded locally. A popular jingle described the local attitude to Musgrave's take-over:

> Dark was the day for Carrick
> When Tom Connolly's estates
> were purchased by the Musgraves
> manufacturers of grates.

Through their agent, Arthur Brooke, they seemed more bent on asserting their authority than in improving the conditions of tenants. Letters to tenants commanded them to stop building additions to their houses, ordering them to tear down fences, control their dogs, geese and cows. Tenants were refused permission to buy neighbouring farms and a child, Charles Gillespie, was summoned for fishing in a local river! A further conflict emerged between the Teelin fishermen and Musgrave who claimed sole rights over fishing in the bay. The biggest conflict was with a local priest Fr McGroarty who persisted, together with some other farmers in fencing off commonage.[32] There is some irony in this incident in that McGroarty and his group, seemingly bent on enclosing land for their own benefit, were doing just what landlords like Connolly and Musgrave had been doing all along.

As is evidenced by the McGroarty case, it would be a mistake to view the indigenous land tenure system as egalitarian. Communal land tenure does not necessarily imply a completely egalitarian society. Even at clachan level there was considerable social differentiation and variations in wealth. Significant differences in access to land and other resources existed within townlands or balibeos, as they were called in Donegal. These differences led to different attitudes towards enclosure. As land became scarcer and population increased, these differences became more critical. Those who had rights to larger tillage areas and greater grazing rights on the commonages often saw it as being to their own advantage to enclose the land to which they had rights. This was usually facilitated by the landlords or their agents even through it generated opposition from other tenants who now found that the areas to which they had access were even more restricted. Furthermore, many of the tenant farmers themselves rented plots to landless people on which they could grow potatoes or graze a cow. This further increased internal differentiation and conflicting attitudes to land use.

A closer look at one townland, Malin Beg at the western tip of Glencolumbkille (Figures 6.3 and 6.4), illustrates this differentiation within a particular townland. Malin Beg, like most of the other townlands in Glencolumbkille, was enclosed only at the beginning of this century. The townland of Malin Beg consisted of 3,100 acres, most of which was mountain and outfield and for which an annual rent of £125 was paid to Connolly. The clachan settlement, as shown on the 1836 Ordnance Survey map, had between 35 and 40 dwellings and some 30 outhouses or 'offices' for animals, these being shared among families. The entire townland was worked co-operatively in accordance with the rundale system. The land was used jointly by 29 families while a further 14 families owned no land. One of these was a herdsman for the group of 29. Most of the families in this main group were related to each other, there being 10 McGinley families and eight Byrnes. The remaining 11 probably married into the group.

While they farmed the area as a team there was nevertheless considerable internal differential access to and control over resources. This differentiation is illustrated by the varying amounts that each family paid for the rental of land, dwellings, and outhouses. The following figures, based on Griffith's valuation of 1845, show the differences in property valuation within the townland:

5 families	£5.00–£5.10 valuation
7 families	£4.10
4 families	£4.00
6 families	£3.10–3.05
4 families	£2.05
2 families	£1.10–£1.00
14 families	no land

The 14 landless families had moved to Malin Beg during the Famine to take advantage of the additional food supplies from the nearby sea. They created a settlement called 'Fisherman's Row' at the back of the clachan. This shows the flexibility of the system in being able to accommodate an increase of almost half the existing population in a time of severe short-

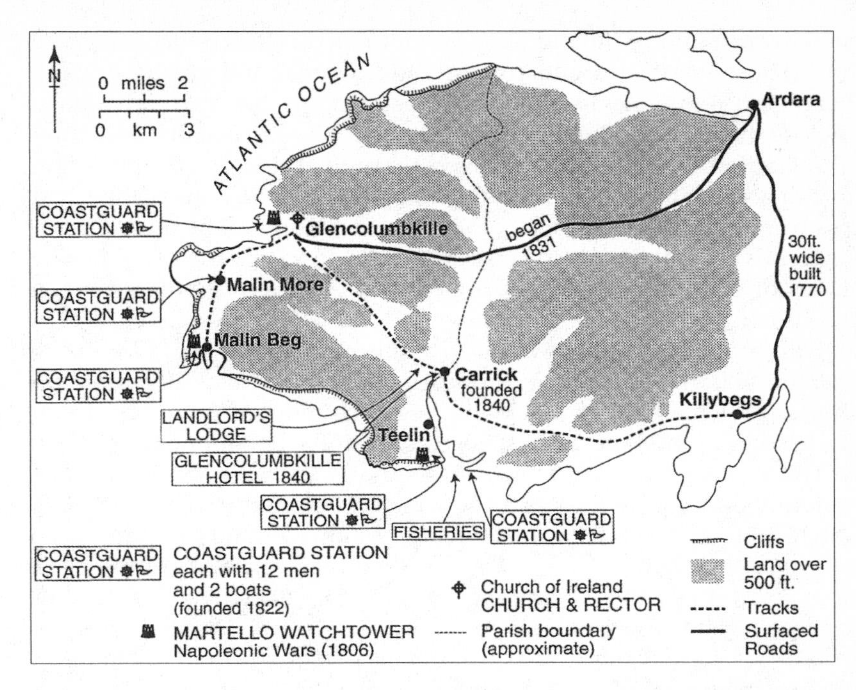

Figure 6.3 Glencolumbkille Parish, outside influences, 1806–40 from a map drawn by Vincent Tucker, redrawn by Ms ML Pringle, Department of Geosciences, the Queen's University of Belfast.

age. This group was not, however, integrated fully into the rundale system, even in 1923, when the land was divided by the Land Commission after independence. They rented tiny plots of land near the seashore to the west of the clachan. Here they grew a few ridges of potatoes. By 1950 this settlement had disappeared.

The rundale system persisted until the end of the 19th century in most parts of Glencolumbkille and this helps to explain the fact that the Famine was not so severe in that area. The co-operative system of tenure had more flexibility than the enclosed systems of tenure. However, because of the exploitative systems of rack-rents combined with population growth, the balance between population and local resources grew ever more precarious. But it was towards the end of the century, and particularly during the famine of 1879, that Glencolumbkille suffered most. In 1880 James Tuke, a Quaker and supporter of the destitute, noted that 600 out of 800 families in the area were on relief. Their only source of support, besides the produce of their farms, was a payment of ninepence a day for working on the roads and one penny a day paid to the women for embroidery.

The process just described was one whereby Glencolumbkille gradually underwent a process of underdevelopment as a result of the break-up of the indigenous system and the consequent extraction of all surplus

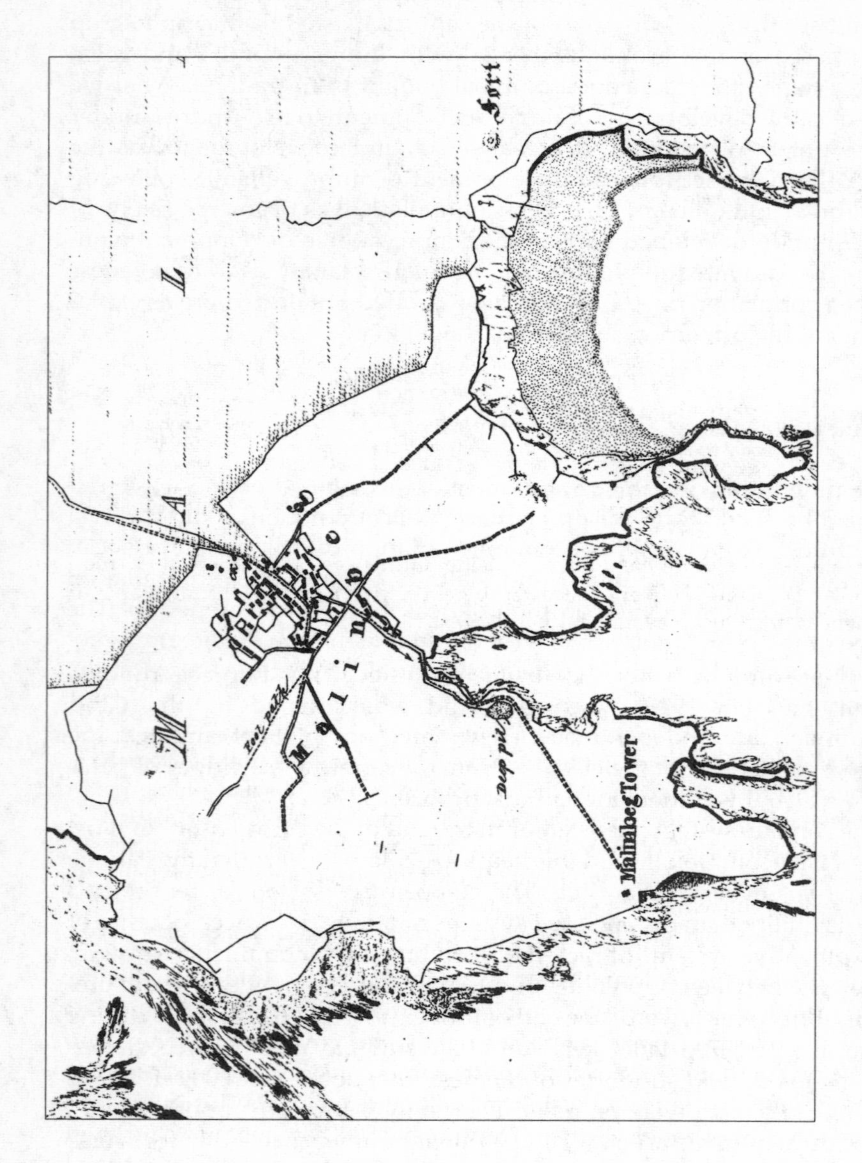

Figure 6.4 Ordnance Survey map, 1835, showing clachan settlement in Malin Beg, Glencolumbkille. At this time there was no enclosure and the land was farmed under rundale.

production in rents and tithes. It was not an instant process as the indigenous system showed remarkable flexibility and adaptability in the face of transformation and exploitation. It was, rather, a gradual process of destabilisation that by the 1880s had reached crisis proportions. The population had, from the early part of the century, existed from crop to crop and from season to season interspersed with 'hungry months' and 'meal months' (when they depended on meal bought from traders). What we see here is the development of underdevelopment, to use Andre Gunder Frank's potent description. In a real sense, underdevelopment was the result of an imposed plan of development or improvement. Following the outbreak of famine in 1879, Glencolumbkille was to emerge as one of the most underdeveloped parts of the country. When development planners again paid attention to the area, the old explanations of remoteness and overpopulation or 'congestion' were trotted out once more as explanations for the underdevelopment of the region.

Community development under colonialism

Development thinking throughout most of the colonial period was characterised by social Darwinism. Herbert Spencer's notion of the survival of the fittest, Adam Smith's economic variation of this notion of social evolution through competition, and Malthus' theories of overpopulation had considerable influence on the political thinking of the period. The decline of the population of the west of Ireland and the disintegration of indigenous society were regarded as natural, even necessary for the development of society.

> Much of this obtuseness sprang from the fanatical faith of mid-nineteenth century British politicians in the economic doctrine of laissez-faire, no interference by government, or meddling with the operation of natural causes. Adherence to laissez-faire was carried to such length that in the midst of one of the major famines of history, the government was perpetually nervous of being too good to Ireland and of corrupting the Irish people with kindness, and so stifling the virtues of self-reliance and industry.[33]

By the 1880s, the colonial state was increasingly under challenge. Agrarian outrages increased from 2500 in 1880 to 4400 in 1881 and 235 'personal protection posts' were set up by the government. The Land League was agitating for reform with some considerable success. The agitation was also felt in Glencolumbkille and when the League asked tenants to withhold their rents in December 1800, few tenants paid their rent to the Musgraves, leading their agent Brooke to report 'It is hard not to be irritated at the stupidity and folly of the poor dupes ... They have no feelings of gratitude ... I think that some (at least in Glen) do not know what they want'.[34]

But the tenants knew exactly what they wanted, they wanted an end to paternalism, exploitation and insecurity of tenure. The home rule movement also had its impact on the colonial administration. Parnell had repeatedly demanded the right of an Irish parliament to erect tariff barriers to protect Irish industry. Joseph Chamberlain, speaking for British industrialists who feared the closure of a market they had long considered their own, opposed home rule. But he was also convinced that coercion in Ireland must be accompanied by reform. It was in this context that a new administrative agency with new ideas about development, the Congested Districts Board, was set up in 1881 under Sir Horace Plunkett, unionist landlord and founder of the Irish Agricultural Co-operative Movement. This was the first government-initiated community development programme and a laboratory for policies and experiments which were later diffused to other colonies.

As the name Congested Districts Board suggests, overpopulation was considered to be the root cause of underdevelopment in areas such as Donegal. It was not the unjust land tenure system nor the siphoning off of surplus through rents which were blamed, but rather, the view that too many people were trying to scratch out a living from land which was too poor to support them all. The main functions of the board were the improvement of agriculture through the amalgamation of uneconomic holdings, the purchase of estates, and their reallocation to tenants under the new land legislation, and the assistance of migration from the 'congested areas'. Plunkett, himself a landlord, was also committed to a solution that involved population reduction.

> Putting aside emigration, which at one period was necessary and ought to have been aided and controlled by the State, but which is now no longer a statesman's remedy, there is obviously no solution except by migration of a portion of occupiers, and the utilisation of the vacated holdings in order to enable the peasants who remain to prosper – much as a forest is thinned to promote the growth of trees. In typical congested districts this operation will have to be carried out on a much larger scale than is generally realised, for a considerable majority of families will have to be removed in order to allow a sufficient margin for the provision of adequate holdings for those who remain ... I do not myself attach much weight to the unwillingness of the people to leave their old holdings for better ones, or to the alleged objection of the clergy to allow their parishioners to go to another parish.[35]

Here we find Plunkett promoting a form of development through 'natural' selection, aided this time by policy measures, in which little weight is attached to the views or wishes of those being 'developed'.

Despite these criticisms there were many positive achievements. The establishment of rural credit banks, of which there were 20 in Donegal in 1901, was an innovative attempt to help overcome the chronic cycle of debt and credit which kept people dependent on the gombeen men. In

1909, however, the rural credit banks came under fire and were ultimately abolished by Plunkett's successor, TW Russell. The board also attempted to revive the fishing industry by building piers in Teelin and Dun Alt. Drying wires and beaches for drying fish were prepared Shetland fashion and the board purchased white fish at fixed prices from the fishermen. Funds were advanced for boats and equipment and Scottish advisors, 'development workers' in contemporary parlance, were appointed to train the young crews. Boats were owned co-operatively and, according to a board report, 'earnings from fishing in 1892 enabled these hard working men to clear off all their debts and to feed and clothe themselves.'[36]

But the improvements were only temporary as the colonial state and economic forces beyond their control impinged once again to undermine local efforts and further peripheralise south-west Donegal. The British Transport Ministry introduced a 120 per cent rise in transport costs making the export of fish from Donegal uneconomical. A British Admiralty prohibition on fishing in Donegal, to prevent any possible collaboration with German submarines, served to ruin all the board's efforts to rebuild the fishing industry. Efforts to build a crafts and textile industry were also of a temporary nature. The modern hand loom was introduced, instructors hired and an export outlet opened. But in 1920, following the war-time boom, the market collapsed and people who had invested in bales of wool or rolls of tweed went broke. In the area of land tenure, the board had no compulsory powers and depended on the goodwill of the landlords. Fewer than 10 per cent of the tenantry had the value of their holdings altered to any significant degree.

The commitment of the colonial administration to the development of the peripheralised areas might be measured by the capital committed to the task. The entire budget of the board was £41,250 drawn from the Church of Ireland surplus. This sum was totally inadequate. In such a context, and despite laudable efforts to develop local resources, teach new skills, and promote self-help, the entire effort was but a hiccup in the decline of the area. This conflict of interests is characteristic of attempts to develop peripheral regions while retaining the structures which created underdevelopment and peripherality in the first place. The efforts of the board became a model for development programmes in other parts of the empire, and in particular in India, where community development was introduced as a means of mitigating existing conditions while avoiding the overthrow of the colonial system.

Epilogue: Development and Underdevelopment in Post-Colonial Ireland

As a newly-independent nation, Ireland was anxious to maintain and emphasise its distinctive cultural heritage and identity and, in particular, its language. The peripheral regions of the west coast, while retaining their image as peripheral underdeveloped regions, also came to be considered as the repository of Irish culture. Between 1925 and 1926, a special commission on the Gaeltacht was set up. It agreed with the diagnosis of the Congested Districts Board which saw overpopulation as the basic problem and it showed little faith in the possibility of developing the western regions. Its solution was to attempt to take the Gaeltacht out of the periphery, where its chances of survival were slim, through the resettlement of large numbers of families in the more fertile areas of the midlands. While plans for mass migration never materialised, some 800 families were resettled at a cost of approximately £5 million. The largest resettlement involved the migration of 122 families (772) persons from Donegal to Meath in 1935. By 1952, only nine families (111 persons) still remained in Meath.

In 1956 a special department was set up and the exact geographical definition of the Gaeltacht agreed on. In 1958 a state-sponsored body, Gaelterra Eireann was established with the social function of keeping the Gaeltacht alive and the economic role of making it more prosperous. In reviewing government policy towards peripheral regions, Commins sums up the overall thrust of Irish development policies:

> ... official policies drifted away from the development of indigenous resources begun a century ago. This early emphasis changed to a concern with land restructuring and settlement during the 1930s and 1940s and was followed in the 1950s and 1960s by a clear change of direction in favour of imported industrial enterprises. While the more recent endeavours of Gaelterra Eireann reflect a renewed interest in the potential of natural resources it has been largely left to co-operatives to emphasise their importance ... The functional terms of reference of statutory authorities do not give much recognition to community based organisations. The position is that while local authorities have permission (as distinct from mandatory) powers to assist local groups in community development the use made of these powers appears to have been slight.[37]

With the introduction of neo-Keynesian orthodoxy to Irish economic planning, the goals of self-sufficiency and the development of indigenous resources, which were the basis of government planning from 1932 until 1958, were abandoned in favour of growth centres and a policy of export-oriented growth. This new vision of development was not, as is generally assumed by conventional accounts of Irish development, the brainchild of Whitaker and Lemass, but simply the introduction into Irish development planning of a programme of modernisation as a condition of support from the Marshall Aid Programme.[38] Modernisation was the flavour of the day in development circles and similar programmes were being promoted by the same development agencies throughout the Third World.

The new policies further peripheralised areas such as south-west Donegal. In 1963, Garret Fitzgerald, a prominent Irish economist, argued that 'there are serious economic dangers in excessive regional or intersectional redistribution of wealth – economic dangers which are rarely stated explicitly and can threaten the success of the whole process of raising the living standards of all our people'.[39] This way of reasoning was evident in the Irish Republic's First Programme for Economic Expansion. In this programme, Whitaker argues that since the objective was to maximise growth in national income, economic development should be concentrated in those parts of the country with most potential for growth. As in most other countries, this concentration of resources in growth centres led to further disparities between regions and to a drain on the human resources of the peripheralised regions through migration and emigration.

At the time, such depopulation was regarded as a positive trend as it would lead to a greater amalgamation of holdings and the creation of more viable holdings. The debate continued throughout the 1960s and was the subject of numerous articles in academic journals. Dr Michael McCarthy, then President of UCC, wrote an article in which he advocated large-scale consolidation of farms and population reduction as a solution to the economic problems of the underdeveloped west. He concluded that 'increased production efficiency must mean less employment on the land'.[40] There were some dissenting voices. General Costello argued that:

> For nearly forty years the West has been 'developing' or, as I would say, 'degenerating' into the kind of farming system which he thinks it should have or at least that it inevitably will have in the future. All that is necessary to do to bring this to full development, to make every farm an economic ranch is to do nothing, to allow rural Ireland to die; to replace the rural community with a small number of ranchers, living in isolation, each requiring for any contact with the world a motor car, TV set and almost certainly a telephone. The extent to which this is the trend of development is evidenced by the fact that almost all vegetables and fruit are brought from Dublin to East Mayo and North Roscommon, that a large proportion originates abroad even if some of it is processed here, that a big proportion of potatoes consumed in the area comes from Dublin, that there is no longer a sufficient labour force to save the turf required in rural areas.[41]

For Costello, underdevelopment was not the result of indigenous factors but of a government vision and policies which had written off the area and its people as outside the ambit of modernisation and development.

There were a few challenges to the bright new vision of modern Ireland with its gleaming industrial centres. Fr McDyer of Glencolumbkille joined forces with General Costello, then director of the Irish Sugar Company. They saw the problem as a loss of human resources through emigration and of underpopulation rather than overpopulation. They mounted a challenge to the government accusing it of neglecting the Western regions. McDyer campaigned for an approach to rural development which would be based on locally initiated pilot development projects. An action committee, the Charlestown Committee, and a 'Save the West Campaign' were launched. McDyer, reacting to the official view of the underdeveloped west, declared that: 'We are unfortunate that we have a regime in the Republic which has become so reliant for progress on state-sponsored projects and foreign industrialists that it tends to view with supercilious scorn the efforts of a purely native community project'.[42]

The government reconvened its committee concerned with the problems of small western farms. The 'Report of the Inter-Departmental Committee on the Problems of Small Western Farms' did not significantly shift from the position stated in a previous report when it concluded that: 'Apart from the work of the Land Commission and anything that can be done to improve hill or bog grazing or to extend intensive forms of production, the weight of future efforts by the State should be directed to the possibilities of non-farm employment through industrialisation, forestry, tourist development or anything else that offers a fair prospect of success'.[43]

McDyer and his supporters were to propose a variety of schemes designed to develop Western regions. The most radical was a communal farming scheme, designed with the help of the Agricultural Institute.[44] It proposed a restructuring of land tenure and land ownership designed to overcome the structural problems which had evolved throughout the colonial period. This proposal, based on communal land use on a townland basis, resembled the rundale system which in Glencolumbkille had withstood all attempts by landlords and developers to transform it until the end of the 19th century. But the scheme was opposed by the government and never materialised. McDyer concluded: 'No such scheme has been undertaken because of the climate of opinion fostered by a group of economists who now openly declare that further dispersal of small communities of the West to be not only in the nature of things, in an expanding economy, but a condition for economic expansion'.[45]

Ireland's membership of the EEC in 1972 further relegated western smallholders to the periphery of the agricultural economy. In 1974, when the Department of Lands instituted the 'Farm Modernisation Scheme,' small farmers in the west were informed that their farms were 'transitional,' ie commercially non-viable, and that they should prepare for early retirement. Resources were to be concentrated on development of 'commercial' farmers who formed only one-fifth of the total farming population.

Conclusion

Dichotomising categories, such as developed/underdeveloped, modern /traditional, periphery/core and even urban/rural, have come to be regarded as natural divisions of the world. Such categories, however, constrain our thinking and obscure the dynamics which create cores and peripheries, margins and centres, developed and underdeveloped regions. Cores and peripheries are not self-evident geographic categories but are constituted through class and power. There is no such thing as a peripheral or marginal society, there are only ways of seeing societies as peripheral or marginal. The colonial project was one whereby certain regions of the world came to be constituted as centres of power and development and others as underdeveloped margins harbouring primitive or pre-modern ways of life.[46] The social and historical construction of margins, peripheries and underdeveloped or disadvantaged regions is the result of military, economic and political processes. But it is also a cultural process which favours the power and knowledge of certain classes and regimes and allows them to hold up their values and ways of life as a norm for others to emulate. The notion of being more advanced or superior is central to most development discourses past and present, whether the language of the discourse be one of civilisation, modernisation or development. It portrays other societies as existing on the margins, not yet integrated into the mainstream of development. In this way, they become objects to be regulated, ordered, improved, modernised or developed as well as artifacts to be gazed upon by tourists from the metropolitan centres.

Glencolumbkille has been consistently portrayed as remote, inaccessible, far-back, marginal, disadvantaged, traditional and underdeveloped. Yet, while the various agents of the colonial state complained about its inaccessibility, Glencolumbkille had long been integrated into the global economy through an extensive sea trade. From the perspective of the local society its inaccessibility to the agents of the colonial state was an advantage and for this reason it was one of the last parts of Ireland to be transformed and regulated. But the colonial state severed Glencolumbkille's links with the wider world and restructured it as a peripheral part of the British Empire. After independence, when the Irish state became integrated into the modern global economy, its peripheral status was reinforced as development was constituted as something which happens only in growth centres. It became inconceivable that development could emanate from peripheral regions – especially forms of development which were not dependent on outside forces, resources or planners. Contemporary EU rural development policies continue this discourse of peripheralisation. In recent times, not only the western areas but the entire country has been designated as peripheral. While these ways of portraying development and underdevelopment hold sway authentic indigenous development will, by definition, remain impossible and processes of social engineering will remain the main tools in the development kit. These discourses, whether in the realm of historical interpretation or in the domain of contemporary policy discussions, must be challenged if rural societies are to become centres of their own development.

Notes

1. VS Mudimbe, *The invention of Africa* (London, 1988).
2. Samir Amin, *Accumulation on a world scale: a critique of the theory of underdevelopment*, vols 1 and 2 (New York, 1974).
3. A good example of this approach is found in the collection edited by Wolfgang Sachs and in the work of Columbian anthropologist Arturo Escobar. See for example Arturo Escobar, *Encountering development* (New Jersey, 1995). Also see Wolfgang Sachs (ed) *The development dictionary* (London, 1993).
4. Quoted in Aidan Manning, *Glencolumbkille: 3000 BC–1885 AD* (Toronto, 1985).
5. Arthur Dobbs, *An essay on the trade and improvements of Ireland* (London, 1846).
6. Lawrence Taylor, 'The merchant in peripheral Ireland: a case from Donegal', in *Anthropology*, vol 4, no 2 (1981) p 69. Lawrence Taylor has carried out extensive anthropological research in south-west Donegal on topics such as fishing, land and religion. See 'Man the fisher: fishing and community in a rural Irish settlement', in *American Ethnologist*, vol 8, no 4 (1981) pp 774–88; and 'Colonialism and community structure in the west of Ireland', in *Ethnohistory*, vol 27, no 2 (1980) pp 169–81. Much of his work is revisited in his recent book *Occasions of faith: an anthropology of Irish Catholics* (Dublin, 1995). This excellent study is noteworthy for the way in which it weaves together political economy, cultural analysis and ethnography. It is an exemplary piece of work in Irish anthropology.
7. Taylor, 'Colonialism and community structure in the west of Ireland', p 69.
8. Ruth Dudley Edwards, *An atlas of Irish history* (London, 1973) p 13.
9. Dobrain, letter to the secretary of the treasury, 23 November 1821, State Papers, Dublin Castle.
10. The Ordnance Survey Memoirs of Ireland, 1824. Reproduced by kind permission of the Royal Irish Academy, as are the extracts relating to notes 11 and 12.
11. Ibid.
12. Ordnance Survey Letters of John O'Donovan, Royal Irish Academy, 1835.
13. Quoted in George Hill, 1877, *A historical account of the plantation in Ulster at the commencement of the seventeenth century 1608–1620* (Shannon, Ireland, 1970).
14. In James Anderson, 'The decay and breakup of the rundale system in the barony of Tirhugh', in *Donegal Annual*, vol VI, no 1 (1964) pp 1–42.
15. Arthur Young, *Young's tour of Ireland (1777–1779)* (ed) AW Hutton (London, 1892).

16. Ibid, p 25.
17. Ibid, p 54.
18. Ibid, p 33.
19. Anderson, 'The decay and breakup of the rundale system', p 21.
20. AR Orme, *The world's landscapes: Ireland* (London, 1970) p 133.
21. Anderson, 'The decay and breakup of the rundale system', p 19.
22. Ibid.
23. Desmond McCourt, 'Infield and outfield in Ireland' in *Economic History Review*, vol 7, (1954) pp 369–76.
24. Lord George Hill, *Facts from Gweedore* (Dublin, 1945).
25. Aidan Manning, *Glencolumbkille*, p 55.
26. Ibid, p 40.
27. Devon Commission Inquiry Into the Occupation of Land in Ireland, 1844, pp 4–9.
28. KH Connell, 'The colonisation of waste land in Ireland 1780–1845', in *Economic and Social History Review*, 1950, pp 44–71.
29. Arthur Young, *Tour of Ireland*, p 320.
30. TC Foster, *Letters on the conditions of the people of Ireland* (London, 1846).
31. Young, *Tour of Ireland*, p 320.
32. Lawrence Taylor, *Occasions of faith.*
33. Cecil Woodham-Smith, *The Great Hunger* (London, 1962).
34. In Manning, *Glencolumbkille*, p 89.
35. Horace Plunkett, *Ireland in the new century* (Irish Academic Press, 1982) p 48.
36. WL Micks, *History of the Congested Districts Board from 1891–1923* (Dublin, 1925) p 36.
37. P Commins, 'Cooperation and community development in the west of Ireland', paper presented to the International Seminar on Marginal Regions, Trinity College, Dublin, 3 August 1979, p 9.
38. Denis O'Hearn has used his studies of the Marshall Aid archives to debunk the myth that Whitaker almost singlehandedly revolutionised Irish development policy. He argues that Whitaker's plans were the flavour of the day and had more to do with the requirements of the Marshall Aid programme than Whitaker's innovativeness. Denis O'Hearn, 'Putting Ireland in a global context', occasional papers series in Irish and world development, Department of Sociology, University College Cork, 1992.
39. GE Fitzgerald, *State-sponsored bodies*, 2nd ed, (Dublin, 1963) p 272.
40. MD McCarthy, 'Some Irish population problems' in *Studies*, vol 56 (1967) pp 237–47.
41. MJ Costello, 'Agriculture in the west of Ireland', in *Studies*, vol 56 (1967) pp 337–48.
42. *Donegal Democrat*, 17 July 1965.
43. Ireland, *Report on the Interdepartmental Committee on the problems of small western farms* (Dublin, 1961).
44. Vincent Tucker, 'State and community: a case study of Glencolumbkille' in Chris Curtin and Thomas Wilson (eds) *Ireland from below: social change and local communities* (Galway, 1989).
45. Ireland, *Report on pilot area development* (Dublin, 1963).
46. Jane Nadel-Klein, 'Occidentalism as a cottage industry: representing the autochonous other in British and Irish rural studies' in JC Carrier (ed) *Occidentalism: images of the west* (Oxford, 1995).

Chapter 7

Farm Succession in Modern Ireland: Elements of a Theory of Inheritance[1]

Liam Kennedy

Introduction

In all property-owning societies, but particularly in agrarian societies, the transmission of property between generations is of primary importance. At the societal level there are likely to be consequences for economic efficiency, social structure, and social inequality; at the level of the individual there may be profound implications for the most intimate areas of life: interpersonal relationships, marriage opportunities, and domestic living arrangements.[2] As in the case of other basic social institutions, of which the family is a good and closely related example,[3] it is the protean character of inheritance that makes its analysis both a daunting and a rewarding task. This chapter confines itself, of necessity, to a limited set of issues: behaviour relating to inheritance and succession within the 'little society' of the household. The empirical evidence presented is drawn from rural Ireland. It relates to two time periods, the first and third quarters of this century, though the theoretical sketch in which this material is embedded has a more general relevance.

The discussion is arranged in five parts. First, there is a preliminary statement, informed by economic reasoning, of the nature of inheritance in farming communities. This suggests a framework of ideas, or what might be loosely termed a model, which is developed further in section two. Some implications of this theoretical perspective are drawn out and then tested against Irish rural experience in section three. In the penultimate section inheritance is related to the wider debate about household versus market provision, with particular reference to such areas of farming life as securing successors and catering for retirement and old age.

The conclusion recalls some of the key themes, according due recognition to the role inheritance plays in the survival of family farming.

THE NATURE OF INHERITANCE

Inheritance appears as a unilateral transfer of goods, taking the form of a pure or non-reciprocal gift relationship.[4] But it may be more realistic to visualise it as a web of exchange relationships, albeit of a highly complex kind. These exchanges are governed by long-term familial considerations, forming in effect a contractual relationship binding different generations of the same family. Using this perspective, one may then go on to identify the benefits and costs accruing to the participants. The benefits to the heir are fairly obvious: the acquisition of assets which he or she values. There may also be psychic benefits in the sense that such transfers reflect publicly the esteem in which the recipient is held by the donor.[5] Relatedly, in some rural societies the assumption of ownership or control of productive resources marks the transition to full adult status in the eyes of the local community.[6] The possible benefits to the property holder or donor are less transparent, mainly because there is a natural tendency to focus on the dramatic moment – the surrender of property rights – to the neglect of earlier and later transactions in time. Still, it becomes clear after a little reflection that the *ability* to confer bequests or legacies will shape behaviour in relation to the donor. It may induce feelings of affection, respect, deference, or even fear on the part of prospective inheritors. In the case of the farm household head this power over offspring may be pronounced, particularly in relation to the designated heir, or heirs. (While multiple heirs were not uncommon in pre Famine Ireland, in this century inheritance by one son has been the norm.) The exercise of direct control, depending on the social context, may extend from such mundane matters as the scheduling of farm tasks to the timing of marriage and choice of spouse.[7] Of special importance on the smaller family farms, the labour power of the prospective heir may be available to the head at less than its opportunity cost.[8] Furthermore, household heads may be in a position to negotiate, informally or otherwise, a variety of entitlements – maintenance allowances, care, and companionship – to enhance their welfare once they have reached a stage of dependency.[9] Finally, there are the rewards of immortality derived from having one's name and progeny established on the land.[10] Variations are obviously possible, but drawing on the historiography and ethnography of rural Ireland the packages of benefits being traded were broadly of the type set out in schematic form in Figure 7.1.

In the dismal world inhabited by economists (and moralists) there is rarely pleasure without penalties. Like the benefits, the costs to the donor of participation in the inheritance exchange are not immediately obvious, but include the loss or deferment of consumption opportunities during stages of the life cycle when children are economically dependent. The process of accumulating assets or of transmitting previously inherited wealth also has an opportunity cost in terms of forgone consumption. Intergenerational transfers of property tend to involve not only a loss of assets but also problems of emotional and status adjustment. In the case of recipients, the costs are most apparent in relation to the farm heir.[11] He (the heir being almost invariably a male child where one was available) pays a time price in waiting for his inheritance.[12] The working relationship with his parents during his period of farm apprenticeship may be more or less irksome depending on the personalities involved and the degree of power sharing (if any) in relation to work organisation and distribution of farm profits. The possibility and timing of marriage are dependent on inheritance, or its promise. The wait may be a lengthy one: in Ireland in 1945 male farmers were marrying, on average, in their thirty-eighth year.[13] In addition, supplying flows of services and income such as maintenance allowances, accommodation and care, what might be loosely called pension rights, is obviously a drain on the heir's economic resources (current or anticipated).[14]

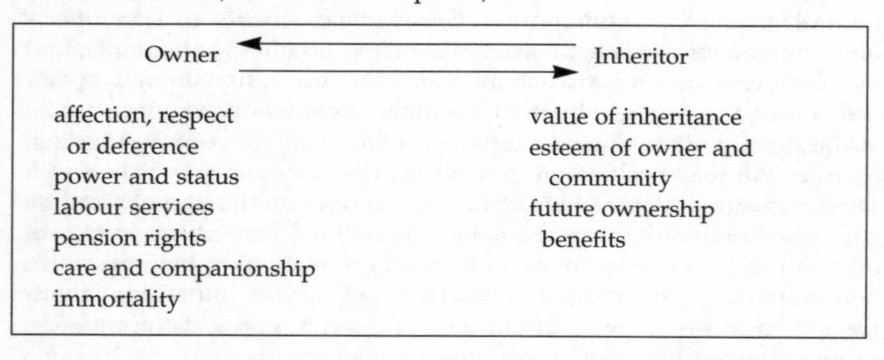

Figure 7.1 The inheritance exchange relationship: benefits to owners and inheritors

SUPPLY OF AND DEMAND FOR HEIRS

The existence of benefits and costs in the inheritance transaction suggests a range of possible practices and outcomes. The property owner may seek multiple heirs (partible inheritance) or indeed no heirs ('non-succession').

Under conditions of natural economy, for example, with property rights vested in kin groups rather than individuals, an egalitarian ethic and partible inheritance are efficient means of ensuring provision for all members of the group, whether economically active or dependent members of the household.[15] In other words, storing consumption claims rather than consumption goods is a more effective means of smoothing lifetime welfare flows and catering for old age. Even with market development and the vesting of property rights in individuals, it may still make sense for those with property endowments to procure multiple heirs. Quite apart from the consumption motives for having children living in close proximity, risk-averse parents may 'overproduce' heirs if mortality rates are high. Furthermore, on holdings which are weakly linked to produce markets or where the terms of trade are unattractive, the value placed on additional produce, and hence on additional units of land, is likely to be low once immediate consumption needs have been met.

In such circumstances, the fragmentation of holdings has a low opportunity cost. The west of Ireland in the pre-Famine period would seem to be an historical case in point. In fact, subdivision and the designation of more than one heir persisted in a few isolated and economically backward districts until well into this century.[16] More complete incorporation into market society, however, may tilt the balance decisively against partible inheritance. Opportunities for earnings through land-intensive production for the market[17] simultaneously raise the value of land and strengthen the incentive for the economically active core of the household to appropriate rights in land to itself.[18] These property rights, and possibly other durable assets accumulated over a working life, can be traded for consumption goods and welfare services in later life. A decline in mortality, rising expectations regarding living standards, and the emergence of alternative employment opportunities strengthen tendencies favouring a reduction in the number of heirs per household. So also do relative price movements which favour labour-extensive farming, such as livestock production. Institutional developments which stretch some minimum safety net under households work in the same direction. All these conditions, it may be noted, applied to post-Famine Irish society,[19] where in the great majority of cases the number of heirs per farm household was pared back to one. The logic linking impartible inheritance, family dispersion, and migration is well captured in the common saying: 'One for the farm, the rest for the road'.[20]

But could the process go even further than this? It is conceivable, and appears to have been the case in post-Famine Ireland, that some farmers were unwilling or unable to purchase direct heirs.[21] Securing an heir is dependent on having children. This in turn implies marriage (for legitimate heirs at any rate),[22] and the demand for marriage is likely to be sensitive to considerations of cost, income, prices of competing goods, age, and culturally determined taste patterns.[23] Whatever the precise mix of reasons, a growing minority of substantial farmers between 1851 and 1911 procured no direct heirs, by virtue of remaining celibate all their lives.[24] In Ireland, as in other rural societies, there were low-cost alternatives such as nephews and cousins.[25] *In extremis*, an unrelated person might be adopted as an heir-substitute.

The demand for heirs has been explored at some length. To complement this discussion it is necessary to look also at the supply side. Pursuing the strained market analogy, it may be presumed that the numbers of heirs offering their services will be responsive to economic considerations. A potential heir, even if he does not pray to Adam Smith every night, may engage in some rough calculus involving perceived costs and benefits. A more formal mimicry of the process of decision making might be as follows: remain in or exit from the role of heir depending on whether the present value of the stream of benefits from farming and inheritance, suitably discounted for risk, uncertainty, and time preference, is greater or less than the returns in the best alternative.[26] The latter might be a non-farming job in Ireland or work opportunities as an emigrant overseas. Our expectation, therefore, is of a conventional upward-sloping supply curve where, as the value of the farming inheritance package increases, the supply of heirs increases, and vice versa.

Equilibrium between the supply of and demand for heirs is possible in principle, though difficult to attain in practice, most particularly under conditions of impartible inheritance and high fertility. In relation to post-Famine Ireland it has been conventional to suggest a disequilibrium in many households and regions, with an excess supply of heirs and consequent disappointment for many.[27] Nonetheless, disequilibrium was not as severe as might appear at first sight. Inheritance transactions constituted a subset of the total of household transactions. Dowry payments, investment in education and emigration, and other forms of compensation for the disinherited moved the family system in the direction of equilibrium.[28] This is a point of major importance in that it helps incorporate inheritance transactions within the broad stream of household activities, allowing for a more elaborate and realistic web of interdependencies in welfare, decision making, and the timing of critical events in the family life cycle. An actual example of a family settlement may illustrate this.[29]

On 1 March 1927 the County Limerick farmer, Edmond Looby, transferred his 132-acre farm, dwelling house, livestock, crops, furniture, and farming implements to his son Michael. As mentioned specifically in the agreement, this intergenerational shift in ownership coincided with Michael's intended marriage to a bride-to-be who was bringing a marriage portion of £600 into the Looby household. Moreover, the agreement stipulated that the retiring owner should receive this sum of £600, as well as 'an annuity of seven pounds per annum during the term of his natural life, said annuity to be payable quarterly, the first quarterly payment of same to be made at the end of three months from the date hereof'. In addition, Edmond was granted rights of coresidence – an example, incidentally, of a stem family household in the process of formation. But what of Ellen, his apparently disinherited daughter? She was to receive an annuity from her brother Michael, the farm heir, and rights of coresidence. (In substance this was an intergenerational transaction, though taking the nominal form of transfer payments between siblings.) The likelihood is that Ellen in due course received a dowry or bequest, broadly similar to the amount secured by Michael's marriage.[30] The income and capital payments are summarised in Figure 7.2. This seems to be a fairly typical pattern of transfers, with the core relationship revolving round the parent(s) and the farm heir, but with provision where possible for non-heirs also. The qualification is important. Compensation for non-heirs could not be allowed to endanger the viability of the farm enterprise; otherwise the pension and other rights negotiated by the senior generation would be placed in jeopardy.[31]

The problem of disequilibrium would appear to be more acute under conditions of excess demand for heirs rather than in cases of excess supply, in that the compensatory mechanisms outlined above could not be readily invoked. For example, in the period since World War II less favourable valuations of farming life relative to urban living have been observed, particularly in the smallholding regions of the west of Ireland.[32] These changes suggest difficulties in recruiting heirs on the smaller farms. This, in fact, is the familiar rising threshold of viability for farms in Irish and other modern agrarian societies, as viewed from the less usual angle of inheritance. Nonetheless, some adaptations to this type of dilemma are possible. Obviously enough, the size of a farm, the land quality, the location, and the amount of farm capital are crucial determinants of the overall value of the heritable assets as well as of earnings in farming. But, from the point of view of the heir, the value or benefit to *him* depends also on the timing of the transfer, and any special conditions attaching to the enjoyment of these resources and their income-bearing potential. In other words, the present value of two identical sets of farm assets can vary appreciably depending on how the landholder structures the package of incentives and positions it in time. There is thus some scope for flexibility in the (implicit) bargaining process involved in the inheritance transactions. Furthermore, heir services, no less than labour services, are divisible. Part-time involvement with the home farm, with or without coresidence, is possible. Both in the Irish Republic and in Northern Ireland in recent decades part-time farming has been on the increase while the phenomenon of the worker-peasant has been widely observed in other European societies.[33]

PREDICTIONS AND EVIDENCE

Conceptualising inheritance and succession in exchange terms, along the lines already discussed, yields a number of implications or predictions. Each, of course, is hedged around by the usual *ceteris paribus* assumptions.

(1) A relationship between the incidence of primogeniture and farm size is likely. On the smaller farms the stock of assets and earning prospects are low. As a result, small farmers are likely to experience greater difficulty in recruiting heirs and thus have less scope for dis-

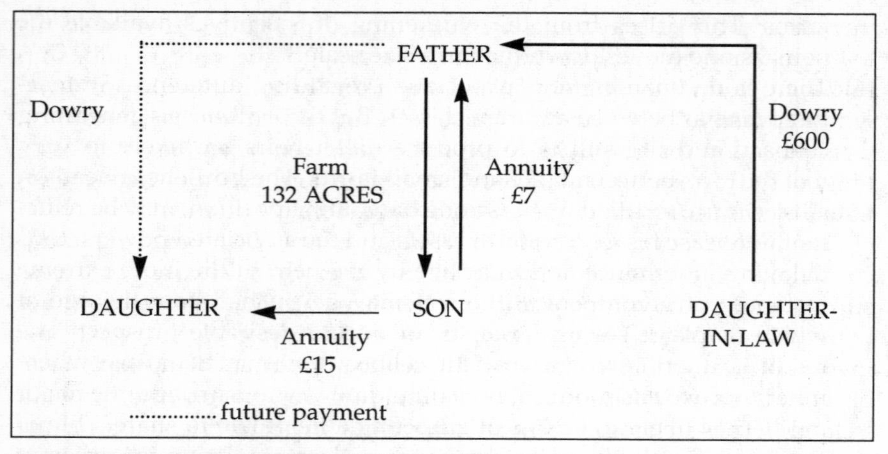

Figure 7.2 The Looby family settlement, 1927
Source: legal documents in the possession of the author.

criminating between sons in the rigid fashion prescribed by the norm of primogeniture. Labour needs are also less; an older son may be more profitably deployed away from the home farm. On the bigger farms, by contrast, there is likely to be an excess supply of heirs. Strong farmers, therefore, are in a sufficiently good bargaining position to indulge a preference for succession by a particular type of son. Underpinning such a preference might be the labour requirements of a larger farm: an older son could be more productively employed at an earlier stage in the developmental cycle of the farm household than would be the case in a smallholding household. The logic of the posited relationship between farm size and incidence of primogeniture would also lead one to presume that primogeniture is unlikely to be the dominant practice under conditions of smallholding agriculture[34] where alternative employment opportunities exist, as was the case in Ireland over the last century and a half.

(2) To the extent that ultimogeniture is practised, one would expect this tendency to be more pronounced on smaller farms. The argument is that the small farmer has a greater need to enhance the value of the inheritance package he is offering. This he can do, without augmenting his existing scanty resources, simply by reducing the waiting element in the transaction. This is effected least painfully, in terms of the surrender of power and status by the household head, through securing a successor who is a younger or youngest son. By the time a younger son has reached manhood the household head will have enjoyed a long period of control, and will be at a fairly advanced age or possibly even dead.

(3) One would expect more direct heirs on large as compared with small

farms. This arises from the weakening of incentives available for heirs as one moves down the farm size scale.

(4) There is no unambiguous expectation regarding differences in marriage *rates* as between agrarian classes. But the *mechanisms* generating celibacy and the failure to produce direct heirs are likely to vary markedly as between large and small farms. The household head on a large farm, fortified by his strong bargaining position, may be reluctant to release his grip on farm assets and the associated powers, thus delaying inheritance and marriage by the heir. In the more extreme instances of gerontocracy, the son may be pushed past the age at which marriage seems a realistic or even a desirable prospect. The result is a drift into permanent celibacy.[35] On small farms, where inheritance (or its promise) is also the gateway to marriage, the major problem is likely to be one of attracting a helpmate to share a life of poverty. Overall, therefore, we have no clear prediction for differential marriage rates. One might speculate, though, that in the long run the problem of securing heirs *and* wives on smallholdings is likely to prove the more intractable problem.

(5) Consistent with the logic of bargaining just elaborated, later *ages* of marriages and inheritance are to be expected on large farms.

(6) Smallholders should be less successful than large farmers in securing for themselves such pension rights as care and companionship in old age. Using, for example, household structure as an indicator, one would expect a larger proportion of social isolates and incomplete households among aged smallholders.

(7) Because the welfare of the older generation is bound up with the fortunes of the family farm, provision for children other than the farm heir will be subject to the constraint of maintaining the viability of the farm. Thus, even if there are egalitarian tendencies present in family ideology, there should be little or no financial compensation on small farms. However, as one journeys through the farm size distribution, the scope for more adequate compensation (or equilibrating measures) emerges. Assuming that the household strives for equity,[36] then, beyond some threshold level, the extent of compensation for non-farm heirs should be positively related to the value of the farm assets being devolved.

The first prediction, relating to the issue of primogeniture, is of particular interest in that the subject has exercised the scholarly imagination in relation to a range of societies and time periods.[37] In mapping areas of Europe by reference to inheritance regime, Thirsk included Ireland (along with Britain, the Scandinavian countries, and south-west France) as zones within which primogeniture predominated by the early modern period.[38] Her evidence related to the upper classes only but such succession norms might well have trickled down to the propertied lower orders over the succeeding generations. Whelan's bold assertion about post-Famine rural society – that 'primogeniture was the standard practice within the nuclear family' – while at variance with the model's prediction is consistent with such a possibility.[39] The prevalence, though not the universality of primogeniture is also suggested by Ó Gráda's ingenious, if indirect, test of the issue using data contained in the household schedules of the 1911 *Census of Ireland*.[40] Drawing on different source materials, the oral testimonies collected by the Irish Folklore Commission during the 1950s, Connell concluded that the heir was traditionally the eldest.[41] Social anthropologists, however, have been more sceptical. Arensberg and Kimball's classic study of west Clare in the 1930s found no fixed rule or norm governing selection of an heir.[42] Harris, writing about a south Ulster parish in the 1950s, claimed that the father was free to select the succeeding son, though, apart from citing a few family histories, she did not indicate what generally happened in practice.[43]

What is needed is direct evidence on actual outcomes in a large number of cases. Table 7.1 presents my findings for four localities in Ireland during the two decades or so after 1911. The study areas were chosen on the basis of their distinctive economic structures. Glencolumbkille, located on the west coast of Donegal, is characterised by extremely poor soil resources, a problem exacerbated by the small size of holdings. Borris-Drom is a district of medium-quality agricultural land, worked in the main by middling-sized and smaller farmers. Athassel is situated in the fertile Golden Vale of Tipperary and, typifying the positive relationship between land quality and farm size in Ireland, held substantial numbers of large farmers. East Meath also contains some of the best farming land on the island, and was dominated by large cattle farms. But clustered on the edges of these grazing farms were many dwarf holdings, worked by a semi-proletariat which depended on supplying labour services to the neighbouring big farmers. The study areas may, therefore, be said to span a wide spectrum of agrarian conditions: the imposing farmsteads on the Meath plains epitomising the highest development of agrarian capitalism in Ireland while Glencolumbkille, with its thatched single-storey cabins, was one of the many marginal economies scattered along the western seaboard.

Table 7.1 Succession practices in four localities in rural Ireland

Locality	County	1st son (%)	not 1st son (%)	N
Glencolumbkille	Donegal	38	62	125
Borris-Drom	Tipperary NR	42	58	150
Athassel	Tipperary SR	44	56	50
East Meath	Meath	43	57	72

Source: datafile for the four study areas; see main text.

The sources used to establish succession practices are, first, the manuscript household schedules from the 1901 and 1911 censuses of Ireland. These are then linked to land valuation records which identify owners and ownership changes through time.[44] The single, most striking fact to emerge from Table 7.1 is that primogeniture was *not* the dominant practice in any of the study areas. Even if one excludes the cottager holdings (the category I to 4 acres),[45] this still holds true for all localities, with the single exception of East Meath. Of further interest, because the sequence of districts adopted in Table 7.1 also reflects an economic ordering of the areas, there is some hint of a relationship between primogeniture and rural wealth.

This issue can be pursued further by disaggregating the data, as in Table 7.2. In Glencolumbkille the expected relationship between farm size and primogeniture seems to emerge, though it should be noted that there is virtually no representation of very large farms. For the other three areas the picture is more complex. As anticipated, primogeniture was uncommon on very small holdings. Intriguingly, though, the practice was also a minority one among very large farmers (those with holdings exceeding 100 acres). On the intermediate-sized holdings primogeniture was more pronounced than at either extreme of the farm-size distribution. If this pattern is representative – the results are suggestive rather than clearcut – this would indicate a curvilinear rather than a simple linear relationship between primogeniture and farm size.

Table 7.2 Primogeniture and farm size

Farm size (acres)	**Glencolumbkille**		**Borris-Drom**		**Athassel**		**E. Meath**	
	1st son (%)	*(N)*	*1st son (%)*	*(N)*	*1st son (%)*	*(N)*	*1st son (%)*	*(N)*
1–4	29	21	37	8	27	11	24	37
5–30	39	88	37	63	55	11	67	15
31–60	33	9	49	45	55	11	70	10
61–100	50	6	56	25	44	9	75	4
101 and over	100	1	11	9	37	8	33	6

Source: datafile for the four study areas.

Why very large farmers should select comparatively few eldest sons as successors is a tantalising question. One plausible line of interpretation is that, unlike smallholders who might lack the resources to retain and maintain an eldest son, the rural bourgeois family could pursue more complex household strategies, securing acceptable economic niches (for example, as doctors, lawyers, clergymen, civil servants) for a variety of sons, depending on aptitude and appropriate investments in human capital.[46] Further, since hired labour was the norm on such farms, the forfeited labour services of an eldest son were amenable to easy substitution.[47] On farms located in the middle-sized categories, however, dependence on family would be more pronounced and the need to economise on wage labour greater.

Strictly speaking, inferences to the rest of rural Ireland are not permissible from the data in Tables 7.1 and 7.2. Still, one may wonder if primogeniture could have been the standard practice, given that two-thirds of the landholdings in 1911 were sized 30 acres or less and that about a quarter of heirs might be expected to be eldest sons on the basis of a purely random process of succession.

For the postwar period we are fortunate in having a national overview of succession practices, based on a stratified random sample of 1221 land-holders.[48] While this does not explore possible relationships between farm size and primogeniture, it is instructive on many other aspects of inheritance during the 1950s and 1960s. Of immediate interest, it shows that only one in every two farm heirs was an eldest son (once allowance is made for only sons). Furthermore, fertility had fallen substantially between 1911 and 1961. Completed rural family size averaged just under five births in 1961, so even in the absence of any succession norm, eldest sons might be expected to inherit in about 40 per cent of cases. The argument for widespread primogeniture, it is clear, cannot be sustained for the modern period either.

Table 7.3 Birth order of male heirs: relative frequency (per cent)

Locality	1st	2nd	3rd	4th	5th[a]	Unknown	Total	N
Glencolumbkille	39	12	10	3	3	33	100	116
Borris-Drom	44	23	5	5	0	23	100	146
Athassel	45	12	12	4	0	27	100	49
East Meath	46	9	15	6	0	24	100	67

Note: [a] fifth and above.

The numbers of cases are different from those in Tables 7.1 and 7.2. This is because of the exclusion of the few instances in each locality in which daughters were 'preferred' to sons (a sub-theme pursued further in section IV).
Source: datafile for the four study areas.

If primogeniture was not the dominant practice, perhaps then ultimogeniture prevailed. This has been suggested for some peripheral areas elsewhere in the British Isles in this century (though English common law tended to favour inheritance by the eldest son).[49] It is also said to be the case among farming families in contemporary Denmark.[50] In relation to smallholding areas in Ireland, one writer believed that emigration siphoned off the older children, leaving 'the floor free for the youngest son, on whom the task of looking after the parent falls'.[51] The evidence from our study areas (Table 7.3) suggests, however, that ultimogeniture was not a majority phenomenon earlier this century.[52] For the postwar period Commins and Kelleher's national sample indicates that a fourth or later son inherited in only 10 per cent of cases.[53] The joint authors did not go on to analyse the incidence of ultimogeniture by farm size. Equally unfortunately, the data from our four study areas, when broken down by birth order and farm size, yield too few observations to warrant anything more than an agnostic position (except perhaps in the case of Glencolumbkille where an association between the two seems to be present). The implication of our model (a negative relationship between farm size and incidence of ultimogeniture) remains, therefore, untested. One small piece of evidence which is consistent with the proposition may be noted, however. On the impoverished smallholdings of mountainous west Kerry, Scheper-Hughes found that 'the last one to escape (usually the *youngest* son) gets stuck by default with an unproductive farm and saddled with a lifestyle of almost certain celibacy and service to the old people' (italics added).[54]

Interestingly, while acknowledging the role of economic factors in structuring succession practices, the author places special emphasis on social psychological elements in her explanatory scheme. The argument in brief is that children underwent quite different socialisation experiences within the family, depending on birth order. Older sons (and daughters) were brought up in a manner which fitted them to seek opportunities outside farming. By contrast, younger or youngest sons were psychologically maimed from childhood, consciously or otherwise, with the aim of tying them to their barren patrimony, and its attendant responsibilities. This pathological interpretation and the economic explanation advanced in this paper are not, of course, mutually exclusive. If Scheper-Hughes's thesis is correct and has some validity for smallholding households elsewhere in Ireland in the postwar period, then such tying devices are best seen perhaps as parental resources sometimes exploited to supplement weak property incentives.[55]

Other predictions of the model relate to success in acquiring farm successors, propensity to marry, and household structure. Contrary to expectations, I did not find that the availability of direct heirs varied by farm size (Table 7.4). Most farm households in fact had one or more coresiding sons. This suggests that the social reproduction of farming families was proceeding fairly smoothly in the earlier 20th century. However, this situation had changed dramatically half a century later. Commins and Kelleher observed that almost one-third of the domestic groups on small farms consisted of non-family households. This proportion fell consistently as size of farm increased.[56] Similarly, in a sample of

Table 7.4 Proportion of rural households within each farm size category with (potential) direct heirs in 1911

Farm size (acres)	Glencolumbkille (%)	Borris-Drom (%)	Athassel (%)	E. Meath (%)
1–4	89	72	64	82
5–30	90	85	82	65
31–60	89	84	67	89
61–100	87	80	75	100
101 and over	100	64	80	100
All farms	89 (N=225)	80 (N=218)	72 (N=58)	79 (N=85)

Source: datafile for the four study areas.

8000 western farmers, mainly smallholders, Scully found that more than 1 in 4 had no apparent heir. Among farmers aged 50 years or more, this proportion rose to an alarming 1 in 2.[57] To take an even more extreme example, Brody concluded that only about 20 per cent of the farms in his isolated seaboard community stood much chance of lasting another generation.[58] In what is clearly a very different world from rural Ireland *c.* 1911, the 1960s witnessed the demise or the imminent demise of the family line on a substantial minority of Irish farms. This was particularly true of small farms, as originally anticipated. Arguably therefore, a tendency towards dynastic failure is present in small-farm economies but this does not manifest itself until a late stage in the evolution of peasant economy.[59]

Table 7.5 Proportion of rural households within each farm size category with a married (or once married) head in 1911

Farm size (acres)	Glencolumbkille (%)	Borris-Drom (%)	Athassel (%)	E. Meath (%)
1–4	89	86	85	81
5-30	90	89	82	72
31–60	93	91	81	72
61–100	83	87	87	100
101 and over	83	79	100	83
All farms	89 (N = 390)	89 (N = 530)	85 (N = 143)	79 (N = 239)

Source: datafile for the four study areas.

The closely related issues of celibacy and marriage rates also yielded findings more complex than those hypothesised earlier. In the democracy of small farms in Glencolumbkille in 1911 there were only 41 unmarried household heads out of a total of 390, which is a celibacy rate among heads of a mere 11 per cent (Table 7.5). In Borris-Drom the position was similar, and in both districts celibacy, if anything, was slightly more evident on the larger farms. In the more affluent farming areas of Athassel and especially East Meath unmarried household heads were considerably more common, though within these areas there was little, if any, association between holding size and celibacy. Half a century later, however, a relationship between economic status and marriage had clearly emerged (Table 7.6), family failure being strongly associated with the lower reaches of the rural class structure. Viewed regionally, the most extreme manifestation of these patterns was to be found in the west of Ireland, with commentators lamenting the 'chronic sexual isolation' of the communities of the Atlantic seaboard.[60]

Table 7.6 Age at marriage of household head and farm size about 1900 (standard errors in brackets)

	Constant	Farm size	Farm size sq.	N	R
Glencolumbkille	31.70	– 0.02	0.05	190	0.05
	(0.77)	(0.04)	(0.18)		
Borris-Drom	34.54	1.90	– 0.39	263	0.06
	(0.76)	(2.03)	(0.70)		
Athassel	29.54	0.12	– 0.42	86	0.34
	(1.25)	(0.04)	(0.17)		
E. Meath	33.18	2.26	– 0.39	112	0.12
	(0.83)	(1.83)	(0.35)		

Source: see text

Attempts to regress age at marriage on farm size and farm size squared (implying a curvilinear relationship between the two variables), using information from the 1911 datafiles, produced no statistically significant results, with the single exception of Athassel (Table 7.6). This was true both when using ages as reported in 1911 (widely known to be subject to systematic bias) and after correcting them by using the ages returned in the immediately preceding census of 1901. Table 7.6 uses corrected age data. Experimenting with simple linear and log linear forms yielded similarly negative findings. This had all changed by mid-century, however. For marriages contracted during 1945–46, the subject of a special official inquiry, a clear relationship between age at marriage and landholding size had become apparent (Table 7.7).

Table 7.7 Age at marriage of male landholders about the mid 20th century, classified by farm size (rateable valuation of the holdings)

	Average age at marriage	N
Rateable valuation of:		
£50 and over	37.7	561
£20–£49	37.3	1123
£10–£19	36.9	1211
£4-£9	35.8	940
Under £4	34.5	717
Other[a]	32.0	1283

Note: [a] valuation not stated and holdings less than one acre (agricultural labourers)
Source: Commission on emigration and other population problems: reports, 1948–54 (Dublin, 1954) p 84.

It was anticipated that at an advanced stage in the life cycle of the senior generation a series of relationships connecting farm resources and household structure would come into focus, indicating in turn varying degrees of success in securing companionship and care in old age. In fact, what is most striking is how *few* elderly couples lived alone and without the benefit of coresiding relatives in 1911. In Glencolumbkille only 5 out of 61 (8 per cent) of couples aged over 60 years formed two-person households. The corresponding levels for Borris-Drom, Athassel, and East Meath were 18 per cent, 5 per cent, and 3 per cent respectively. Moreover, instances of aged persons living alone were quite rare (Table 7.8): there were only 12 isolates out of a total of 533 cases of aged land-

Table 7.8 Isolation and old age: solitary households as a proportion of all households headed by aged persons (over 60 years), arranged by farm size

Farm size (acres)	Glencolumbkille (%)	Borris-Drom (%)	Athassel (%)	E. Meath (%)
1–4	0	7	9	3
5–30	1	1	0	1
531–60	0	0	0	0
61–100	12	0	0	0
101 and over	0	0	0	0
All farms	1 (N=217)	2 (N=199)	2 (N=48)	6 (N=69)

Source: datafile for the four study areas.

holding heads. An incipient connection between social stratification and household structure (as measured by these two indicators) may be present, though the dominant impression is one of family cohesion right across the socio-economic spectrum.

This tableau of family life underwent substantial alteration over the next half-century. In the peculiar circumstances of west Kerry, Scheper-Hughes can speak of postwar social change transforming the community of Ballybran from a healthy conjugal community to a sick and dying celibate one.[61] Viewed nationally, the scene was much less gloomy, but what is particularly significant for our purposes is that the experience of change varied markedly by agrarian class. For example, while there was a general decline in the importance of conjugal family units between 1911 and the 1960s, the proportion of non-family households was twice as great (and of solitary households almost two-and-a-half times as great) on small as compared to large farms.[62] Reflecting and reinforcing this differential experience, older unmarried farmers were concentrated disproportionately on smaller farms, the share declining systematically with increasing farm size.[63]

In our sketch of the family transactions surrounding inheritance we anticipated some relationship between household resources (crudely indicated by farm size) and the extent to which non-heirs were compensated. A recent analysis of wills and probate records by Ó Gráda for the late 19th and early 20th centuries lends support to the expectation of an association between means and equity.[64] My own evidence for the post-war period, based on a sample of farmers in East Meath is presented in Table 7.9.[65] The very low rate of compensation on small farms (a frequent comment by heirs on such farms was, 'There was nothing to give the others') is consistent with the view that the primary exchange being safeguarded was that between the senior generation and the farm heir. Where family resources permitted, as on the more substantial holdings, an impulse towards equity could be indulged.

Table 7.9 Frequency with which non-heirs in East Meath received compensation, classified by landholding size

Farm size (acres)	Some compensation (%)	No compensation (%)	N
5-30	15	85	59
31–60	34	66	91
61–100	30	70	56
101–200	71	29	34
201 and over	85	15	46
All farms	42	58	286

Source: East Meath survey, 1985 (see text).

It may be helpful at this stage, having matched the implications of the model with empirical evidence, to summarise the various findings.[66] This is done in Table 7.10 for the two time periods. A plus sign indicates confirmation, a negative sign refutation, while mixed results are shown by a combined plus and minus sign. In relation to the overall pattern what is most striking is the fact that the 'anomalies' (in terms of the model) had all disappeared by the postwar period. This would suggest that the underlying rationale of the inheritance system has been identified, at least in an approximate form, and that certain latent tendencies and problems only become manifest when small-farm agriculture is in economic retreat. In the Irish case this has been due to the accelerating pace of agricultural commercialisation in the decades after 1945, increasingly visible gaps in living standards between farming and non-farming occupations, and enhanced opportunities for employment during the long postwar boom in the western world. The 1950s in particular witnessed a massive rural exodus as the British labour market offered the youth of rural Ireland effective economic alternatives, in the process devaluing the benefits of land inheritance and squeezing the supply of heirs.

Table 7.10 The model and the evidence: confirmation (+) or rejection (–) of the predictions

Predictions		Time periods	
		c.1910–30	c.1950–70
(1)	primogeniture	+	+
(2)	ultimogeniture	?	+
(3)	direct heirs	-	+
(4)	marriage rates	-	+
(5)	age of marriage	+-	+
(6)	pension rights etc.	+-	+
(7)	compensation & equity	+	+

Source: see text.

Beyond the Market

Our understanding of the exchange perspective on inheritance can be deepened by considering a fundamental question which, so far, has been treated as unproblematic. This is the reliance on family and kinship rather than market mechanisms for producing the goods and services which make up the inheritance package.[67] Most of the goods were also available (to varying degrees) as commodities through the market. In 20th-century Ireland non-family labour could be hired, land could be rented, purchased, or sold, insurance and pension schemes existed, as did nursing and domestic services. One may wonder therefore why the market had not displaced these traditional functions of the family farm (more especially as we have been using market analogies for the study of inheritance and its ramifications). Yet dependence on family as compared to hired labour has become more, rather than less, pronounced during the past century and more. Kin have been, and still are, preferred to non-kin as farm successors. The bulk of land transfers, now as in past times, involve kin, and take place outside the orbit of the market.[68] Why?

Part of the answer seems to lie in the lower cost of family labour, in the context of a secular rise in agricultural wages. The farm heir in particular experienced a lengthy apprenticeship during which his money earnings were probably less than his marginal product over much of the apprenticeship period. In effect, he was paid to a small extent in cash but primarily through payments-in-kind and *future claims* to productive assets.[69] This strategy reduced current cash outlays and helped smooth the cost of labour over several stages in the life cycle of the family. The fact that membership of the family was for life facilitated wage sacrifices and commitment by the heir to long-term goals. The family farm also possessed important advantages over, say, capitalist farming, in terms of motivating and monitoring its own members' work performance.[70] More speculatively, family members may have accumulated farm-specific capital, in the sense of productive skills and knowledge peculiar to the home farm, which gave them an efficiency advantage over non-kin.[71] Moreover, because the owner-heir relationship typically involved a work partnership and coresidence, compatibility of temperament and personality traits was desirable. Strangers, virtually by definition, were riskier propositions in this respect.[72]

These considerations may also help to explain the preference for male over female heirs. In theory it would have been possible for farm owners to nominate a daughter rather than a son as successor, achieving farm continuity and labour services through the medium of an incoming son-in-law. But succession by a daughter in circumstances where she had one or more brothers was most unusual. Only four cases were observed in Glencolumbkille, a similar number in Borris-Drom, one in Athassel, and five in East Meath (1911 datafile). The rarity of daughter succession and the fact that it was confined to smaller farms suggests that it occurred by default rather than by preference.[73] It is not hard to see why sons-in-law were poor substitutes for son-heirs. Quite apart from potential problems centring on skills, personality, and household harmony, there was the additional drawback that the labour services of a son-in-law would not be available until a late stage in the life cycle of the farm household.

So much for labour and heir services. The family also possessed certain transactional advantages in the production of such services as insurance and pension rights.[74] Information and monitoring costs were bound to be lower than for non-family farms. Furthermore, these activities were time rather than cash intensive, and money resources were likely to have been the more severe constraint on most Irish farms.

More fundamentally, it could be argued that the family offered a particularly good *organisational structure* for handling complicated, long-term exchanges.[75] The sheer complexity and fragility of family processes revolving round inheritance (Figure 7.1) merit closer attention. Transactions extended over a long time span, with the constituent elements widely spaced in time. These intergenerational agreements involved not only asymmetric power relations; in so far as power was a function of labour productivity, the distribution of power within the family was subject to shifts over time. (The senior generation progressed from high to low productivity states, while the converse was true of the younger generation.) Additionally, the vicissitudes of family and farm life, as well as uncertainty over the precise content and quality of mutual obligations, meant that breakdown or default was a real possibility. It is little wonder, therefore, that there was no perfect counterpart in the market capable of handling such subtle processes and interdependencies. In a world of imperfect information and high transaction costs, as Ben-Porath puts it, agreements between persons well known to each other who expect to be connected for a long time 'may be more efficient because the behaviour of the partners is based on self-enforcement of implicit contracts'.[76] Trust (based on intimate knowledge) and family loyalty, buttressed by customary norms, limited the scope for arbitrary or exploitative practices. Two other forces conferred robustness on family inheritance arrangements. Most importantly perhaps, control over productive assets compensated for waning productive powers on the part of the older generation; promises (or threats) regarding their disposal were thus a means of enforcing earlier agreements. Furthermore, private legal settlements were sometimes invoked to reinforce specific family arrangements.[77]

Nonetheless, the family had characteristic weaknesses as well as strengths as an institution responsible for producing services such as insurance and pension rights. Because the kinship and economic spheres interpenetrated, there was an ever-present danger that conflict in one might overflow into the other, thereby rupturing production as well as personal relationships.[78] Also, the family could not easily spread risks, nor could it, with the unfolding of new technological possibilities, avail itself of major economies of scale. For these reasons, we find the market and the state encroaching on some of the diverse functions originally performed by families. But, despite the shifting boundaries between family, market, and state provision, what is most remarkable perhaps is the persistence in rural society of the ancient, kinship-impregnated institution of inheritance in modified, though still robust form into the late 20th century.[79]

THE SURVIVAL OF FAMILY FARMING

In conclusion the model of rural inheritance and succession presented here has been developed primarily with reference to conditions of impartible inheritance, though it is apparent that, *mutatis mutandis,* it could be applied to partible inheritance regimes also. It is applicable to tenant farming systems, as in 19th-century Ireland, as well as owner occupancy. In testing this framework of ideas within the context of 20th-century Irish rural society I have largely abstracted from regional, institutional, and cultural factors. Such parsimony confers a greater degree of generality but it also means that a richer analysis of inheritance and succession practices would seek to incorporate these further elements.

Some of the implications of the inheritance-exchange perspective were realised already by the early 20th century. Others, however, did not materialise fully until the postwar period (Table 7.10). Over time regional or class deviations seem to have been eliminated, resulting in a high degree of consistency between predicted and actual behaviour. The existence of time lags in relation to the emergence of some effects suggests that the primary role of the model is to indicate *directions* of social change (rather than to prescribe outcomes in each and every region and time period). As Leibenstein notes, one of the important functions of theory is 'to show what is latent in a set of circumstances although the facts appear to show otherwise'.[80]

It is worth repeating that the intergenerational transmission of landed property has to be viewed against a larger backdrop of household strategies which seek to provide, not only for household heads and heirs, but for family members more generally. Many of the critical transactions which compose household strategies connect, directly or indirectly, with the institution of inheritance. The complexity of these transactions, and the risks involved, have meant that the state and the market have displaced the household only slowly and unevenly. This brings us naturally, if unexpectedly, to an issue of major historical and contemporary significance: that is, the survival of family farming itself. Contrary to the expectations of early marxist (and some non-marxist) writers, large-scale capitalist farming (agri-business) has failed to displace family farm production.[81] Marx's 'laws' of concentration and centralisation –so potent in the realm of manufacturing – have been frustrated in the world of agriculture. A variety of explanations might be proffered, ranging from limited economies of scale in important branches of farming to the providential role of the state in relation to rural communities in most western societies since the time of the 'Great Agricultural Depression'. But arguably the most neglected element in explaining the persistence of the family farm economy is also the most significant: the role of inheritance, and its associated institutions of family and kinship. Farm property flows along kinship lines according to criteria dictated by corporate (family) and individual members' strategies. This closed system of transactions insulates heirs from the full play of market forces in competing for land and related productive resources. Thus, by endowing kinfolk with agricultural assets at little cost, in money terms at least, the institution of inheritance has acted as a breakwater against market pressures and the ultimate triumph of agro-capitalism.

Notes

1. This chapter was previously published in *Economic History Review*, XLIV, 3 (1991) pp 477–99. It is based on the author's longer 'Inheritance patterns in Irish farming areas', a report submitted to the Economic and Social Research Council, London, in 1986.
2. For some elaboration see: J Wedgwood, *The economics of inheritance* (1929); CM Meade, *Efficiency, equality and the ownership of property* (1964); CD Harbury and DW Hitchens, *Inheritance and wealth inequality in Britain* (1979); WD Rubinstein, *Men and property* (1981); J Goody, J Thirsk, and EP Thompson (eds) *Family and inheritance: rural society in western Europe, 1200–1800* (1979).
3. EA Wrigley, 'Reflections on the history of the family', in *Daedalus*, vol 106 (1977) pp 71–85.
4. The classic discussion of gift relationships is to be found in M Mauss, *The gift: forms and functions of exchange in archaic societies* (1954).
5. EH Leyton, *The one blood: kinship and class in an Irish village* (Toronto, 1975).
6. J Goody, 'Inheritance, property and women: some comparative considerations', in J Goody, J Thirsk, and EP Thompson (eds) *Family and inheritance: rural society in western Europe, 1200–1800* (1979) p 28; CM Arensberg and ST Kimball, *Family and community in Ireland* (Cambridge, Mass, 1940); R Harris, *Prejudice and tolerance in Ulster* (Manchester, 1972) pp 62–4.
7. In the Irish case one might note the description of intergenerational relationships contained in KH Connell, *Irish peasant society* (Oxford, 1968) pp 117–8; Arensberg and Kimball, *Family and community*, pp 54–8; RE Kennedy, *The Irish: emigration, marriage and fertility* (Berkeley, 1973) pp 151–7; KA Miller, *Emigrants and exiles: Ireland and the Irish exodus to North America* (New York, 1985) p 125.
8. See, for example, HS Barron, *Those who stayed behind: rural society in nineteenth century New England* (New York, 1987) p 106; D Jenkins, *The agricultural community in south-west Wales at the turn of the century* (Cardiff, 1971) pp 119, 124; Harris, *Prejudice and tolerance*, pp 63–4
9. PA Neher, 'Peasants, procreation and pensions', *American Economic Review*, vol 61 (1971) pp 380–9.
10. 'This ideal is reported in virtually every ethnography of rural Ireland': R Breen, 'Dowry payments and the Irish case', in *Comparative Studies in Society and History*, vol 26 (1984) p 290.
11. Sometimes in fact the heir was considered to be less rather than more fortunate than his brothers. See, for example, Jenkins, *Agricultural community*, p 154; Connell, *Peasant society*, p 118; E Weber, *Peasants into Frenchmen: the modernisation of rural France, 1870–1914* (1979) pp 188–91.

12. This has been and continues to be true of family farming communities, not only in Ireland but in Britain, continental Europe, and North America. See, for example, Jenkins, *Agricultural community*; G Dallas, *The imperfect peasant economy* (Cambridge, 1982); M Segalen, *Love and power in the peasant family* (Oxford, 1983); Barron, *Those who stayed behind*; LJ Alston and MO Schapiro, 'Inheritance laws across colonies: causes and consequences', *Journal of Economic History*, XLIV (1984) pp 277–87.
    While female heirs were unusual, except under conditions of widowhood or in the absence of male children, exceptions to this generalisation do, of course, exist. For an instance of an Irish locality where daughters as well as sons enjoyed substantial rights in land see R Fox, *The Tory islanders* (Cambridge, 1978). An economic basis for male preference is explored briefly in section IV of this chapter.
13. *Commission on emigration and other population problems: reports, 1948–54*, p 78.
14. For a graphic account of resentment on this score see Weber, *Peasants into Frenchmen*, pp 174–6.
15. Neher, 'Peasants, procreation and pensions', p 386. Some suggestive ideas on the existence and persistence of different types of inheritance regimes are contained in C Creighton, 'Family, property and relationships of production in western Europe', *Econony and Society*, vol ix (1980) pp 129–67.
16. Fox, *Tory islanders*; J Lee, *The modernisation of Irish society, 1848–1918* (Dublin, 1973) pp 8, 82.
17. This careful formulation is necessary. The emergence of labour markets, either locally or in regions to which labour might migrate on a temporary or seasonal basis, could strengthen 'archaic' patterns, including partible inheritance. Opportunities for labour–intensive production, such as in cottage industry, might have a similar effect.
18. One should not necessarily assume a sharp transition from inheritance by multiple heirs to inheritance by a single heir. In parts of County Down, for example, it was reported in 1845 that division of holdings between the *two* eldest sons was commonplace. See *Evidence taken before Her Majesty's commissioners of inquiry into the state of the law and practice in respect of the occupation of land in Ireland* (PP 1845, xix) p 462.
19. Thus, there was ready access to the great labour markets of Britain and North America, the relative price structure discouraged labour-intensive tillage farming, and institutional innovations included the extension of the British poor law system to Ireland in 1838 and the introduction of state-financed old age pensions in 1908.
20. K Whelan, 'The Famine and post-Famine adjustment', in W Nolan (ed) *The shaping of Ireland* (Cork, 1986) p 160.
21. T Guinnane, 'Migration, marriage, and household formation: the Irish at the turn of the century' (abstract of PhD thesis), *Irish Economic and Social History*, vol 25 (1988) pp 105–6.
22. For the general observation that some goods, for instance children, are demanded not simply for themselves but also as inputs into the production of more basic household commodities see M Keeley, 'A comment on "an interpretation of the economic theory of fertility"', in *Journal of Economic Literature*, vol 13 (1975) p 462. Note also G Becker, 'A theory of the allocation of time', *Economic Journal*, vol 65 (1965) pp 494–6.

23. J Mokyr, 'Malthusian models and Irish history', in *Journal of Economic History*, vol 40 (1980) pp 161–3. For particular subgroups marriage may have been a low-valued good, or perhaps not even a good at all. One thinks of homosexual, asexual, or misogynistic persons, for example.
24. In 1851 less than one in eight Irish males in the age group *45–54* years was unmarried. This proportion had more than doubled to one in four by 1911. The ratio in 1961, using the same measure of celibacy, was virtually unchanged by comparison with 1911. Calculated from WE Vaughan and AJ Fitzpatrick, *Irish historical statistics: population, 1821–1971* (Dublin, 1978).
25. P Commins and C Kelleher, *Farm inheritance and succession* (Dublin, 1973) p 22; Guinane, 'Migration', p 105; BA Hanawalt, *The ties that bound: peasant families in medieval England* (Oxford, 1986) p 233. For a detailed anthropological study of surrogate heirs in contemporary rural Ireland see C Bloodworth, 'Talking past differences: conflicts, community and history in an Irish parish' (unpublished PhD thesis, Cornell University, 1988).
26. This does not, of course, purport to be an actual description of how an individual in past time made such a decision. The intention behind the model-building approach used in this section is rather to identify *tendencies* in social behaviour which may be true of large numbers of people, taken as a whole, though not necessarily of particular individuals within that aggregate.
27. Connell, *Peasant society*, pp 116–7; Miller, *Emigrants*, pp 403–5
28. Ó Gráda argues for a propensity to treat children equitably in Irish farm households; C Ó Gráda, *Ireland before and after the Famine: explorations in economic history, 1800–1925* (Manchester, 1988) pp 156–63. For a somewhat different emphasis, see L Kennedy, 'Inheritance patterns in Irish farming areas' (report to ESRC, 1986) pp 33–6.
29. Indenture made between Edmond Looby, Michael and Ellen Looby, and Mary Kelly, 1 March 1927, one of several dozen family agreements in the possession of the author.
30. On the circulation and size of dowries see Breen, 'Dowry payments', p 288; Ó Gráda, *Ireland before and after the Famine*, pp 165–8. Goody calls dowry a type of premortem inheritance to the bride; J Goody and SJ Tambiah, *Bride wealth and dowry* (1975) p 1.
31. Kennedy, 'Inheritance', pp 19–21.
32. JJ Scully, *Agriculture in the west of Ireland* (Dublin, 1971). For similar observations on other regions of rural Europe see SH Franklin, *The European peasantry: the final phase* (1969).
33. P Commins, 'Land policies and agricultural development', in PJ Drudy (ed) *Ireland: land, policies and people* (1982) pp 218–34.
34. Seven out of every 10 farm holdings in the Irish Republic did not exceed 50 acres as late as 1960.
35. For an interesting, new interpretation of non-marriage among large farmers see Guinnane, 'Migration', p 106.
36. Ó Gráda, *Ireland before and after the Famine*, p 163. See also D Fitzpatrick, 'Irish farming families before the First World War', *Comparative Studies in Society and History*, vol 23 (1983) p 369.
37. See for example Hanawalt, *Ties that bound*, pp 67–78; Alston and Schapiro, 'Inheritance laws'; the essays by Le Roy Ladurie, Howell, and Thirsk in Goody *et al* (eds) *Family and inheritance*; J Hutson, 'Fathers and sons: family

farms, family business and the farming industry', *Sociology*, vol 21 (1987) pp 215–29.

38. J Thirsk, 'The European debate on customs of inheritance, 1500–1700', in J Goody, J Thirsk, and EP Thompson (eds) *Family and inheritance: rural society in western Europe, 1200–1800* (1979) pp 177–91.
39. Whelan, 'Famine and post-Famine adjustment', p 160.
40. Ó Gráda concludes that in three out of the four areas studied by him it is *probable* that inheritance by the eldest son was a majority phenomenon. See his 'Primogeniture and ultimogeniture in rural Ireland', *Journal of Interdisciplinary History*, vol 10 (1980) pp 491–7.
41. Connell, *Peasant society*, p 116.
42. Arensberg and Kimball, *Family and community*, pp 64–5.
43. Harris, *Prejudice and tolerance*, p 62. Similarly Leyton finds no rigid prescriptions regarding the birth order of heirs in his east Ulster study area (though there is some suggestion of a preference for primogeniture among the small local elite of substantial property holders). See Leyton, *One blood*, pp 74–5; EH Leyton, 'Spheres of inheritance in Aughnaboy', *American Anthropology*, vol 72 (1970) pp 1378–88.
44. Land records are held at the Valuation Office, Dublin, while the household census schedules are housed at the National Archives, Dublin.
45. The levels of primogeniture in this case become 39, 42, 49, and 63 per cent respectively. It is interesting and significant that even in Glencolumbkille, where dwarf holdings proliferated, the tiniest landholders defined themselves as farmers when filling in the census form.
46. There is some limited evidence on this point in Kennedy, 'Inheritance', pp 27–8.
47. While Ireland generally had comparatively few farm labourers by the early 20th century, there were strong concentrations of labourers in Tipperary (South Riding) and especially in County Meath. See Department of Industry and Commerce, *Agricultural statistics 1871–1926* (Dublin, 1928); D Bradley, *Farm labourers* (Belfast, 1988).
48. Commins and Kelleher, *Farm succession*.
49. AD Rees, *Life in a Welsh countryside* (Cardiff, 1950) pp 71–2; Jenkins, *Agricultural community*, p 153; Hutson, 'Fathers and sons', p 219.
50. Commins and Kelleher, *Farm succession*, p 121.
51. P O'Donnell, 'De Valera's speech on emigration: a comment', *The Bell*, 17 (1951) p 56 (quoted in Ó Gráda, 'Primogeniture', p 492). The logic of the situation mirrors that reflected by Barron (*Those who stayed*, p 97) in his rural New England study: 'all the sons were sure to move on, "except for the youngest, perhaps, who remained to inherit a worn-out farm – and the worn-out parents"'.
52. Birth order refers to male births only. The 'unknown' column refers to cases where it is clear from the census schedules that the heir (as identified in the land valuation records) could not have been the eldest son. However, because one or more of his siblings had left the family household by 1911, it is not possible to determine with confidence his precise placing in the sequence of births. My impression is that the 'unknowns' are not evenly distributed, being somewhat biased towards the lower birth orders. Nonetheless, the conclusion that ultimogeniture was not the dominant prac-

tice is likely to hold, even in the improbable event that virtually all of the unknowns were last sons.

53. Commins and Kelleher, *Farm succession*, p 30.
54. N Scheper-Hughes, *Saints, sinners and schizophrenics: mental illness in rural Ireland* (California, 1979) 41–2.
55. My feeling, however, is that the pathological interpretation has limited scope, being confined to exceptional rural communities in a terminal stage of demographic and social decay. Scheper-Hughes subscribes to the school of thought which proclaims the imminent 'death' of rural Ireland, through a failure of social and biological reproduction. For some sceptical comments on this thesis see my 'Social change in middle Ireland', *Studies*, LXXIV (1985) pp 242–51.
56. Commins and Kelleher, *Farm succession*, p 19.
57. Scully, *Agriculture*, p 38.
58. H Brody, *Inishkillane: change and decline in the west of Ireland* (1973) p 90.
59. There are also counter-forces at play. The role of expanding dynasties – families who succeed in establishing two or more sons in farming, either through indirect inheritance or farm purchase – should not be overlooked.
60. See, for example, JA O'Brien (ed) *The vanishing Irish* (New York, 1954); J Healy, *Death of an Irish town* (Cork, 1968); J Messenger, *Inis Beag: isle of Ireland* (New York, 1969) pp 67–71; Brody, *Inishkillane*, pp 86–99.
61. Scheper-Hughes, *Saints*, p 37.
62. Commins and Kelleher, *Farm succession*, p 20.
63. *Census of population of Ireland, 1961*, v (Dublin, 1963)
64. Ó Gráda, *Ireland before and after the Famine*, pp 159–60.
65. Social survey conducted by the author in 1985, and described more fully in Kennedy, 'Inheritance', pp 23–5. Similar results, based on a larger sample, are to be found in Commins and Kelleher, *Farm succession*, p 40.
66. The convenience of a summary should not obscure the fact that the strength of evidence for different hypotheses varies. Thus, while most of the postwar evidence is based firmly on census or large-scale survey data, the hypothesis of an association between ultimogeniture and farm size rests on a single small-area study.
67. See Table 7.1. The argument that follows is influenced by G Becker, *A treatise on the family* (Cambridge, Mass, 1981); Y Ben-Porath, 'Economics and the family: match or mismatch?', *Journal of Economic Literature*, vol 20 (1982) pp 52–64; and, in particular, R Pollak, 'A transaction cost approach to families and households', *Journal of Economic Literature*, vol 23 (1985) pp 581–608.
68. According to a recent report four out of every *five* Irish land transfers involved inheritance; only 15 per cent were market transactions. On the continuing importance of kinship and inheritance in gaining access to farm land in Britain also, see A Harrison, *Farmers and farm business in England* (University of Reading, 1974) pp 27–8; T Marsden, 'Capitalist farming and the farm family: a case study', *Sociology*, 18 (1984) pp 209–10.
69. This is either explicit or implicit in much of the ethnography on rural Ireland. On the subject of pocket money, or rather its absence, see the archives of the Irish Folklore Commission (hereafter IFC), kept at University College, Dublin, MS 354, p 385.
70. Pollak, 'Transaction cost', pp 588–90.

71. This is a point sometimes made in the literature of development economics; see, for example, MR Rosenzweig and KI Wolpin, 'Specific experience, household structure, and intergenerational transfers: farm, family, land and labour arrangements in developing countries', *Quarterly Journal of Economics*, vol 100, Supp (1985) pp 961–87.
The following autobiographical reflections on growing up on a Leicestershire farm are suggestive: 'Our farm was like some vast apprenticeship school with skills and attitudes handed down from Father, the masterman at the top'. See H St G Cramp, *A yeoman farmer's son* (Oxford, 1986) p 38. How relevant the notion of farm-specific (human) capital formation is to small-scale farming in Ireland is an open question.
72. This seems to have been taken to extremes on Tory Island, off the Donegal coast. There, according to Fox (*Tory islanders*, p 161), such was the aversion to in-laws of any kind that marriage was seen as 'treason' against the family. This hostility had its material base in the archaic inheritance practices of the islanders.
73. For the more recent period see R Crotty, *Irish agricultural production* (Cork, 1966) pp 104–5. On the preferential treatment of male as against female children, on a range of issues (from nutrition to inheritance), across a wide spread of cultures see United Nations, *The state of world population* (New York, 1989) pp 1–14.
74. Pollak, 'Transaction cost', pp 590–2.
75. Ibid, p 590; Ben-Porath, 'Economics and the family'.
76. Ben-Porath, 'Economics and the family', p 61.
77. A specific and fairly typical example illustrates the point. In an indenture dated 14 February 1896 Eliza Hinchey, illiterate widow of Ballybricken, County Limerick, agreed to transfer her land rights, 10 cows, one horse, two yearlings, and other farm assets to her son James, in view of his forthcoming marriage. In turn, James promised to 'support and maintain the said Eliza Hinchey in the dwelling house on said lands in the same manner in which she has heretofore supported and maintained herself. The agreement then specifies that 'in the event of the said Eliza Hinchey being at any time hereafter dissatisfied with such support the said James Hinchey hereby agrees to pay her the annual sum of Ten Pounds in lieu of such support same to be paid by quarterly payments and shall also allow her the said Eliza Hinchey the use of the bed room in said house now occupied by her and the furniture therein together with the use of the kitchen in common with the other members of the family.' Nor was this all. James was also obliged to 'maintain and keep his sister Bridget Hinchey in said house for the term of three years. Provided the said Bridget Hinchey makes herself generally useful about the business of the said house and farm as heretofore.' (The original document, uncatalogued, is held at the Regional Archive Centre, Limerick.)
78. Fictional accounts of Irish life are a rich, if sometimes treacherous source on intra-family conflict. The most famous treatment perhaps is JM Synge, *The playboy of the western world* (Dublin, 1907). Folklore is a further extensive source; see, for example, IFC, MS 39, p 189 and MS 968, pp 464–8.
79. Marsden in fact seems to suggest that family and kinship are becoming more rather than less important in determining access to land, especially in regions dominated by capitalist agriculture in contemporary Britain ('Capitalist

farming', pp 210–21).

80. H Leibenstein, 'An interpretation of the economic theory of fertility: promising path or blind alley', *Journal of Economic Literature*, vol 12 (1974) p 468.
81. The literature is an extensive one. As points of entry into the debate see J Harris (ed) *Rural development: theories of peasant economic and agrarian change* (1982); M Friedberger, *Farm families and change in twentieth-century America* (Lexington, 1988); Hutson, 'Fathers and sons'. For Ireland, E Hazelkorn, 'Some problems with Marx's theory of capitalist penetration into agriculture: the case of Ireland', *Economy and Society*, vol 10 (1981) pp 284–315.

Chapter 8

Current Issues in Rural Development

Mary Cawley and Michael J Keane

INTRODUCTION

Rural underdevelopment and measures for its alleviation have a long history in the Republic of Ireland, dating back, at least, to the efforts of the Congested Districts Board at the end of the 19th century. This chapter focuses on the years since the early 1980s. During this recent period the definition of problems of underdevelopment and the methods adopted for offsetting those problems have been modified considerably. One of the more notable changes is that from an emphasis on sectoral to integrated approaches in the design and application of measures to counteract rural social and economic decline. Other changes of policy and strategies relating to rural development may be identified and are reviewed here. In addition, perceived shortcomings of efforts to date are discussed as are issues that clearly merit additional attention.

The chapter falls into six sections. First, the underlying dimensions of rural underdevelopment in the Republic of Ireland are discussed briefly and key remedial measures introduced since the late 1980s are identified. Second, some of the shortcomings of these efforts, as revealed in recent evaluation exercises, are discussed. Employment creation, which is a key objective of development efforts, is then addressed. Fourth, arguments for the adoption of an area-based approach to development are presented. Underlying dimensions of change in the size and distribution of population, which are related closely to the long-term social and economic viability of rural areas, are reviewed in the fifth section. Finally, the chapter concludes by discussing the potential role of rural-urban relationships and of geographical localities as underlying elements in the support of viable social and economic structures in the countryside.

Symptoms of rural underdevelopment and objectives of development efforts

Population loss, especially among the younger age groups, has for long been recognised as a key symptom of rural underdevelopment in Ireland, although outmigration among some rural school leavers to large centres for further education, training and employment is inevitable. Trends for the 1980s, as expressed in net patterns of change for counties and rural districts, reflected large-scale and widely distributed losses. The underlying reasons for these losses included the limited employment potential of many small farms under conventional farming systems, and the absence of adequate non-farm employment opportunities to absorb outmigration from agriculture. The factors contributing to these circumstances lay in part in local resource endowment, existing farm structures and the reduced social and financial capital of farm families. They also derived in large part from the major restructuring of economies that took place during the 1980s arising from: (i) a need to control the prices and outputs of farm products in response to the costs of maintaining guaranteed prices and supporting overproduction through storage and export subsidies; (ii) moves towards restriction of high-intensity methods of production because of their deleterious environmental effects; and (iii) restructuring in manufacturing industry, which had negative implications for the low-skill activities that traditionally tended to locate in small towns and rural locations.[1] The severity of market disruption in the rural economies of much of the western part of the Republic of Ireland is reflected in the large expanse of the Less Favoured Areas recognised by the EU, where livestock headage payments serve as an important income supplement for many farm families. Within these areas, low incomes, rising levels of under- and un-employment and increasing dependence on state transfers are issues for considerable concern.[2]

Population decline and relatively low income levels arising from reductions in farm prices and from limited opportunities for off-farm employment, have also contributed to the erosion of basic service structures in many sparsely populated areas.[3] Geographical access to primary education, primary health care and retail outlets has been severely curtailed in areas where public transport systems are either non-existent or infrequent along low density networks.[4] Rural postal services have come under threat of closure in many areas in recent years and few rural garda stations remain open on a full-time basis. Apart from the increased distances that must be travelled to access basic services and the increased expenditure of time and money that result, the gradual erosion of the service base removes key institutions which contribute to a sense of community identity and function as a context for social organisation in the countryside. The erosion of the service base is not limited to village settlements: small and medium-size urban centres (of up 3000–4000 population) outside the zone of influence of larger towns and cities have also experienced reductions in their populations, services and employment in recent years.[5]

Overcoming the symptoms of social and economic fragility that exist in large areas of rural Ireland has involved action through a series of policies and agencies introduced during the later 1980s and the 1990s. These include the EU-assisted Operational Programmes for Rural Development, Forestry, Tourism, Fisheries and Local Urban and Rural Development, which formed parts of the National Development Programmes of 1989–93 and 1994–99, the Social Fund-supported Forum initiative in north-west Connemara, LEADER I and LEADER II, area-based partnership initiatives, integrated measures for rural development, the establishment of 36 County Enterprise Boards to support small-scale enterprise in 1994 and, most recently, the establishment of a Western Development Commission.[6] Remedial measures include supports for the diversification of sources of farm income through the pursuit of novel on-farm and off-farm enterprises as means of using human, monetary and physical resources more effectively.

The methods by which development efforts were orchestrated changed markedly during the late 1980s. Advances in the design of remedial policies included recognition of: (i) the multi-dimensional nature of rural economies, as reflected in integrated development measures introduced on a pilot basis between 1988 and 1990; (ii) the contribution that the recipients of development initiatives may make to their design and implementation, through principles of subsidiarity, as applied in the LEADER programmes; (iii) the need for collaboration between the different actors involved in the development process, from EU to local level as reflected in partnership arrangements funded under the Area Development Management (ADM) global grant and under LEADER.[7]

Monitoring and evaluation

Monitoring and evaluation have been incorporated increasingly into rural development practice with the result that weaknesses in policy and actions are being identified and addressed on an ongoing basis. One weakness that has received considerable attention is the need for capacity building through training and support to enable communities to define their own needs, to design strategies to enable them to use their available resources more effectively and to support them in the development of those resources. Capacity-building of this type is accorded recognition in a number of EU-funded programmes. The monitoring of expenditure through various state and EU programmes to ensure accountability receives particular emphasis, as illustrated in the guidelines issued by the Office of the Irish Comptroller and Auditor General in association with LEADER I and II.[8]

Monitoring and evaluation have served to identify weaknesses in the strategies that are being implemented, at least in the short term. Thus, experience shows that truly multi-dimensional approaches are difficult to operationalise effectively at a local level. Within the context of LEADER I, which promoted integration actively, a series of multi-sectoral projects has been identified by evaluators as being present at the level of broad LEADER areas but, at a local level, multi-dimensionality was considered to be less than desirable.[9] In a policy context, more generally, it has been found that whereas local co-ordination is sought, individual government departments continue, for the most part, to operate independently at national level.[10] The experience of partnerships, while in many respects positive in finding common ground between disparate institutional elements, pertinent to the promotion of development, has not been without difficulties. In particular, a need has been identified to renegotiate power relationships between different social, economic and political interest groups in local contexts.[11] In pursuing development activities, farmers and rural entrepreneurs also continue to have to negotiate with a range of different agencies which operate at varying spatial scales.

As a result of LEADER and the operational programmes there is currently a wide range of institutions and initiatives in place to support rural and area-based development. However, official commitment is tempered somewhat by a series of doubts or questions about what is feasible and sensible in economic terms in this area, within the framework of existing preoccupations and priorities which constrain the pace and direction of overall national development. This tension has been described by Matthews, 'In the light of the macroeconomic forces at work shaping the spatial distribution of economic activity, and the various sectoral policies (eg, industrial, tourism, mining, fishing) already in place, it must be asked what these measures can hope to achieve'.[12] He goes on to suggest that it makes sense to invest in rural development initiatives only if they can contribute added value in ways which are not available to mainstream agencies. Clearly a key issue, and an important agenda item for research, must be to demonstrate if/how this added value can be generated. This search can be theory-led but, we suggest, only if it uses an approach in which questions as to 'what is to be done' outweigh, yet do not overwhelm, the attention to theoretical comprehensiveness.[13]

Local economic development is a realm in which competing ideologies, theories and practices are playing themselves out in complex ways.[14] Much of what is happening has originated as local responses to particular problems. Much of the knowledge base is idiographic: specific stories about the economic successes of individual projects or areas. Ultimately it is a situation where everybody can invent their own path to development. Clearly some objective perspectives are needed if we are to address the effectiveness of rural development practices. This can help to give the different elements some coherence but, more importantly, such an exercise can be of enormous help to the local economic development (LED) planner. The challenge for the LED planner is not only to assist the community to be effective in the approach it takes but also to help it think about why it is choosing that approach, and to consider the consequences and the alternatives.[15] Careful assessment of the effectiveness of the various practical development elements in local and rural development, apart from some official evaluations, has not been done to any great extent. Area-based approaches are widely favoured but, as has been suggested, there is little evidence that the approach to problem analysis and policy design has been adequately worked out. Some of these issues are addressed in the following sections of the chapter.

Added value in local development: process versus projects

Development actions must start with local conditions, as it is out of these conditions that change will occur. The particular emphasis in actions will depend on (a) where the area is at in term of factors like the strength and diversity of the local economy, its level of social infrastructure, its institutional capacity and the degree of social cohesion present in the area, and (b) the goals and objectives that are set as part of the proposed development actions. Some of the dimensions just mentioned are not particularly economic, they may have little to do with efforts to generate employment and income opportunities in local areas but they are important if we are interested in the context of creating a development process. One view of this process is summarised in Table 8.1. The classifications shown in Table 8.1 help to describe areas and different kinds of development actions. The attributes listed in the first column might be interpreted as a hierarchy of area goals. The descriptions across the rows indicate where an area might be *vis-à-vis* particular goals. Thus, a local area that is internally fragmented and feels a sense of powerlessness relative to outside agencies lacks social coherence. Creating this local coherence is, in turn, a precondition for institutional capacity and so on towards higher level goals.

What this classification scheme of Stern's describes is a series of stages in a development process. This encourages us to think about the different competencies in a local area and of how we might design suitable incentives and supports to complement these competencies and to encourage effectiveness. In a complex decision-making system the challenge in encouraging effectiveness is to identify and test procedures that rely less on control and more on incentives. Control and co-ordination are widely used, but we all know that they are the least effective instruments of influencing decisions and behaviour.

Table 8.1 Continuum of social development

Major attributes	Underdeveloped	Unevenly developed	Self-sustaining
Quality of life (socio-economic base)	Deprivation. High unemployment and poor quality jobs.	Segmented local labour markets. Pockets of affluence.	Full employment. Higher than average income levels.
Social infra-structure	Neglected and / or non-existent amenities.	Isolated schemes. Sometimes amenities not supported.	Many amenities well supported. Others being planned and implemented.
Institutional capacity	Little or no leadership or capacity to initiate development.	Limited and confined local leadership.	Widely dispersed capacity to lead, initiate and manage local development.
Social coherence	Sense of power-lessness regarding outsiders and internal fragmentation.	Partial coherence internally. Ad hoc liaison with external agencies.	Shared sense of development priorities. Co-operative link externally.

Source: Personal communication, Eliot Stern, Tavistock Institute, London.

For example, stating accountability in terms of inputs – 'through detailed guidelines and controls on objects of expenditure' – simply spawns red tape, and creates layers of bureaucrats and rigidity without introducing any incentives to encourage good performance. A preferred approach is one that states the accountability in terms of outputs and that rewards those who do things more effectively and efficiently. This procedure would liberate groups and communities from the straitjacket of input controls and could promote vigorous and imaginative attempts to improve results on the ground.[16]

This idea of accountability certainly sounds simple and sensible and right. Implementing it is harder. Most local initiatives have vague and diverse goals, and agreement on how to measure their success is far from complete. Unfortunately, there has not been enough serious work done to develop the objective measures of performance that are needed to implement a concept of accountability. There are, at a minimum, two general rules that must be followed if we are to develop performance measures that are suitable for judging and rewarding effectiveness in local development. First, single measures of performance should be avoided and second, performance measures must reflect the difficulty of the problem. It may be difficult to get agreement on measures of achievement. Even in conventional economics, with its strong positivist perspective, there is only limited guidance on how we might understand and assess local development.

The assumption that an area-based approach to rural and local development can make a genuinely additional impact in creating sustainable employment in rural areas is yet 'an open question'.[17] There are clear-cut and universally agreed performance measures that we can use to assess employment and other economic outcomes. The measures include notions of project viability, of additionality, absence of dead weight and no displacement. They do represent the rather narrow end in the spectrum of evaluation methods which helps if we want to avoid difficult issues. In addition, these measures do, in a sense, subdivide the total realm of economic action thereby qualifying only certain actors and actions as relevant for local economic development practice.[18] Some legitimate and valuable actions get left out.

Generally speaking the 'manoeuvring space' for local initiatives is not *a priori* terribly clear-cut. A LEADER, group, or indeed any local group, finds itself positioned somewhere between an existing set of EU and state policies and their related delivery mechanism and an equally heterogeneous set of local needs, aspirations and actions (reflecting, perhaps, a position somewhere in Stern's classification scheme, see Table 8.1). It can be argued that the contribution or 'value added' in a local initiative is somehow linked to (a) the 'localness' of the actions, and (b) the way in which this 'localness' helps to promote participation and partnership to achieve various synergies and other, what we might loosely refer to as, 'costless improvements in efficiency'. The critical issue, we suspect, is not necessarily the concept of 'localness' itself but the way in which the local strategy is structured and operated. The use of a market failures framework has been suggested[19] to help us identify and define various roles in local economic development. Such a framework offers a number of worthwhile possibilities for guiding local economic development that are not picked up by the conventional performance measures mentioned above. It is worth pointing out that some of these ideas found their way in to the ex-post LEADER I evaluation[20] but because of their institutional and qualitative nature they were overshadowed by the conventional measures. It is no great surprise that what was picked up from the LEADER I evaluation was the high incidence of deadweight and of displacement that was reported.[21] Here it is worth remembering that some researchers argue that, in reality, all local economic policy is simply about redistributing, rather than creating, jobs.[22] What chances then for a LEADER group trying to operate with meagre financial resources and in the interstices of the market. There has to be some honesty about what can be expected in local situations.

Experience in a few instances suggests that the real 'manoeuvring space' for local initiative resides in the way the local strategy is structured and how programmes are put into practice. Local strategies which appear to offer the best prospects in terms of effectiveness and innovation are those which have the following features:

(a) They are designed to try and make gains for the community through a process of productivity enhancement and creation of assets within local populations (rather than, for example, indulging in games of redistributive transfers and rent seeking).
(b) They try to identify and address instances of market failure in the local economy.
(c) They give attention to the process through which resources are developed as well as utilised.
(d) They include an accurate and complete economic perspective, which helps explain more about the complexity of one's area about internal dynamics and about the linkages between the local and the larger economy.
(e) They include new forms of planning such as adjunctive and strategic planning; these are forms of planning that seek to facilitate decision-making among a wide variety of organisations and interests in the society. They focus attention on solving remediable aspects of known problems and identify courses of action that move marginally, incrementally and through successive approximations away from unsatisfactory social and economic conditions, even when 'optimal' or ideal goals cannot be agreed upon, and explore alternatives on which diverse interests can act jointly.[23]

This, of course, is a conclusion which would have to be systematically examined. Some work on this topic is currently underway within the framework of the European Observatory for Innovation and Rural Development.[24] What impact such strategies can make to genuine additional employment creation is also, to quote Matthew[25] 'an open question'. For the European Commission it is an important political question.

THE LOCAL AREA UNIT AS A BASIS FOR ACTION

Rural areas and local economies do not reproduce in isolation but as a part of the whole. This is an important theme and it is one that suggests that we should think about a framework for action that has at least two dimensions, the local dimension and an external dimension. The various programmes, ie LEADER and the Operational Programmes, appear to completely ignore this second dimension. The report by the National Economic and Social Council, *New Approaches to Rural Development*, sought to introduce a perspective on spatial organisation and reorganisation as a way of going about issues of management and making choices in rural areas. Just as crises of accumulation in capitalist societies necessitate the periodic and radical restructuring of production processes in order to establish new opportunities for profitable investment, it may be the case that spatial arrangements also become outmoded. This perspective gives an active role to space and to spatial considerations in the context of development issues. It defines the development process as one of spatial reorganisation, because a given set of spatial arrangements can become outmoded and unsuitable due to the kind of socio-economic transformations taking place in the society. Thus, in order to adapt to, or to accommodate a new set of social goals, it becomes necessary to have some kind of spatial adjustment or reorganisation. This reorganisation will seek to make the system better able to respond to the new demands for better efficiency and equity.

The practical aspects of this question concern how we might respond to the ongoing functional shifts in rural space – shifts which make it difficult to see how all smaller places can offer the kinds of diversified communities which are needed if we are to have a truly rural society. An economic issue associated with this is the ability of small centres to capture the benefits of any rural development programmes and in preventing income leaking from the local area. Most commonly, income leakage occurs as a result of spending on consumer goods in centres outside the local economy, or because of savings and profits being transferred out of the local area.[26] Leakages mean that the economic benefits, in terms of induced incomes and added employment, are not realised locally.

A statistical investigation, using the ordinary least squares technique, into towns' economic performance in the Republic is reported in Table 8.2. This analysis helps to illustrate the functional shifts and competitive responses that are occurring within the structure of the settlement system. In particular it illustrates the negative effects which these shifts appear to be having on the lower layers of the system. A vital part of the rural fabric is the system of towns and villages; and many of the smaller and locationally disadvantaged centres would appear to be under threat. A basic requirement, if we are to be serious about an area-based integrated approach, is that we address and try to understand the processes that are going on in rural areas. For the design of rural development policies, Saraceno[27] cites some important rules. One is that we should acknowledge what is going on; and another is that policies should not try to 'invent' anything. Rural Ireland is a mosaic of manifold area units with different problems and possibilities. To a greater or lesser extent, all rural areas are being absorbed into an urbanised economy. Even within the urban system, as suggested in Table 8.2, there are patterns of strengths

Table 8.2 A model of town economic performance

Commercial performance = f	**(functional status, size, location)**		
Parameter signs*	**+**	**+**	**+**
t values	**(2.55)**	**(1.79)**	**(2.71)**
			R^2 = 0.56

Performance:	Change in retail sales, 1979–88.
Functional status:	The commercial attractiveness (number of functions) of a place relative to other competing places.
Size:	A dummy variable; large > 5,000, small < 5,000.
Location:	A measure that reflects how well positioned a place is relative to the competing places from which shoppers can choose.
Number of observations:	134

* The parameter signs indicate that commercial performance is positively related to functional status, size and location.

and weaknesses. If the economies of rural areas are to be sustained, then it will be necessary to manage this process of integration; so that within the kinds of relationships and systems that are being created around urban centres, it will be possible to articulate different roles, and identify how various economic, social and infrastructural objectives can be achieved. The question of how a territorial approach might be designed is an important one. One overarching issue is whether it is possible to design such an approach when there is an institutional vacuum, in the sense that there is no planning framework for resolving the higher level issues relating to spatial management. The planning focus of local authorities does not provide the kind of forum that is needed. Furthermore, there is a need to follow a comprehensive national approach rather than continue with a series of disparate pilot and geographically scattered programmes or projects which 'ration out' resources. These practices are inefficient and help to create unwieldy and unworkable bureaucratic structures.

Dynamics of change at an area level: population distribution and composition

The relationships between urban places and their hinterlands are viewed as being a pertinent but, as yet, neglected component of the drive for rural development in the Republic of Ireland. In the absence of any detailed information which would illuminate the mechanics of the relationships referred to earlier, one of the most satisfactory starting points is to examine patterns of population change in both absolute terms and in terms of composition and to relate these changes to size of place. While, ideally, one might approach this exercise at the level of the District Electoral Division (and such exercises have been conducted by both of the authors, and by other researchers in the past), a higher level of resolution, that of the Rural District (RD) has merit as a basis of analysis for the state as a whole. Studies, based on some 160 combined Urban and Rural Districts (UDs and RDs) and more than 600 towns suggest that a retreat of population from the countryside occurred on a widespread scale throughout the state during the 1980s and that concentration took place in selected urban centres. Some reversal of these trends has occurred during the early 1990s, but certain underlying features of population distribution between urban and rural areas continue to have major implications for area-based rural planning.

Small population size districts dominate in the Republic of Ireland even at the level of the 160 combined UDs and RDs. This small size reflects a weak employment base and creates difficulties in terms of capacity to provide basic services in proximity to the distribution of consumer demand. With the exception of the County Boroughs (CBs – Dublin, Dun Laoghaire, Cork, Limerick, Galway and Waterford), few districts contain a population in excess of 50,000 (Table 8.3). Most UDs have populations between 30,000–50,000 and 20,000–30,000 and approximately one-half of the districts have populations of 10,000–20,000. Where UDs are absent the population tends to fall below 10,000. Such RDs occupy peripheral positions outside the zones of influence of larger centres and also coincide with areas of poor quality land.

The national trend in population change over the past 15 years has been one of slow growth during the years 1981–86 (of 0.56 per cent per annum), low decline between 1981 and 1991 (of -0.1 per cent per annum) and recovery during the first half of the 1990s (+0.57 per cent per annum). Losses in population during the 1980s, as expressed in annualised rates, were associated in particular with the smaller size districts (Figure 8.1a and b).[28] The annual percentage change in population for 1981–86 and 1986–91, recorded by size of district in 1981 and 1986, respectively (for all districts other than the CBs), illustrates that a positive relationship existed between population size in the initial census year and change over the subsequent inter-censal period. A limited number of large size districts registered some of the highest rates of growth over the years 1981–86 and the greatest losses in population were registered by the smallest size places (Table 8.3). Forty-nine districts registered decline between 1981 and 1986, 39 of which had a population of less than 10,000. During the second half of the 1980s the most marked rates of decline

Table 8.3 Combined urban and rural districts classified by size grouping 1971, 1981, 1986, 1991

Population	Number of RDs+CBs				Number of RDs containing UDs (excluding CBs)				Number of districts registering decline		
	1971	1981	1986	1991	1971	1981	1986	1991	1971–81	1981–86	1986–91
<10,000	78	73	72	71	4	4	4	4	24	39	62
10,000–20,000	52	47	45	49	26	21	20	22	4	7	27
>20,000–30,000	20	20	21	18	17	14	15	13	-	-	17
>30,000–50,000	6	13	15	15	5	11	11	11	-	-	7
>50,000	6	9	9	9	-	2	2	2	1	3	5
Total	162	162	162	162	52	52	52	52	29	49	118

Sources: Census of Population of Ireland, 1971, 1981, 1986, 1991, Volume 1, Areas, Government Publications, Dublin. See Cawley (1995), note no 29.

(A)

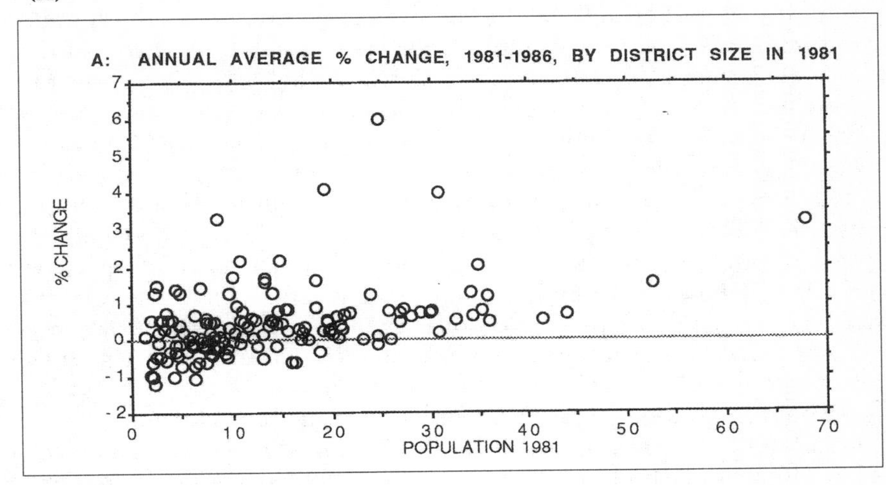

(B)

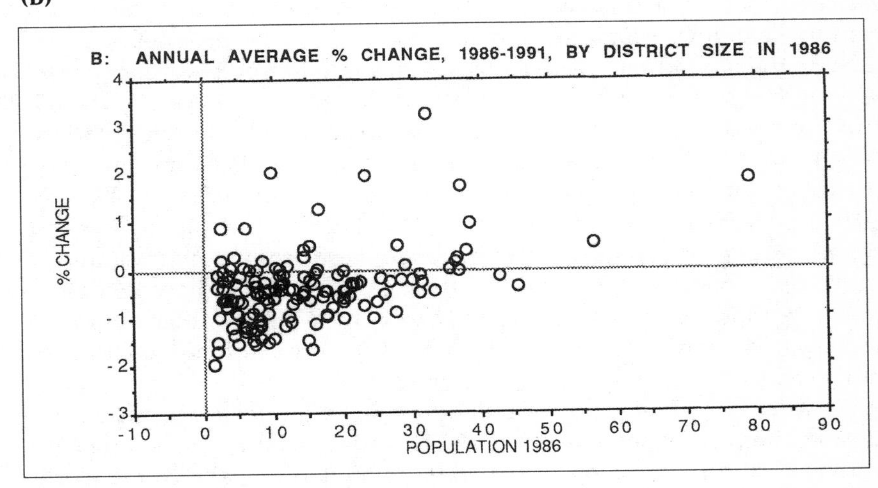

Figure 8.1 Annual average percentage change in population for combined Urban and Rural Districts (County Boroughs excluded) by population size in initial census year: A 1981–86; B 1986–91

were registered by the smallest places but, in fact, losses took place across a wide range of population size places (Figure 8.1b): 118 or 73 per cent of all districts experienced decline during these five years (Table 8.3). These comprised 87 per cent of all districts with less than 10,000 population as well as substantial proportions of all other district size classes. Their geographical distribution reflects the increase in decline in the north and south midlands. The universality of decline in small size districts has been reversed somewhat during the first half of the 1990s in response to a wide variety of area-based development oriented measures. Nevertheless, decline continues in areas which have remained outside the ambit of remedial actions.

Evidence from local studies in peripheral areas in the past has illustrated that losses are experienced from the school-leaving and young working age groups, in particular, a phenomenon that is not unexpected given the limited opportunities for higher education and employment that exist in such locations. This problem became widespread during the 1980s as employment opportunities deteriorated, as study of net migration trends reveals.[29] The main trends emerging during the first half of the 1980s were continued outmovement from small size districts to larger districts and widespread losses of both males and females across a range of age groups in districts of varying size. The ability of districts to attract persons in their 30s and 40s involved factors other than size *per se* and pointed to the uncertain economic conditions of the time. Employment retention and creation were becoming increasingly dependent on rapidly-changing economic circumstances at an international level. During the second half of the 1980s, net migration patterns for school-leaving and young working age groups reflected losses in small size districts and some gains in larger size districts.[30] The underlying pattern was, however, one of widespread losses across districts of varying sizes. Increasing numbers of districts with populations of 20,000–30,000 and 30,000–50,000 were involved, pointing to a deterioration of employment opportunities for young workers in general at that time. A substantially improved economic climate and a growing range of area-based employment creation measures during the 1990s have helped to reverse the widespread outmigration of the 1980s. The former trends continued, however, in smaller population size areas.[31]

If we relate changes in population numbers and age composition during inter-censal periods to population mass, we can see a relationship between critical mass and ability to retain population in the young working age groups. As the 1980s progressed, the threshold levels at which these age groups could be retained increased, pointing to a gradual weakening of the employment base. Districts of 10,000 population or less were particularly vulnerable to losses. At this time the retention of investment in and the attraction of new investment to smaller settlements and rural areas became increasingly difficult. Implications followed for service structures and for the delivery of basic educational, medical and retail services which impinge on the quality of life experienced by rural populations; and which require critical population thresholds within particular spatial ranges for their maintenance. There were also implications for capacities of development-orientated organisations. The presence of a business and professional component at local level traditionally provided much-valued skills and knowledge of external institutions and organisational mechanisms. Increasingly, animateurs had to be introduced to provide such skills and knowledge. The professionalisation of rural development became even more marked during the early 1990s in response to a need for specialist advice to prepare applications for submission for funding to the EU and state agencies. The emergence of new spatial entities has been a further feature of the availability of new policy measures and enhanced sources of financial and other assistance for development. While some of these entities have a basis in past local association and have become strengthened as a result of recent developments, others lack continuity.[32] As a result, while some exceptions undoubtedly exist, administrative structures at a sub-county level in the Republic of Ireland remain poorly articulated and to-date lack a statutory basis.[33]

CONCLUSION

This chapter has focused on the 1980s and the early 1990s in discussing rural underdevelopment problems, remedial measures and their impacts in the Republic of Ireland. The review has identified both strengths and weaknesses that merit further attention from researchers and policy makers. Much progress has been made over the past two decades. The multi-dimensional nature of rural economies and the need for integrated action at a local level is recognised. The involvement of the people who form the focus of action in the design and implementation of development measures is pursued increasingly, as is the merit of joint-funding ventures in which local and institutional actors work together through partnerships. The necessity for pre-development advice and support is receiving attention. Particular geographical areas in both urban and rural settings have been identified as meriting special initiatives.

Review of the impacts of recent remedial measures and of the changing distribution of population reveals that while current approaches are responding to the needs of some areas and some groups of people, they may not have the capacity to address effectively the broad range of social and economic weaknesses that persist over extensive areas of rural Ireland. A particular lacuna exists in relation to the lack of statutory structures at a sub-county level which would provide a basis for the democratic representation of interests, for the orchestration of area-based initiatives in a comprehensive way across the national space and for the maintenance of community identity. There is also an absence of recognition of the interrelationships between towns and the rural populations which they serve, as sources of employment and of services, and of the broader implications of these relationships for reducing leakages from local economies. A policy of targeting selected groups and areas that have particular social and economic needs at specific points in time, as defined by outside agencies, by the people themselves, or by the latter with professional consultancy advice, is currently pursued. While such an approach may offset severe aspects of deprivation, it is unlikely in the longer term to provide a sustainable basis for the maintenance of viable social and economic structures in rural Ireland.

Notes

1. David Goodman and Michael Redclift discuss underlying contributory factors to agricultural restructuring in *The international farm crisis* (London, 1989).
2. Key aspects of poverty in Ireland are addressed in a publication on behalf of the Conference of Major Religious Superiors, Bridget Reynolds and Sean Healy (eds) *Rural development policy: what future for rural Ireland?* (Dublin, 1991).
3. Euradvice, *A crusade for survival: final report of study of the west of Ireland* (Galway, 1994), which received EU and Irish government funding and was conducted at the request of the Catholic bishops of Connaught and Donegal delineates processes of desertification in operation.
4. Anne Byrne with colleagues in *North-west Connemara: a baseline study of poverty* (Galway, 1991) illustrates the local experience of low levels of access to services.
5. Mary Cawley, 'Town population change 1971–1986: patterns and distributional effects', in *Irish Geography*, vol 24, no 2 (1991) pp 106–16. Michael Keane, 'The significance of spatial dependencies in small area income determination models', in *Regional Studies*, vol 23, no 5 (1989) pp 455–62.
6. See Patrick Commins and MJ Keane, *New approaches to rural development*, National Economic and Social Council, report No 97, Government Publications (Dublin, 1994). A Western Development Commission was established in 1997 with a remit for seven western counties, Clare, Donegal, Galway, Leitrim, Mayo, Roscommon and Sligo.
7. Ibid.
8. Government of Ireland, Office of the Comptroller and Auditor General, *The LEADER Programme* (Dublin, 1995).
9. A review of the operation of LEADER I in Ireland was conducted by Brendan Kearney, Gerry Boyle and Jim Walsh, *EU LEADER I Initiative in Ireland: evaluation and recommendations* (Dublin, 1994).
10. Tony Varley, 'On the fringes: community groups in rural Ireland', in Tony Varley, Thomas Boylan and Michael Cuddy (eds) *Rural crisis: perspectives on Irish rural development* (Galway, 1991) pp 48–76.

11. Sally Shorthall, 'The Irish rural development paradigm: an exploratory analysis', in *Economic and Social Review*, vol 25, no 3 (1994) pp 233–60.
12. Alan Matthews, 'Agricultural competitiveness and rural development' in John O'Hagan (ed) *The economy of Ireland* (Dublin, 1995) pp 350–55.
13. Akin Mabogunje, *The development process* (London, 1980).
14. Michael Teitz, 'Changes in economic development theory and practice', in *International Regional Science Review*, vol 16 (1994) pp 101–6, provides an interesting review of the issues from a US perspective.
15. David Douglas, *Community economic development in Canada* (Toronto, 1994).
16. Alice Rivlin, *Systematic thinking for social action* (Washington, 1970).
17. Matthews, 'Agricultural competitiveness and rural development'.
18. RA Beauregard, 'Constituting economic development: a theoretical perspective' in RD Bingham and R Mier (eds) *Theories of local economic development* (London, 1993) discusses some interesting implications that follow from this subdivision of actions.
19. Michael Keane's paper 'Economic issues in local development' presented to a symposium organised by the Agricultural Economics Society of Ireland in Dublin (May 1992) outlines this market failures framework.
20. Brendan Kearney, Gerry Boyle and Jim Walsh, *EU LEADER I Initiative in Ireland*.
21. Ibid. For example, Brendan Kearny *et al*, in their evaluation report on LEADER 1 say that about 40 per cent of the project respondents indicated that their projects would have gone ahead in the absence of LEADER finance.
22. For some of these arguments see KG Willis and CM Saunders, 'The impact of a development agency on employment: resurrection discounted?', in *Applied Economics*, vol 20 (1988) pp 81–96; and A Eisenchitz and J Gough, *The politics of local economic policy* (London, 1993).
23. For a discussion on this form of planning see Dennis Rondinelli, *Development projects as policy experiments* (London, 1993).
24. For information on the LEADER programme and on the European Observatory see Yves Champetier, 'In a word', in *LEADER Magazine*, no 9, 1995, p 2.
25. Matthews, 'Agricultural competitiveness and rural development'.
26. Keane, 'The significance of spatial dependencies in small area income determination models'.
27. Rural policy design, using some of the experiences from Italy, is discussed by Elena Saraceno in her paper, 'Recent trends in rural development and their conceptualisation', in *Journal of Rural Studies*, vol l0, no 4 (1994) pp 321–30. ME Cawley, 'Desertification: measuring population decline in rural Ireland', in *Journal of Rural Studies*, vol 10, no 4 (1994) pp 395–407.
28. ME Cawley, 'Town population change 1971–1986: patterns and distributional effects'; ME Cawley, 'Desertification: measuring population decline in rural Ireland'. James Walsh, 'The turn-around of the turn-around in the population of the Republic of Ireland', in *Irish Geography*, vol 24, no 2 (1991) pp 117–25.
29. ME Cawley, 'Desertification: measuring population decline in rural Ireland'. See also ME Cawley, 'Migration trends in rural Ireland: 1971–1991', paper presented at the International Seminar on Marginal Regions, St Patrick's College, Maynooth, July, 1995. A series of Pearson Product Moment correlation values and accompanying plots of net migration by size of place,

derived from the above papers, was provided to illustrate the discussion in this chapter.

30. Ibid.
31. Central Statistics Office, annual population estimates for various years.
32. Some LEADER I areas, for example, were modified in the preparation of applications for LEADER II funding.
33. A number of important documents on possible administrative reorganisation have been published in recent years, see particularly Department of the Environment, *Better local government: a programme for change* (Dublin, 1996), and Department of the Environment and Local Government, *Report of the task force on integration of local government and local development systems* (Dublin, 1998).

Chapter 9

Changing Patterns of Rural Planning and Development in Northern Ireland

John Greer and Michael Murray

INTRODUCTION

While Northern Ireland is synonymous with particular societal divisions, its experience of a longstanding rural–urban dialectic is shared in common with other parts of Europe and North America. In part, this is a problem born out of definitional uncertainty which categorises the rural as either open countryside, or a combination of nucleated and dispersed settlement at the sub regional scale. In each case, however, the spatial baseline remains the pattern of major urban locales and as a classification[1] of rural areas illustrates, using distance as a key variable, that the hegemony of the urban is difficult to undo. The identification of pressured rural areas, accessible rural areas and remote rural areas mirrors the conventional codification of core and periphery in regional planning practice and takes the urban as the essential departure point for analysis.

But the rural–urban dialectic can also be traced back to the now discredited orthodoxy of what constitutes good planning. This view supports the dominant role of planning experts embedded in the technocracy of government, whose toolkit of procedure and method is applied in a manner which is largely independent of the planned for. In a context where the rural has been perceived as residual, planners have sought to minimise wasted public effort by grasping the economies of scale offered by urban concentration. Northern Ireland is no stranger to that mode of policy prescription where a strong urban bias in planning and development has been conjoined with a protectionist imperative for the Ulster countryside over the period since the 1960s. This chapter begins, therefore, by more fully interpreting the rural dimension in Northern Ireland and its relationship with planning policy.

Arguments of equity, capacity and empowerment as expressed through community-led local development and area-based partnership governance have sought to challenge the marginalising of rural society. One effect has been that government policy makers have had to adjust their perceived wisdom on differential patterns of locational advantage and adopt a more interactive mode of planning and investment allocation. But harnessing the capacity of rural people to engage effectively and on a sustained basis with public officials requires the adoption of collaborative strategy building and initiative-based development processes. These lie at the heart of a social capital formation perspective on rural development. Accordingly, the chapter moves on to examine critically the progress of participatory rural development which has blossomed in Northern Ireland during the 1990s. This bottom-up perspective on creating change stands in stark contrast to the centrist, top-down style of planning pursued earlier, though certainly the 'rules of the game' remain set from above.

It is a truism that the future is often reinvented from the past and with work having commenced in 1997 on a new regional strategy for Northern Ireland, it is not difficult to conceive the re-emergence of the planning expert whose popular catch phrase 'value for money' is a cloak for urban preference. The contemporary political and economic context is very much different from previous decades, but the fundamental concerns of rural society have, arguably, changed little. Thus, in the final section of this chapter some of the implications of this regional strategic framework for future rural development patterns in Northern Ireland are explored.

INTERPRETING THE RURAL IN NORTHERN IRELAND

Rural imagery

The rural in Northern Ireland, as elsewhere, is very much a social construction whose meaning varies across individuals and across interest groups. For some it is the simplistic essence of everything that is good in society – neighbourliness, fresh air, or great scenery. It is thus the antithesis of everything that is perceived as less wholesome (and urban) – high density housing and anonymity, traffic congestion, poverty and violence. As a social construct the rural comprises a complex melange of place, culture, and identity and which, as suggested by Duffy,[2] may for most people be more myth than reality. Such representations, however, do serve to set it apart. The accompanying imagery, filtered from historical and contemporary realities, can invoke a romanticism and nostalgia, which at best is but a partial illustration of circumstance. Photographs can be an especially powerful influence on perception and behaviour as portrayed for tourism promotion purposes by the branding of Northern Ireland as a place of bucolic harmony. But behind this gentle illusion of a normal society, alternative and unstated interpretations of rural living are equally feasible: the isolation of the elderly, the marginal viability of the small farm, the depletion of community services.

The cultural landscape, therefore, is a potent reservoir for informing analysis and policy prescription with a similar iconography capable of being used for different public agendas. The case of rural housing in Northern Ireland is a useful example of this multiple meaning. In a richly illustrated investigation into the constructional and typological aspects of rural houses, Gailey makes a genuine plea for the conservation and restoration of vernacular dwellings for their own sake.[3] But a subsequent and again richly illustrated publication from the Northern Ireland Housing Executive,[4] as part of its rural housing policy review, questions the picturesque postcard view of the thatched cottage which masks a lack of amenities and isolation. Its research identified a litany of rural housing problems at that time, for example, approximately 1 dwelling in 12 lacking basic amenities, more than 3000 dwellings without mains electricity and a similar number not connected to a mains water supply, and some 68 per cent of all vacant rural dwellings regarded as unfit. In 1991, a policy statement *The Way Ahead* argued not only for refurbishment aid, but also replacement grants.[5] This differential commodification of rural housing into built heritage and unfit shelter is a depiction of broader debates about the nature of rurality in Northern Ireland which pitch environmental conservation against social deprivation. A deeply divided society provides an overlay of contested territory and relationships.

Rural planning and landscape protection

The environmental conservation ethic in Northern Ireland has a lineage extending back over 50 years. In 1946 the Planning Advisory Board published a report, *The Ulster Countryside*, which stated that the countryside was one of the region's most valuable assets and in view of what was regarded as 'irreparable damage caused by thoughtless and careless development' recommended that: (1) public and private development should aim to preserve and improve amenities and rural architecture; (2) certain areas of particular beauty and interest should be protected and national parks designated as appropriate; (3) the preservation of the coast should be a matter of national concern, with strict control of ribbon development; and (4) main roads should be protected from ribbon development. The subsequent passage of the Amenity Lands Act, 1965 provided the legislative base for the designation of national parks and the appointment of an advisory body to government (the Ulster Countryside Committee) on these and related conservation matters. Proposals were made for national parks during the late 1960s in Fermanagh, south Armagh and the Sperrins but political opposition deterred the government from following through. However, eight Areas of Outstanding Natural Beauty were confirmed, the Ulster Countryside Committee believing that strict development control would at least ensure a degree of landscape protection until national parks were finally designated.[6] In short, this formative period underlines an incomplete perception of the personality of rural Ulster which was weighted more towards a negative, regulatory concern for amenity and the preservation of the landscape.[7]

These precepts, when linked with the adoption of growth centre principles, were carried forward in a series of regional planning frameworks extending from the Matthew Plan of 1963, through the Northern Ireland Development Programme 1970–75, to the Regional Physical Development Strategy 1975–95. A telling judgement from Estyn Evans was quietly ignored as physical and economic planning policy continued to shackle rural society with a relentless urban preference:

> The personality of Ulster is too strong for solutions to its problems to be found in economic planning alone. However much its people are advised to forget the past and their entrenched myths and attitudes, the realities of social history and geography cannot be overlooked. Even at the level of economic planning these factors must be taken into account. Solutions for the highly urbanised and on the whole successfully urbanised English community are not likely to succeed in this environment.[8]

Even though the number of country towns and larger villages selected for growth in subsequent local plans did increase, this expansion could only be achieved by considerable population movement from the smaller settlements and families living in the open countryside, a settlement pattern which personifies rural Northern Ireland. Development control policies exercised a presumption against new housing outside selected settlements, unless need could be proven, and became a necessary adjunct to achieving the targets set for these growth centres.

A short-term relaxation of strict control did occur in the aftermath of the 1978 review of rural planning policy by the Cockcroft Committee. But this so dismayed the conservation lobby that the Department of the Environment was prompted to introduce a further policy adjustment in the 1980s with an emphasis on the criteria of suitable location, siting and design of new development in the countryside. Housing availability and a freedom to build are at the centre of the rural debate, not least for the implications which arise for the sustainability of rural communities and their service infrastructure, and thus when government published *A Planning Strategy for Rural Northern Ireland* in 1993 it is not surprising that the language used was conciliatory to all interests. It is unfortunate that this document with its 117 policies, some quite detailed in nature, was quickly adopted for the framing of planning permission refusals, since perhaps for the first time there was an opportunity to give rural planning a new set of credentials. That document, unlike its predecessors, seeks to reconcile the diverse and conflicting aspirations of different groups in society, abandons a rigid hierarchy of settlements and the related direction of population and development, promises generous development limits around smaller settlements and promotes rural regeneration in circumstances of economic and social disadvantage.[9] But with the emphasis in the *Planning Strategy* firmly on development control policies, it is scarcely surprising that strong opposition was spawned, which has received high level support from the House of Commons Northern Ireland Affairs Committee in an authoritative review of planning in the region.[10] In short, there is little convincing evidence that landscape amenity considerations have reduced their stranglehold on contemporary planning practice.

In recent years a different and arguably more enlightened policy agenda has sought to mediate the excesses of the conservation ethic in rural areas by highlighting the benefits of good stewardship by land owners. The enactment of the Nature Conservation and Amenity Lands (Northern Ireland) Order 1985 provides a new impetus for innovative landscape management which can bring benefit to farmers and the public, not least through the funding of enhancement initiatives in redesignated Areas of Outstanding Natural Beauty.[11] Moreover, a suite of Environmentally Sensitive Area designations over the period since 1987 has provided incentive payments on an annual basis to landholders on the basis that farming operations are integrated with sympathetic landscape maintenance.[12] The important point here is that this spatial pattern of environmental policy succession (Figure 9.1) is remarkably consistent with the geography of rural disadvantage.

Rural deprivation and targeting social need

As an alternative discourse in the interpretation of rural Northern Ireland, social deprivation is not only more recent, but also represents a cultural iconography representative of more fundamental perceived power imbalances between Belfast with its hinterland and the rest of the region. This has been poignantly embodied in the slogan 'West of the Bann' which signifies a separation of the disadvantaged rural sub-region from its more prosperous and urban counterpart. Unravelling the spatial configuration and complexity of this disadvantage has moved on from days when the rural problem was solely aligned to the hardship of the small farmer, whose interests were represented by a union with

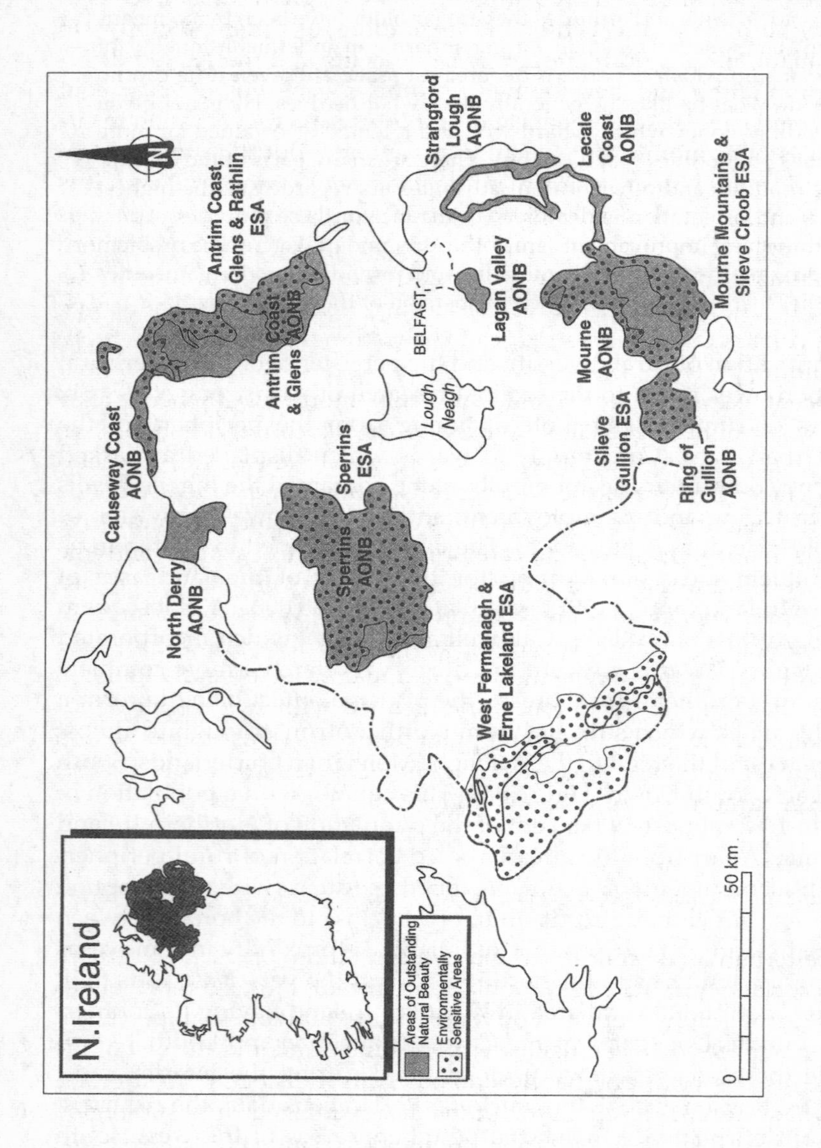

Figure 9.1 Areas of Outstanding Natural Beauty and Environmentally Sensitive Areas in Northern Ireland 1998

credentials for entry into the policy community of government. A conventional analysis ran as follows:

> Finally, it should be borne in mind that while commercial farming and state regulation of agriculture have been the dominant trends in the last few decades, skills and attitudes that are far older have been by no means lost or abandoned. The small farmer inherits an indefinable quality of stockmanship which is perhaps his greatest asset, and even if he can no longer do what he likes he generally likes what he does. He is not given to spending money which is hard-won and it tends to be valued far more than the commodities that it can buy. There are many parts of the country where modesty and other peasant attributes are regarded as the highest virtues and ostentation is deplored. In the face of these attitudes capital investment and improvements are not readily undertaken ... The problem of improving the quality of rural living and providing modern amenities is further increased by the extreme dispersion of the farmsteads.[13]

The identification of rural diversity and the persistence of a broader rural deprivation owes much to the seminal research of Armstrong *et al.*[14] Six categories of rurality were noted ranging from the periphery of the Belfast Urban Area (Category 1) to wards which displayed a marked dependency on primary sector employment, contained the highest levels of over-crowding and unemployment, and had the lowest provision of household amenities (Category 6). The latter are defined in the report as 'rural problem areas', accounting for two-thirds of the land area of Northern Ireland and a 1971 population of 230,000. A subsequent reworking of this analysis by Caldwell and Greer[15] which incorporated those Category 5 wards adjacent to Category 6 offered a more complete portrayal of 'peripheral rural areas', the principal effect being to form a monolithic block which stretches from North Antrim, through to almost the entire west of the region, the Armagh/Monaghan borderlands, South Armagh and South Down (Figure 9.2). This equates with a population of 276,830 in 1981, almost 19 per cent of the population of Northern Ireland at that time. Apart from the already noted correlation of rural peripherality with scenic amenity, it is notable that these areas (with the exception of North Antrim) either directly abut, or run close to the border between Northern Ireland and the Republic of Ireland. Its proximity in some cases creates peripherality, as in the north-west, or at the very least adds to it, with every peripheral rural area in Northern Ireland having its counterpart in Counties Donegal, Leitrim, Cavan, Monaghan and Louth.[16]

While these analyses have been updated during the interim, most recently by Robson *et al*[17] using *inter alia* 1991 census data, the recurrent pattern of deprivation remains the peripheral areas of the west, south and north-east of the region, together with a suite of wards in Belfast and Derry. At an aggregate scale, analysis of the 1991 census also suggests an ethnic geography of Northern Ireland which has become more sharply

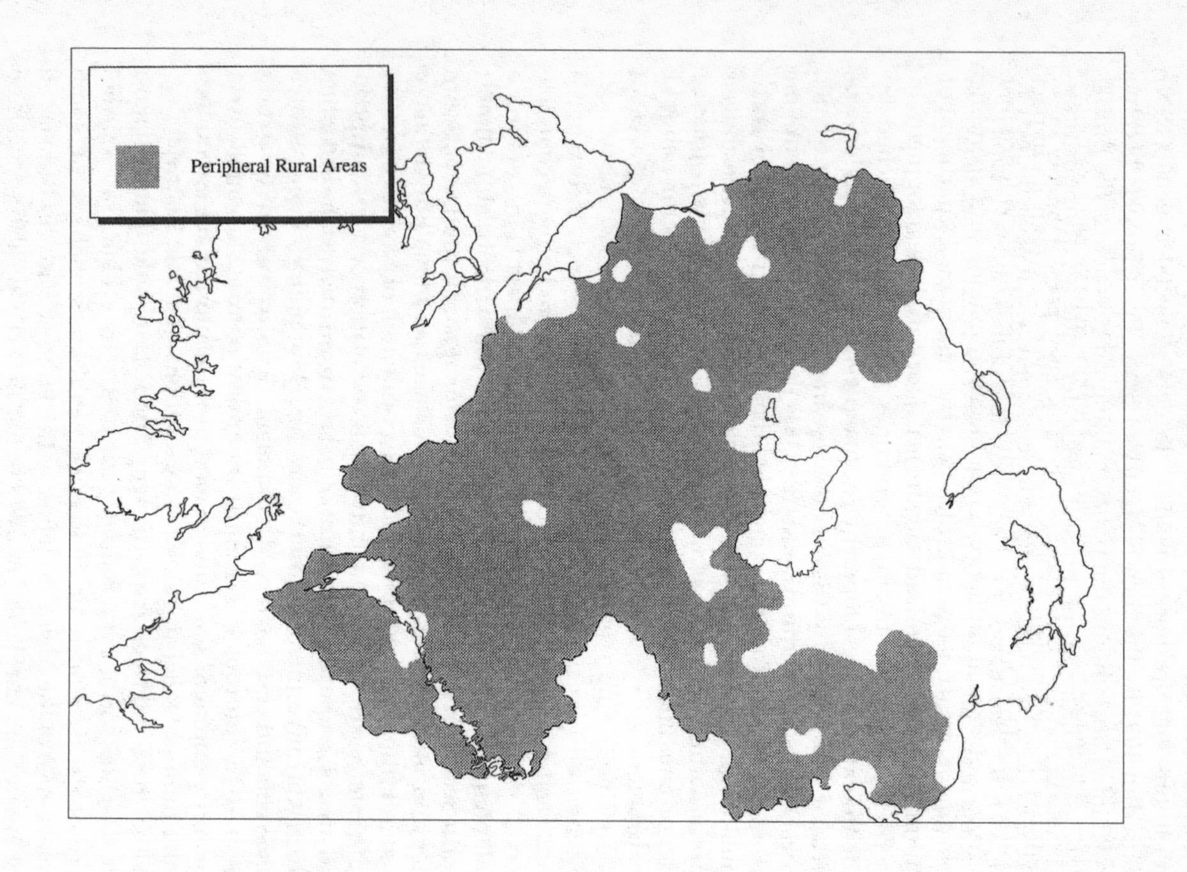

Figure 9.2 Peripheral rural areas in Northern Ireland

demarcated with Catholics forming a substantial majority in all of Counties Fermanagh, Tyrone, and Londonderry, north-east Antrim and parts of Down.[18]

The public discourse on rural disadvantage as conveyed by its spatial representation has thus become a powerful metaphor of key socio-economic differentials which have built up over time between the competing traditions of Northern Ireland. 'Targeting Social Need' (TSN) announced in 1991 by the then Secretary of State, Peter Brooke, became one tool aimed at changing the policy-making process across the profile of public expenditure in the pursuit of greater equality of opportunity and equity. The symbolism of TSN may, however, outweigh its impact since, as reported by Quirk and McLaughlin,[19] there is little evidence that it has had a substantial influence on the decision making and spending of government departments. Specifically in the case of the Department of Agriculture (DANI), the lead department for rural development in Northern Ireland, mainstream programmes have been untouched by TSN, with only rural development, 'a small new area of activity' in any way related to this priority. Given, however, that this accounts for 6.5 per cent of DANI's expenditure and depends heavily (75 per cent) on European Union funding, it is concluded that this 'programme is clearly marginal and separate from the department's overall activities'.[20] It is within this context of rural circumstance and government performance that the progression of rural development beyond mere rhetoric should be located.

Rurality and a divided society

A final interpretation of the rural in Northern Ireland must also acknowledge that sectarian tension and violence have created a rural geography of inter and intra-settlement apartheid. Villages and small towns have been cut off from their natural hinterlands by cross-border road closures, housing estates display sharp reminders of community territoriality, and central areas have carried the brunt of property destruction and an aversion to private investment. Recent research by Murtagh[21, 22] demonstrates that the social processes which have created 14 'peacelines' in Belfast do not stop at the greenbelt and that community attitudes in small town Northern Ireland need to be understood in the context of the experience of living through violence as well as perceptions of ethnic sustainability. Life on the rural interface involving two villages, one mile apart and with little contact between them, is described thus:

> People in Catholic 'Whiteville' travel mainly to Newry, the biggest town in the region, for most of their shopping and service requirements. Indeed, there is some evidence that people will travel across the border for enter-

> tainment purposes. This contrasts strongly with the residents of Protestant 'Glendale', who look to mainly Protestant towns to the north of the region such as Markethill, Portadown and Armagh for the same service.[23]

In short, the regeneration challenges facing many small towns, villages and dispersed rural communities in the disadvantaged rural periphery of Northern Ireland are both complex and multi-dimensional. There are contested policy agendas and priorities, contested spaces and contested traditions which point to the existence of different rurals for different people. As discussed in the following section of this chapter, rural development policy has belatedly sought to make a contribution to the wider quest of restoring community confidence and building stability in these highly vulnerable locales. Against a backcloth of contestation it may be that the singular merit of rural development is its potential boundary spanning inclusiveness based on participation.

Participatory rural planning and development in Northern Ireland

Northern Ireland is marked by a large and vibrant community/voluntary sector. Birrell and Murie[24] have pointed to some 500 community groups and associations in existence in 1975, while more recently the Northern Ireland Council for Voluntary Action[25] has estimated the current combined total of voluntary organisations, community groups and charitable bodies at some 5000. Their interests are wide ranging and embrace planning, advocacy, service delivery and job creation in a manner which is complementary to the work of public bodies and the private sector. Community development processes have been central to these tasks and in the difficult context of Northern Ireland these have sought additionally to construct necessary bridges across a deeply divided society.

As noted by Lovett *et al*[26] the community development movement emerged during the 1970s out of a more radical action-based ethos which proclaimed that people should have a greater say in the decisions affecting their everyday lives. In Belfast and Derry, for example, successful campaigns were mounted against housing redevelopment and road proposals. By the 1980s many community groups had been absorbed as part of the broader state welfare system, with earlier oppositional stances to public policy tempered by a co-optive engagement based on responsibility and funding. While the initial locus of activity was essentially urban, this has been dramatically counterbalanced during the past decade by an increasingly organised rural constituency which has suffered equally from the worst effects of deprivation and violence. Herein, perhaps, is one of the paradoxes of Northern Ireland: the coexistence of a blossoming civil society in the mire of deep societal division. A defining characteristic of this participative democracy is that it involves people in decision making thus nurturing a social ability to collaborate for shared interests. Robert Putnam in his seminal 1993 book *Making Democracy Work* expresses this concept in a more prosaic form: 'I'll do this for you now knowing that somewhere down the road you'll do something for me'.[27] He argues that without these norms of local reciprocity and networks of engagement the outlook in any society is bleak. Outcomes include clientelism, lawlessness, economic stagnation, and ineffective government. Strong participatory citizenship whereby people are involved in planning and in implementation, in facilitative leadership roles and in creating better futures for their own communities is a necessary condition for avoidance of those ills. A benign institutional environment is, however, an overarching requirement. The recent experience of community-led local development and local partnership governance is illustrative of this linkage between rural development and civil society.

Community-led local development in rural Northern Ireland

Increased interest by the European Commission and lobbying at a local level prompted by the recommendations from a pilot rural community action project led the then Secretary of State for Northern Ireland, Peter Brooke, to appoint an Inter-Departmental Committee on Rural Development (IDCRD) in 1989. Its brief was to advise him on the best way of carrying forward action to tackle the social and economic problems in the most deprived rural areas in Northern Ireland. The committee reported in December 1990 with a panel of recommendations. In summary these were: (1) DANI should become the lead department with responsibility for promoting the development of the most deprived rural areas; (2) a permanent inter-agency forum should continue in operation to oversee progress; (3) an independent Rural Development Council (RDC) should be established, sponsored and funded, at least in its early years, by government. Its staff would be charged with responsibility for community-led rural development and the organisation would also provide a forum for discussion between communities; (4) DANI should appoint a small team of local co-ordinators from across the public sector to bring together the responses from all public sector agencies to plans and projects located in the most deprived rural areas; and (5) a specific but relatively small fund for rural development should be set up to supplement mainline programme expenditure.

These recommendations were accepted in principle by government and formed the basis of its Rural Development Initiative launched in 1991. Thus from the outset, a new agency, outside government but dependent upon it for funding, assumed a pivotal role in facilitating community-based social and economic regeneration. The RDC determined that its entry to this field had to be through generic community development in the first instance and in late 1991 commenced the process of appointing a team of six community officers. The 1992–95 Strategic Plan of the RDC defined their role as: stimulating awareness of the value of collective action at local levels; building confidence in ability to bring about improvement; encouraging marginalised groups to participate; and promoting the adoption of good working practices. This community development support was accompanied by financial assistance to facilitate group formation, to participate in training and education activities and to purchase technical services, for example, in regard to development strategies and project business plans. The RDC also articulated in its first strategic plan a commitment to providing a research and information service, and a willingness for co-operation and consultation with a wide range of rural interests. However, there is no mention in the documentation of the role identified by the IDCRD for RDC to provide a discussion forum between communities. This task was addressed by the establishment in 1991 of Rural Community Network (RCN), a voluntary organisation which emerged out of the earlier Rural Action Project with a mission to identify and voice issues of concern to rural communities in relation to poverty, disadvantage and community development.

In November 1996 DANI published a review of progress over the period since 1990. With specific reference to the government's rural development programme, it notes the involvement of over 450 community organisations in regeneration activities; more than 700 people have been trained in community economic development and the management of rural development initiatives; commitments of support totalling £24 million have been given to 42 locally-based projects, and some 375 jobs, concentrated in disadvantaged rural areas, are claimed to have been created. The evidence is that an energised rural constituency has responded to the opportunities held before it, although an annual expenditure of some £8 billion by the government in Northern Ireland sets the modest commitment of the rural development programme in context.

Partnership governance and rural development in Northern Ireland

Partnerships are increasingly being embraced in advanced capitalist societies as a service delivery mechanism. A study by the Organisation for Economic Co-operation and Development (OECD) in 1990 defined partnerships as: '... systems of formalised co-operation, grounded in legally binding arrangements or informal understandings, co-operative working relationships, and mutually adopted plans among a number of institutions. They involve agreements on policy and programme objectives and the sharing of responsibility, resources, risks and benefits over a specified period of time'.[28]

While not being a panacea for solving local development problems, partnerships can be effective mechanisms to improve relationships among multiple stakeholders and to bring together human and financial resources from a variety of funders to achieve common objectives. The concept implies a change in the nature of governance, not as an alternative to elected representation, but with the state taking a less pronounced role in dealing with complex problems such as urban and rural disadvantage or social exclusion. Moreover, the notion of partnerships converges easily with political pressures for a reduction in state activity and increased responsibility at the local level.

The emergence of partnerships is a recognition of the multi-faceted nature of public policy and administration and the inter-connectedness of regeneration decisions taken at the local, regional and international levels. Bryson and Crosby have usefully described this as a shared power or a 'no one in charge' world in which: '... no one organisation or institution is in a position to find and implement solutions to the problems that confront us in society. In this world, organisations and institutions that share objectives must also partly share resources and authority to achieve goals'.[29]

It is not surprising, therefore, that the corporate strategies, operational plans and annual reports of government departments and agencies within Northern Ireland should resound with approaches to creative collaboration. Indeed the rural development arena abounds with local partnerships. These extend well beyond the direct influence of DANI and are located additionally, for example, under the Department of the Environment and the Department of Economic Development. Elected representatives, public officials, the business and trade union sector, and community and voluntary interests are collectively engaged in a more grass roots approach to resolving local problems. The sheer scale of partnership governance for rural development is highlighted by the following structures.

(a) Under DANI's Rural Development Programme, in place since 1991, there are eight Area-Based Strategy Action Groups, each of which is resourced with a budget of £1million in order to lever in additional funding for regeneration projects within disadvantaged rural areas. The first Area-Based Strategy was launched in south Armagh in December 1995 within a border region which has suffered a negative image due to terrorism. The strategy covers small business development, agriculture, environmental management and tourism development and is being implemented in association with a locally-based cross-community regeneration group.

(b) There are 15 Leader II local action groups in which district councils have a prominent leadership role and whose brief comprises the giving of support to innovative, demonstrative and transferable rural development initiatives.

(c) Within each local authority area there is a district partnership established under the EU Special Support Programme for Peace and Reconciliation and with a funding remit which comprises social inclusion, rural and urban development, productive investment and employment (for a further discussion see Hughes *et al*).[30]
(d) Furthermore, each district council has a local economic development partnership which is concerned with the delivery of economic development measures contained within the current EU Structural Funds Northern Ireland Single Programme for the period 1994–99.
(e) The Department of the Environment, in partnership with the International Fund for Ireland (IFI), district councils and rural communities is contributing to small town and village renewal through a portfolio of 51 Community Regeneration and Improvement Special Programme (CRISP) projects. These comprise the blending of a core community business scheme, environmental improvements, and grant aid for private sector development (for a further discussion see Murray and Greer).[31]

Common to all these illustrations of partnership governance-in-action is: (1) the critical involvement of district councils in lead or support roles; (2) the preparation and implementation of locally prepared strategic plans; (3) a dependency upon public funding from EU, IFI and mainstream sources; (4) a high level of voluntary participation; (5) an appreciation that the rural development challenge is multi-dimensional, extending across economic, social, environmental and infrastructure needs; and (6) a policy preference, thus far, for a project-driven implementation approach in which community groups are a central delivery mechanism. There is, however, growing acceptance that this highly differentiated rural development arena is rapidly 'crowding out' through the presence of multiple delivery agents which extend beyond the partnerships identified above, to include other organisations such as Local Enterprise Agencies, the Rural Development Council and Rural Community Network. Moreover, with the benefit of hindsight, serious questions are beginning to be posed about the wisdom of a policy imperative which almost exclusively has advocated large-scale capital support for community-led projects. Difficulties related to project management, profitability and the repayment of loan capital have surfaced in a number of instances. A revised preference is now emerging for more emphasis to be placed on delivery of services and advocacy support, linked with continued capacity building. The bottom line questions to be posed after almost 10 years of activity are the sustainability of this local scale participatory planning and development effort and its future effectiveness when set against the prospect of a normal Northern Ireland; which increasingly will be driven by private sector investment and the quest for regional competitiveness.

In the latter part of 1998, the government released a suite of prominent statements on regional physical and economic planning in Northern Ireland, which include proposals for housing growth, transportation infrastructure and hospital services. The future wellbeing of rural society is inextricably bound up with this portfolio of policy directions and, while space in this chapter does not permit a discussion of each topic, brief consideration is given below to the new draft regional planning strategy for Northern Ireland. This declaration and its preparation is evidence of an enduring policy contestation connected with rural planning and development, but whose mediation, on the evidence above, now requires that policy makers engage with a much more active, better organised and astute rural constituency.

RECASTING THE RURAL: THE REGIONAL STRATEGIC FRAMEWORK FOR NORTHERN IRELAND

In June 1997 the Secretary of State for Northern Ireland, Dr Marjorie Mowlam, initiated the process of preparing a regional strategic framework for Northern Ireland. Over the previous 18 months work had been carried out by the Department of the Environment on a new strategy for the Belfast City Region; but rather than bring the latter to a conclusion it was sensibly decided to merge it with the formulation of a more coherent Northern Ireland-wide analysis and plan. In November 1997 a discussion paper titled *Shaping Our Future: Towards a Strategy for the Development of the Region* was published by the Department of the Environment (NI) to stimulate public debate and to facilitate input to the planning process from multiple interests.[32] The rural constituency responded with energy to that invitation not least on the suspicion that the essential thrust of the Department's thinking at that time was a thinly disguised urban preference which favoured greater development over the next 25 years in the more densely populated eastern part of the region. A popular perception in rural Northern Ireland was that the ghost of the 1960s Matthew Plan had been re-awakened. The discussion paper argued for conformity with 'sustainable urban development principles' comprising proximity, accessibility, vitality, amenity, identity and quality but, in its assessment of rurality, progressed little beyond the identification of environmental resources and the inevitability of agricultural change.

Rural advocacy was facilitated by the broadly-based Rural Policy Forum, and by the Rural Community Network[33] through an intensive programme of public meetings and clinics; but arguably it was the initiative of five district councils in Counties Fermanagh and Tyrone to form a planning compact that has helped to raise the profile of rural development in Northern Ireland to a new level. In making its response, the five district councils, of what became known as the West Rural Region, took the view that any meaningful input into a Northern Ireland strategy could best be represented through a collective voice. The councils were, in addition, mindful of other policy frameworks being devised within the context of *Well into 2000* by the Department of Health and Social Services, an *Economic Strategy for Northern Ireland* by the Department of Economic Development, and a new EU Structural Funds bid by the Department of Finance and Personnel. Accordingly, the Councils commissioned the University of Ulster and the Queen's University of Belfast to prepare an audit of the West Rural Region and to assist with the identification of development principles and themes. The completed strategy was presented to government in April 1998.

In summary, the West Rural Region has the following characteristics:

(i) it covers some 38 per cent of Northern Ireland and, with a 1991 population of 232,000, comprises some 14 per cent of its population;
(ii) fast population growth coexists with high rates of net out-migration; the latter is highly selective which raises issues about the skill base of the region and the quality of education and training provision for those who choose to remain;
(iii) high male and female employment rates are accompanied by high rates of non employment and, in particular, high rates of long-term unemployment among the under 25s;
(iv) the West Rural Region accounts for 35 per cent of all farms in Northern Ireland but 56 per cent of all farms classified as mainly located in Severely Disadvantaged Areas. Some 87 per cent of all farms in the West Rural Region are located within Less Favoured Areas;
(v) the small firm sector is relatively strong, there has been above average growth in public sector employment, but the track record of the Industrial Development Board in promoting jobs within the West Rural Region has been disappointing;
(vi) the settlement pattern comprises a complementarity of towns, villages, townland groupings and houses in open countryside which lends support to a diversified rural economy where pluriactivity is an important feature;
(vii) the West Rural Region contains a diversity of landscapes, a significant proportion of which enjoy protected status. This resource is important for the tourism sector in the region which accounts for some 11 per cent of all tourism expenditure in Northern Ireland.

The important point here is that this type of analysis probed much deeper into the living and working patterns of rural people than was attempted by the Department of the Environment and, moreover, allowed for the crafting of a sub-regional strategic framework which commanded multi-lateral local political support for its content. Thus in its vision for the future the local authorities outline a suite of measures which are designed to strengthen communities, develop business and invest in people.[34] It is not appropriate to dwell on the detail within the limitations of this chapter except to note that these measures fit well with the government's intention to go beyond land use planning, to create joined-up policy initiatives and to engage an active citizenry in the quest for growth and development in Northern Ireland as a whole. These measures also capture the essence of what rural development should champion.

The input of the West Rural Region into the strategic planning process has thus been significant and at the very least has helped to deliver a draft framework which in its tone and content is at pains to be conciliatory to rural interests.[35] For example, the elevation of Omagh and Enniskillen from designated medium growth settlements in the November 1997 discussion paper to Major Service Centres in the December 1998 draft Regional Strategic Framework (Figure 9.3) is an interesting insight into the outcome of contested power relationships which were worked through during that 12-month period. The latter document provides valuable locational guidance for future housing development across the regional cities and towns in Northern Ireland, but in so far as the distribution across lower order settlements and open countryside is concerned, it is content to rely on future Area Plans and development control policy. That clearly, in the Department of the Environment's view, is work for another day but with fundamental implications for the future of rural society.

Conclusion

The analysis in this chapter has sought to unravel the multiple threads of meaning which are wrapped around the concept of *the rural* in Northern Ireland. What is clear is that rurality has become a powerful metaphor for claims related to spatial equity, bottom-up development processes, and intergenerational sustainability. An outside perception of rural areas as solely an environmental resource is being increasingly confronted by the internal reality of active community interests for whom place, culture and identity are powerful signifiers. Within the sphere of public policy there are disturbing tensions which pitch rural development against environmental protection and which surface within the contested arena of statutory town and country planning. This point may be underlined by the fact that many proposals related to rural development do require planning permission. Regional strategies, area plans, development control advice notes and policy statements thus become decision-making aids of first resort in this dialectic of approval versus refusal.

Northern Ireland has the potential to act as a global exemplar in con-

(i) Discussion paper proposals - November 1997

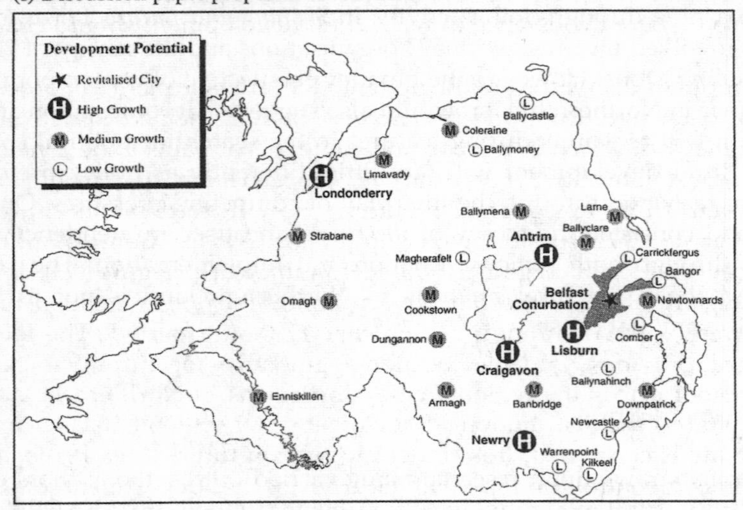

(ii) Draft Regional Strategic Framework - December 1998

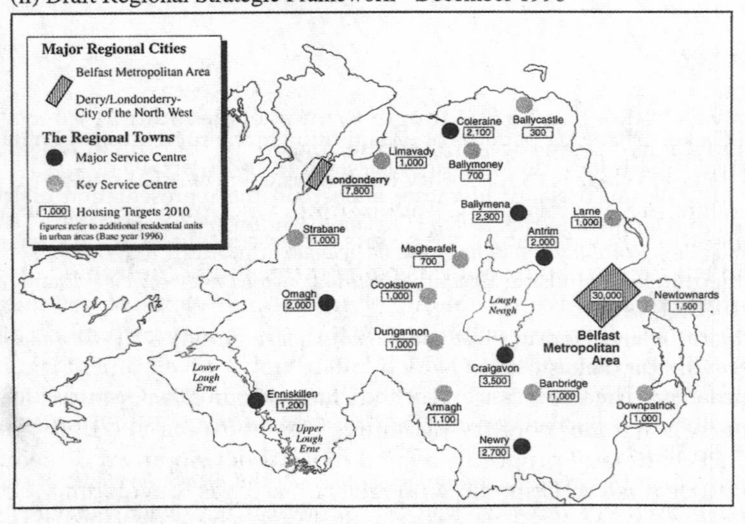

Figure 9.3 Northern Ireland settlements spatial strategy

flict resolution in the way that an accommodation has been forged through discussion, understanding and inclusiveness; and there is little doubt that critical insights from this democratic experimentation in the search for constitutional and institutional agreement have spilled over into the devising of a new consensus for spatial patterns of development. The sheer extent of the many consultative processes embarked on over the past few years in regard to strategic planning initiatives are evidence of that learning through doing activity. In *Shaping Our Future*, for example, this involved meetings with 593 organisations and the receipt of 207 formal submissions. However, the broader perspective of contemporary governance in Northern Ireland would also suggest that contestation and mediation will remain enduring features in the search for political consensus. Rural development will fare little differently as policy preferences are reshaped through the interplay of competing pressures. Only strong and consistent advocacy of *the rural* can offset any tendency to muddle through with policy formation and implementation. The key challenge ahead for rural interests in Northern Ireland is not to be deflected from that cause.

Acknowledgement

This chapter draws upon research being carried out by the authors on participatory rural planning which is being funded by LEADER II through the Queen's University of Belfast/Rural Development Council for Northern Ireland Action Research Partnership.

Notes

1. Paul Cloke, 'Changing patterns of urbanisation in the rural areas of England and Wales 1961–1971', in *Regional Studies*, vol 12 (1978) pp 603–17.
2. P Duffy, 'Writing Ireland: literature and art in the representation of Irish place', in B Graham (ed) *In search of Ireland* (London, 1997) pp 64–83.
3. Alan Gailey, *Rural houses of the North of Ireland* (Edinburgh, 1984).
4. Northern Ireland Housing Executive, *Rural housing policy review – leading the way* (Belfast, 1990).
5. Northern Ireland Housing Executive, *Rural housing policy – the way ahead: a policy statement* (Belfast, 1991).
6. R Buchanan, 'The Ulster Society for the Preservation of the Countryside', in J Forsyth and R Buchanan (eds) *The Ulster countryside in the 1980s* (Belfast, 1982) pp 87–94.
7. J Caldwell and J Greer, *Planning for peripheral rural areas: the effects of policy change in Northern Ireland*, Social Science Research Council Final Report (Belfast, 1983)
8. EE Evans, 'The personality of Ulster', *Belfast Telegraph* Centenary Edition, 1 September (Belfast, 1970).

9. Michael Murray and John Greer, 'Planning and community-led rural development in Northern Ireland', in *Planning Practice and Research*, vol 12, no 4 (1997) pp 393–400.
10. House of Commons Northern Ireland Affairs Committee, *The planning system in Northern Ireland* (London, 1996).
11. Michael Murray and John Greer, 'Prized landscapes and recreation policy in Northern Ireland: the Mournes exemplar', in *Irish Geography*, vol 23, no 1 (1990) pp 43–9.
12. JE Moss and SM Chilton, 'Agriculture and the environmentally sensitive area scheme', in Michael Murray and John Greer (eds) *Rural development in Ireland: a challenge for the 1990s* (Aldershot, 1993).
13. L Symons, *Land use in Northern Ireland* (London, 1963).
14. J Armstrong, D McClelland and T O'Brien, *A policy for rural problem areas in Northern Ireland: a discussion document* (Belfast, 1980).
15. J Caldwell and John Greer, *Planning for peripheral rural areas.*
16. T Haase, K McKeown and S Rourke, *Local development strategies for disadvantaged areas* (Dublin, 1996).
17. B Robson, M Bradford and I Deas, *Relative deprivation in Northern Ireland*, occasional paper no 28, Policy Planning and Research Unit, Department of Finance and Personnel (Belfast, 1994).
18. B Graham, 'The imagining of place', in B Graham (ed) *In search of Ireland* (London, 1997) pp 192–212.
19. P Quirk and E McLaughlin, 'Targeting social need', in E McLaughlin and P Quirk (eds) *Policy aspects of employment equality in Northern Ireland* (Belfast, 1996) pp 153–85.
20. Ibid.
21. B Murtagh, *Community and conflict in rural Ulster* (Belfast, 1996).
22. B Murtagh, 'Community, conflict and rural planning in Northern Ireland', in *Journal of Rural Studies*, vol 14, no 2 (1998) pp 221–31.
23. B Murtagh, *Community and conflict in rural Ulster*.
24. D Birrell and A Murie, *Policy and government in Northern Ireland: lessons of devolution* (Dublin, 1980).
25. Northern Ireland Council for Voluntary Action, *The state of the sector* (Belfast, 1998).
26. T Lovett, D Gunn, and T Robson, 'Education, conflict and community development in Northern Ireland', in *Community Development Journal*, vol 29, no 2 (1994) pp 11–18.
27. R Putnam, *Making democracy work* (Princeton, 1993).
28. OECD, *Partnerships for rural development* (Paris, 1990).
29. J Bryson and B Crosby, *Leadership for the common good: tackling public problems in a shared power world* (San Francisco, 1992).
30. J Hughes, C Knox, Michael Murray, and John Greer (1998) *Partnership governance in Northern Ireland: the path to peace* (Dublin, 1998).
31. Michael Murray and John Greer, 'Evaluation insights from village and small town regeneration in Northern Ireland: a community perspective?' in *Pleanail: The Journal of the Irish Planning Institute*, vol 14 (1997–98) pp 154–70.
32. Department of the Environment for Northern Ireland, *Shaping our future: towards a strategy for the development of the region* (Belfast, 1997).
33. Rural Community Network, *Directory of Rural Community Network members* (Cookstown, 1996).

34. Cookstown District Council, Dungannon District Council, Fermanagh District Council, Omagh District Council and Strabane District Council, *The west rural region: a strategy for people, partnership and prosperity* (1998).
35. Department of the Environment for Northern Ireland, *Draft regional strategic framework for Northern Ireland* (Belfast, 1998).

Chapter 10

Towards a Brave Liberal World? Living with European Rural Policies

John Davis and Sally Shortall

INTRODUCTION

Rural affairs traditionally have played a very prominent role in the economic and cultural life of Northern Ireland. With the exception of the Greater Belfast and Derry areas the region remains almost entirely rural. Within the European Union* agricultural and rural policies have been a cornerstone (some might say a millstone) in the development of common policy frameworks. The Common Agricultural Policy (CAP), including structural funds measures to promote rural development, remains by far the largest common policy programme in the EU: expenditure under CAP accounted for about 55 per cent of the total EU budget in 1996.[1] Thus the CAP is a very important source of support for the region's agricultural sector and rural society. It remains very much an agricultural support mechanism, indeed its primary goal in practice is to redistribute income in favour of farmers; over 90 per cent of CAP spending is for this purpose. The CAP has been rightly criticised for, among other things, the narrowness of its support and adverse distributional effects within agriculture, the large costs it imposes on EU consumers and taxpayers and for the price depressing effects it has had on the traditional markets of agricultural exporting nations such as New Zealand and Argentina.

This chapter looks at some aspects of agricultural and rural change in Northern Ireland within the context of the EU's policy framework. Thus, the starting point is 1973, the year in which the United Kingdom became a member of the European Economic Community (EEC). Agriculture and rural development are treated as analytically distinct topics although obviously both are part of the same rural reality. This approach is used partly for ease of treatment but also to reflect the fact that the activities have tended to be compartmentalised from an EU policy standpoint. The chapter has three main aims. First, to explore the role of agriculture and its ancillary industries in the region and some of the key changes since EEC accession. Second, to provide an overview of the consequences of EC membership for the farm sector, for farm households and the wider rural society. Third, to examine the emergence of EU-promoted rural development policy and practice in Northern Ireland and to identify important issues related to the implementation of this policy in the region. After establishing the nature and role of the agri-food sector in Northern Ireland the chapter goes on to examine experiences within the main farm commodity sectors: included in this section is a look at agri-environmental issues, the agri-money system and the effects of the CAP on agricultural land prices. We then provide an overview of some of the consequences of 25 years of EU membership for the farm sector. The chapter goes on to look at the emergence of rural development in the region and discusses some theoretical and practical issues which we believe have implications for future rural policy and practice.

AGRI-FOOD IN NORTHERN IRELAND

Agriculture and its ancillary industries, increasingly referred to as the agri-food sector, makes a significant contribution to the economy of Northern Ireland: in terms of its importance to the economy the sector lies somewhere between its counterparts in the Republic of Ireland and Great Britain. At the time of accession agriculture on its own contributed about 8 per cent of gross domestic product (GDP) in Northern Ireland. By 1996 its contribution had fallen to 5 per cent; this latter figure may be compared with 8 per cent in the Republic of Ireland and about 2 per cent in Great Britain. The agricultural workforce at accession represented about 11 per cent of the total regional workforce; by 1996 this had fallen to 6 per cent. Again, we can compare the latter with about 13 per cent in the Republic and just over 2 per cent in Great Britain. Taking agri-food in the region as a whole, the contributions to GDP and employment declined from 12 and 15 per cent respectively at accession to 8 and 10 per cent in 1996.[2]

It is frequently argued by the farming lobby that agri-food constitutes the single most important sector of the economy of Northern Ireland. There is some justification for this assertion, even though its relative importance has diminished over time. For example in the 'countryside' it contributes between 20 and 30 per cent of the rural economy.[3] Moreover, it remains an important source of exports from the region: about two-thirds of its output is currently 'exported' (sold outside the region) and this represents about one-quarter of total external sales of the region's manufacturing sector.[4]

Farms in Northern Ireland are largely owner-occupied family businesses. Since 1973 there has been consolidation of farm holdings: the total number declined from 42,000 to 28,000 between 1973 and 1998 and the average size of holding increased from 25 to 36 hectares. Of course, it may be questioned whether, over a 25–year period, this degree of structural change has been adequate to develop international competitiveness in the region's agriculture; and thus to maintain the livelihoods of those remaining in the industry. Evidence presented later in the chapter will suggest that structural improvements have not progressed sufficiently fast. The highly protectionist nature of EU farm policy embedded in the CAP must be viewed as a very important if unquantified factor contributing to such a modest rate of structural adjustment, ie well under 2 per cent per year.

The average size of agricultural holding in 1998 was above that in the Republic (29 hectares) but only about one-half the size of farms in Great Britain (70 hectares). It is sometimes said that the scale of agriculture in Northern Ireland is very close to the EU average but this is somewhat misleading. It is true that the contribution to employment is broadly similar: but agriculture in the EU as a whole contributes less than 3 per cent of GDP and the average size of holding (about 15 hectares) is much smaller.[5] Indeed, dairy enterprises in Northern Ireland are larger on average than in any other EU state.

However, it is worth emphasising the structural differences and weaknesses of agriculture in the region compared with the rest of the United Kingdom. For example, about 61 per cent of cattle and sheep farms are classified as 'very small' compared with about 40 per cent in Great Britain: dairy herds have about 47 cows on average compared with around 70 in Britain. These structural contrasts can create problems and dilemmas when it comes to representing the interests of Northern Ireland in policy formation within an EU/UK negotiating framework. For example, attempts by the EU to modulate CAP support towards smaller farms have, in the past, been resisted by the UK government. The much heavier dependence on food exports in the region can also create unique pressures not experienced to the same extent in the rest of the country, as the EU-imposed 1996 beef export ban illustrated.

The relatively mild and moist climate of the region creates strong comparative advantage for grazing livestock enterprises, ie these enterprises, especially dairying, have low opportunity costs relative to other regional and international competitors. Over 80 per cent of the value-added in agriculture is accounted for by dairying and beef and sheep-meat/wool production: dairying is the largest single element at the farm and processing levels. The intensive sector – pigs and poultry – has a relatively small share of on-farm value-added. However, the poultrymeat industry is the largest employer in food processing and in terms of product development and innovation is probably the most successful part of the food sector. Arguably, its success is due in no small measure to the fact that it has operated with minimum intervention and support under CAP over the last 25 years and has been forced to develop its international competitiveness in order to survive. Crops are relatively minor in Northern Ireland. Indeed, the potato, once synonymous with farming in Ireland, now contributes only 2 per cent of the industry's output.

In the search for future growth and development opportunities in the regional and rural economy the agri-food sector will continue to make an important contribution. These opportunities are most likely to occur in the post-farm processing industries as they continue to professionalise their operations, incorporate more advanced quality control measures and move towards the production of higher added-value products. However, it is questionable whether these industries will be able to make a significant contribution to future growth in rural employment. In the dairy processing industry, for example, Davis[6] identified substantial inefficiencies and the need for rationalisation; this could result in significant job losses in the medium to longer term. Moreover, the EU agricultural policy environment is probably entering an era of relatively constrained support for farm production and so further growth in farm output is likely to be severely restrained. In short, although the agri-food sector must continue to develop its international competitiveness, its contribution to future growth of the rural economy will be limited and its overall importance will probably decline in relative terms.

Finally, some brief comments about trends in rural society. In Northern Ireland about 41 per cent of total employment is located in rural areas: this is much higher than the UK average of 15 per cent and well above the figures of 31 per cent for Wales and 22 per cent for Scotland. There has also been a degree of 'urban to rural shift' of population and employment within the region. Of the 26 district council areas, only Belfast has a declining population. During the 1970s and 1980s rural areas were the only parts of the United Kingdom to experience significant total employment gains. In Northern Ireland this amounted to over 15 per cent; compared with 8 per cent in Scotland and under 12 per cent in Wales. The structure of rural society has changed significantly: it is no longer linked directly or indirectly with agriculture to the extent it was in the pre-EEC accession era. These points are made simply to illustrate that rural change is a dynamic and complex process and that it is difficult to generalise about problems often associated with rural areas, such as depopulation and deprivation. A fuller discussion of some of these issues is included later in the chapter. The reader may also wish to refer to a House of Lords report on the Future of Rural Society.[7]

Experiences under the CAP

Farm households in the region had quite high expectations at the time of EEC accession, as their farm businesses came gradually under the powerful influences of the CAP. Any attempt at evaluating whether these hopes were realised, and indeed the wider implications of the CAP for the region, raises some very difficult questions. There is not the space in this chapter to do justice to all the issues: and there are inherent problems in trying to establish links in any precise way between the development of a sector of the economy and the operation of a particular policy framework, even one as powerful as the CAP. For example, we do not know the counterfactual position, ie the policy regime which would have existed in the absence of the CAP. Therefore, this section restricts itself to establishing some facts about changes in agriculture and the wider rural economy, some of which can be linked directly or indirectly to the CAP.

Dairy sector

At the time of accession in 1973 it was expected that agriculture in the region would benefit from the high price productivist policies of the EEC. This hope was probably fulfilled most clearly in the case of the dairy sector. Following generous increases in institutional support prices for milk, especially in the early 1980s, dairy cow numbers and milk output expanded rapidly; by 1983 milk production was about 90 per cent higher than the immediate pre-accession level.[8] In 1984, the European Commission imposed EC-wide milk production quotas in order to halt the very rapid growth in dairy support expenditure within CAP. Expansion of milk output in Northern Ireland was brought to a halt at just below the 1983 level of production. This was followed by various downward adjustments in quotas; although recent imports of quota to the region have returned production to about the 1983 level. Dairying remains by far the most competitive and profitable farming enterprise in Northern Ireland; as reflected partly in its ability to import production quotas from other regions of the United Kingdom.

One 'casualty' within the dairy sector which can be attributed more or less directly to the EC's policy framework was the Milk Marketing Scheme which provided the statutory powers under which the Milk Marketing Board operated. This scheme had been established, as in other regions of the United Kingdom, in the 1930s: it enabled the producer-dominated boards to sell milk to processors on behalf of dairy farmers. The statutory powers of the boards gave them almost complete monopoly powers in the first-hand milk market. Although their powers were increasingly circumscribed by government they were nevertheless regarded by milk producers as the bulwark of their industry. However, by the early 1990s the boards found it increasingly difficult to defend those powers within an EC policy regime which was promoting trade and integration between member states, ie the European Single Market, and which had a strong presumption against monopoly powers. There was a particular problem for the board in Northern Ireland in that the land frontier with another member state facilitated increasing trade in milk, thus undermining the scheme's regional administered pricing structures. These pressures inevitably led to the abolition of the board in 1995 and to the creation of a voluntary marketing framework; about 70 per cent of producers remained loyal to the new producer organisation, United Dairy Farmers, while the remaining 30 per cent exercised their new freedom to sell milk directly to processors. Without a Milk Board able to operate as a monopolist, processors could no longer shelter behind the administered pricing and profit margins of the old regime. The change in the competitive environment in the region's milk sector was sudden and dramatic; producers and processors are still trying to come to terms with the new situation.

Beef sector

Experiences in the beef sector following accession were disappointing, as this was the main area where expansion had been expected; in anticipation of EEC membership and higher profitability there had been a period of very rapid growth in production prior to 1974. Accession unfortunately coincided with depression in demand and prices following the 1973–74 oil crisis. The transitional arrangements to full adoption of the CAP support measures were not adequate to maintain farm returns and this precipitated a crisis in the industry and a decline in the beef herd which actually continued until 1983. Following reductions in the dairy herd in the years following milk quotas, the beef herd entered an expansionary phase in 1987 which lasted until 1994. However, because of a marked reduction in imports of store cattle from the Republic of Ireland the total number of finished cattle marketed in 1994 was about 15 per cent lower than a decade earlier. Beef enterprises are small scale compared with dairying and tend to be concentrated in the more remote and deprived areas. Their profitability is also weak by comparison with dairying and is highly sensitive to fluctuations in beef market prices.

In early 1996 a crisis in the beef sector was precipitated by a worldwide ban on UK beef exports imposed by the European Council of Ministers. This followed the 20 March 1996 announcement by the British Minister for Health of a probable link between the consumption of beef products, prior to the 1989 ban on the use of specified bovine offal in foodstuffs, and new variant Creutzfeldt-Jakob's Disease (CJD) (the human form of BSE). The ban was a very clear example of the power of the EU in regulating the trade of a member state. There was a sharp fall in consumer confidence in beef in both domestic and export markets and the ban meant that export demand for the region's beef was effectively reduced to zero. The impact was particularly detrimental to the beef industry in Northern Ireland as about 68 per cent of production was being sold outside the region and about 50 per cent by volume exported from the United Kingdom.

During 1997 a major study of the economic impact of the BSE crisis on the UK and its regional economies was undertaken on behalf of the Ministry of Agriculture, Fisheries and Food. The work in Northern Ireland by Caskie *et al*[9] analysed the overall effects of the export ban on the regional economy. They concluded that the various measures introduced by the British government and the EU to compensate beef producers had been successful in stabilising the market in the short term: direct payments under these measures in 1996 alone amounted to about £130 million. The results of their modelling exercise showed the very severe income and employment consequences for the regional economy of any sustained loss in export demand. About 20 per cent of the jobs supported by beef farming were predicted to be under threat. Moreover, the losses would be concentrated in those farming enterprises which were already generating relatively low incomes, often located in the more disadvantaged areas.

It is interesting to speculate about whether and how the BSE saga would have developed if the UK had been outside the EU. It could be argued that the high EU prices for milk compared to the world price provided incentives, in a region with very strong comparative advantage in dairying, for the feeding of dairy cows with relatively high levels of protein derived from animal offal: and indeed there was an increasing supply of this material due to the policy-induced build up in sheep numbers in the region. Another important contributing factor seems to have been the UK government's decision in the early 1980s to deregulate the processing of this offal, thus allowing the infective material to enter the food chain. These issues are currently the subject of a major enquiry. Would the world-wide ban on the UK beef exports have been imposed by the UK government? It is extremely unlikely: although a *de facto* ban may well have been imposed by a substantial number of export customers. Nevertheless, a region such as Northern Ireland, with a relatively low incidence of BSE and a highly developed animal traceability system, would probably have begun to re-establish export markets much faster than was possible within the EU/UK framework.

Sheepmeat sector

This is one area which clearly benefited from EEC accession. Although a common support regime was not introduced until 1980 the breeding flock increased in every year from 1975 to 1993. The attractiveness of the sheep enterprise increased substantially following the introduction of a sheepmeat support regime in 1980: production has now more or less stabilised. The limitations placed on dairy farmers by EU imposed production quotas also gave a boost to sheep production as an alternative enterprise in the 1980s. The total volume of sheepmeat output almost doubled in the decade to 1997. The sector was one beneficiary of the BSE crisis as demand switched to alternative meats, with prices in 1996 about 24 per cent higher than in 1995.

Beef and sheep farming both benefited from the introduction in 1975 of Directive EC 268 which authorised member states to introduce special aids in so-called Less Favoured Areas (LFAs). These aids were intended mainly to compensate hill farmers for natural disadvantages suffered as a result of location and topography. The LFA areas were extended in 1984: in Northern Ireland about 70 per cent of the total land area is now designated LFA. The Hill Livestock Compensatory Allowances (HLCAs) payable to beef and sheep farmers in the LFAs help to maintain the unique character of farming in the hills and uplands. In 1996, about 17,000 holdings in the region benefited from HLCA payments which totalled over £14 million. At time of writing the scheme is under review by the UK government.[10] It seems likely to be replaced by one which places greater emphasis on conserving the fragile ecosystems found in many hill areas.

Pigmeat and eggs

This sector arguably was the most adversely affected by EEC entry. A major influence on its competitiveness is the cost of cereal-based feed inputs. Following entry, much greater reliance had to be placed on relatively high price cereals within the EEC, as access to cheaper grains on the world market was cut off. There was also the problem for producers that the EEC was self-sufficient in pigmeat and eggs and they were not well supported under the CAP: of significance also was the fact that their consumption was in long-term decline at the time of accession. Although pigmeat output recovered from a dip immediately following accession it still remains well below the levels of the early 1970s. The BSE-induced switch to alternative meats also benefited this sector and producer prices in 1996 were 18 per cent higher than the previous year. Egg production declined more dramatically especially in the decade following accession, after which it stabilised: output is now only about 50 per cent of the level at time of entry.

Poultrymeat

This industry by contrast has been a remarkable success story within the intensive sector. It is one of the most interesting cases in the rural economy of Northern Ireland. Unlike pigmeat and egg producers, the industry has been operating in a favourable market environment as a result of rapidly expanding demand: stimulated by a fall in the price of poultrymeat, relative to red meat and shifts in consumer preferences in favour of white meat. Output has increased almost four-fold since the time of EEC entry. A key factor in this industry has been the relatively rapid improvement in technical efficiency in production, resulting in a 40 per cent real terms fall in poultrymeat prices in the decade to 1996. Coupled with this has been very effective vertical integration, quality control, product development and aggressive marketing: these features are in marked contrast to much of the remainder of agri-food which has been heavily protected under CAP. As with beef substitutes the poultry industry benefited from the BSE crisis with output value 18 per cent higher in 1996 than the previous year.

Agriculture and environment

The interaction between agriculture and the natural environment raises a number of complex questions. On the one hand agriculture may be seen as having a positive impact through providing a form of stewardship or conservation of the countryside. On the other hand, the intensification of agriculture brought about by the high price productivist policies of the EU has been associated with, among other things, increased pollution of waterways, destruction of plant and animal habitats and reductions in biodiversity. For example, the HLCA payments to LFA farmers have been blamed for overgrazing of hill land and fundamental changes in certain moorland landscapes. It is difficult to generalise about these issues as there are quite different views in society, for example about the preferred types of natural landscape and the priorities to be given to different environmental enhancement measures. Moreover, it can be quite difficult to discern the preferences and priorities of the general public on these matters as distinct from the views of environmental elite groups.

The first important formal recognition by the EU of the potential environmental problems associated with the CAP was in the 1992 MacSharry reforms which introduced the so-called Accompanying Measurers: Agri-Environment, Regulation (EEC) 2078/92, as well as stocking rate limits on eligibility for the new cattle and sheep headage-based direct compensation payments. The agri-environment programme provides support in member states for a range of measures designed to enhance the environmental impacts of agriculture. In Northern Ireland a notable example is the Environmentally Sensitive Area (ESA) Scheme. The ESAs are location-specific schemes tailored to enhance the environmental features of defined geographic areas: there are now five of these in Northern Ireland. The reader is referred to a comprehensive evaluation by Moss and Chilton[11] of the original ESA in the Mourne Mountains and Slieve Croob. Their study showed that the ESA scheme was one model of how farmers could be compensated for the delivery of environmental improvements, many of which had a public good value. The scheme was shown to provide very good value for money especially when the non-market or public good benefits of the improvements were taken into account. It is likely that agri-environment schemes of this nature will play a more significant role in the future CAP framework. This issue is discussed later in the chapter.

Agri-money

No review of the impact of EU membership on the agri-food sector in the region would be complete without reference to the notorious EU 'agri-money' or 'green money' system. The system itself is horrendously complex, especially as it has operated within the region, and so what follows is very much a simplified account. For more detailed explanations of the current system see Stainer[12] and its earlier incarnations.[13]

The 'green money' system was first devised as a means of countering the effects of currency instability within the EU on farm commodity and retail food prices. The reader should note that all internal EU support prices for farm commodities are set in ECU (or previously using an 'agricultural unit of account'). In the early days of the CAP (1960s) these prices were translated into national currency terms at the then prevailing fixed exchange rates. However, with the currency instability of the late 1960s and the 1970s this would have resulted in substantial fluctuations in farm and retail food prices: the reason for this is that EU support prices have typically been well above world market prices and therefore have effectively determined EU market prices.

The first manifestation of this problem was in 1969 when the French franc was devalued. This would automatically have increased French farm and retail food prices. Rather than allow this to happen, the French government retained the pre-devaluation rate of exchange for the purpose of determining farm prices: thus there appeared the notional 'green' currency rate of exchange. However, there would have been an immediate problem if accompanying trade measures had not been taken. French farmers and traders had an incentive to sell their production in the German market, receive payment in Deutschmarks and convert these to francs at the new advantageous market exchange rate. This had the potential seriously to undermine the German agri-food market. In c to counter this a frontier tax was imposed on French exports which was related to the currency differential: equally other EEC exporters to the French market were entitled to a refund or export subsidy. These taxes and refunds came to be known as Monetary Compensatory Amounts or MCAs. Although it was intended that the system would be phased out over a number of years, the currency instability of the 1970s meant that it became a permanent feature and applied to all member states.

During certain periods over the last 25 years the operation of the 'green money' system has had fairly profound effects on the agri-food sector in Northern Ireland. The problems arose mainly because of the different farm price policies pursued by the UK and Irish governments and, of course, because of the fact that the land frontier could not be adequately policed to prevent smuggling of farm commodities. The 'green money' problems in the region were probably at their height in the second half of the 1970s. Sterling had been substantially devalued against other major European currencies. However, in order to shield consumers from food price increases the UK government was unwilling to devalue the 'green' rate sufficiently to bridge the gap between it and the market rate of exchange. At times there were very large gaps between the market and the 'green' rates, of the order of 25 to 30 per cent. In Ireland, the government was much more farmer oriented and did not allow such large monetary gaps to develop. This created huge incentives to smuggle farm products from Northern Ireland to the Republic, thus avoiding MCA payments. Allegedly, some of this produce was reimported legally, attracting a refund, and then smuggled out again! This practice became known as the 'carousel'. In one two-week period in 1976 virtually all of the cattle marketed in Northern Ireland 'disappeared': the competitiveness of the meat processing sector had been completely undermined. In order to counter the effects the UK government was forced to introduce costly rescue measures, the Meat Industry Employment Scheme. This amounted to payments to meat processors of about £35 million in 1977/78 and £40 million in 1978/79 in order to restore their competitiveness. These monetary problems continued throughout the 1980s but to a lesser extent than in the 1970s (although there was a serious smuggling problem in the mid 1980s). The 'green money' system still exists but, with the introduction of the Single European Market (SEM) in 1992, strict limits were placed on the level of permissible divergence between the 'green' and market rates. This means that farm commodity prices now reflect currency movements much more directly. This was illustrated in the large windfall gains to farmers following the exit of sterling from the Exchange Rate Mechanism (ERM) and the subsequent reversals following the appreciation of sterling in 1996 and 1997. The 'green money' episodes illustrate in a very stark way the dire consequences which can arise from differential rates of implementation of common policies by member states.

The agricultural land market

Finally, one of the most interesting aspects of accession was the impact on the region's land market. The real prices of agricultural land in Northern Ireland from 1959 to 1995 are shown in Figure 10.1. It would be easy to over-simplify the factors underlying these price trends: a more in-depth analysis will be available following the completion of work which is currently being carried out by Myles Patton, Department of Agricultural and Food Economics, The Queen's University of Belfast.

It has always been assumed that rational behaviour on the part of farmers would result in the price of agricultural land being driven mainly by its productive value, ie prices for different categories of land would reflect the profitability of farming enterprises carried out on that land. During the 1960s real land prices increased steadily, reflecting a steady upward trend in farming incomes. However, after 1970 the link between farm incomes and land prices was broken. It would seem that the immediate pre-accession period was one of optimism in agriculture as farmers expected to gain from the high levels of support under the CAP. This gave rise to increased demand for land both prior to and following accession. Land prices rose at unprecedented rates during the 1970s: by 1979 prices reached an all time high, an almost three-fold increase in real value compared with the pre-accession period. During

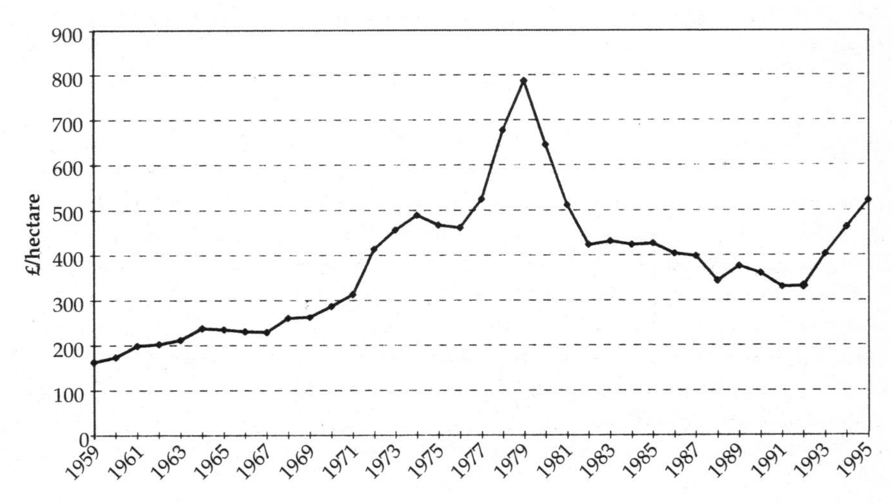

Figure 10.1 Real prices of owner-occupied agricultural land in Northern Ireland (1959 prices)

this period we also witnessed a definite breaking of the link between land prices and farming incomes: indeed, following accession incomes entered a downward trend which lasted until 1980, despite earlier expectations.

After 1979 the land price 'bubble' burst and prices fell sharply over the next three years. Although the rapid decline was halted in 1982, prices continued to decline throughout the 1980s. This trend was probably linked to a change in direction within the CAP, signalled by the introduction of milk production quotas in 1984. There was also an expectation that similar quotas would be introduced for the other major farm commodities; although this did not actually happen until the 1992 CAP reforms. Interestingly, the steady downward trend in land prices during the 1980s was associated with a definite upward trend in farming incomes during the same period. In short, it can be argued plausibly that behaviour in the land market in the 1980s was conditioned by sober reflection on the excesses of the 1970s, fuelled by the over-optimistic expectations of a CAP cornucopia.

The first half of the 1990s saw a return to what seemed to be more rational behaviour in the land market. As described below, this was a period of rapidly rising farming incomes which, in 1995, reached their highest level since accession. Land prices rose very rapidly during this period: indeed in 1993 the price of agricultural land in Northern Ireland moved significantly ahead of the price of owner-occupied land in England, thus reversing an historic price relativity. It remains to be seen whether this apparent return to rationality in the land market is sustained.

AN OVERVIEW

How should we view the overall impact of 25 years of EU membership and the CAP on agri-food and the wider rural economy? It is very difficult to quantify this in any precise way. We have no way of knowing the counterfactual policy or how the sector would have responded to competitive pressures under such a regime. What we can say is that there have been very large financial transfers into the sector; yet partly because of the very unsophisticated nature of the CAP, significant economic and social problems persist in rural areas.

Subsidies, dependence and instability

It seems fairly clear that the differential effects of the CAP commodity regimes have resulted in an agri-food sector which now looks significantly different from what it might otherwise have been. The level of support to the sector has been high, probably considerably above what would have been paid if the UK had stayed outside the EC. For example, over the four years to 1995 transfer payments (farm subsidies) averaged about 50 per cent of total income from farming. In 1996, the additional payments to counter the BSE crisis meant that these transfers accounted for virtually the entire income from farming. During much of the first half of the 1990s farm incomes were buoyant; by 1995 they were at their highest level in real terms since 1973. This situation was due to a fortuitous coincidence of events, linked directly to EU policies, rather than to any significant improvement in performance. First, there was the devaluation of sterling against the ECU following its exit from the ERM in 1992, thus giving farmers higher sterling returns for their commodities whose prices were set in ECUs. Second, world prices for agricultural commodities remained relatively high during much of the first half of the 1990s. Third, the CAP reforms of 1992 introduced new direct headage payments to beef and sheep farmers. These were supposedly to compensate them for the reductions in institutional support prices introduced by the reform package. However, they continued to be paid despite the rise in world commodity prices and their value was enhanced by sterling's devaluation: in effect, farmers were over-compensated.

However, farm incomes are notoriously unstable and in 1996 and 1997 suffered dramatic turnarounds in virtually all farm types. These sharp reversals were due to a combination of factors: a total of six 'green' rate revaluations after mid-1996 which effectively reduced internal support prices by about 19 per cent; falls in world market prices for milk and cereals; and of course the BSE crisis. It is perhaps just worth noting the typical levels of some of these farm incomes and the magnitudes of the swings. In 1995 a typical dairy farm's net income was around £23,000 but by 1997 this had fallen to about £8000. On cattle and sheep farms the already meagre net income of about £6500 in 1995 had fallen to under £5000 in 1997. These figures help to illustrate the very fragile nature and fluctuating fortunes of agriculture in the region. With the possible exception of some elements of dairying, much of agriculture, especially in the more marginal areas, would not be viable without subsidies. On many of the smaller cattle and sheep farms, usually located in the more disadvantaged areas, net farming income consists almost entirely of compensatory (subsidy) payments. This may come as a surprise to the reader. It is a fairly startling fact about the industry's competitive position, when one considers the very high level of EU support over the last 25 years.

Farm households

While the situation in the farm business sector is important in any overview, we would argue that the position in farm households as a whole also needs to be considered: indeed in many ways this is the more appropriate unit of analysis. At the farm household level the picture becomes more complex and, due to data problems, somewhat less complete. It is widely known, for example, that farm households have been increasingly allocating their labour to a range of new activities both on and off their farms and often at the same time retaining their land and some form of active involvement in agriculture. This diversification of household labour is sometimes referred to as pluriactivity: it has brought about a quiet revolution in the nature of farming and the farm household, assisted by various EU farm diversification programmes.

Research by Davis *et al* has produced new perspectives on the incomes of farm households in the region.[14] They analysed the sources and overall levels of incomes in a large sample of households engaged in agriculture in three peripheral regions of the EU – Northern Ireland, Republic of Ireland and Greece. First, they established a Minimum Income Requirement (MIR) or 'poverty line' for each household in the sample which reflected household composition and stage in the household's reproductive cycle. Households were then allocated to one of six groups; three above MIR and three below. The groups above MIR were differentiated according to the relative importance of farm income to total household income. In the case of Northern Ireland they found that while farming provided the major source of income overall (54 per cent), only about one-third of households could be described as 'farm-based', ie were above MIR and generated virtually all of their income from farming. The frequency of 'poor' households was high. About 35 per cent of active households in Northern Ireland were in this category; although this was much lower than the Republic of Ireland figure of 70 per cent. Interestingly, although farming was the single most important source of income for 'poor' households in Northern Ireland, it contributed less than 50 per cent of their total income: welfare payments was the second most important source. These findings highlight the wide variety of circumstances in households engaged in agriculture; and the fact that the CAP has certainly not eliminated the income problems of a large number of these households.

Many of the problems identified above are endemic in agri-food and rural areas of Northern Ireland. They are extremely intractable and may continue to prove fairly resistant to EU policy interventions. It is partly for these reasons that new thinking and approaches to the development problems of rural areas have gradually been taking shape during the 1990s. These have shifted the emphasis slightly within the traditional CAP framework from a mainly sectoral towards a more spatial approach to intervention in rural areas. The rationale for this shift was given initially in the Commission report 'The Future of Rural Society'.[15] These new policy strands have come to be known collectively as rural development.

THE EMERGENCE OF RURAL DEVELOPMENT

While there are now many policy documents and reports on rural development in Northern Ireland and beyond, there is still no agreed definition. It is generally assumed to embody social, economic and environmental advancement. This starts to break down, however, when we debate the relative importance of social, economic and environmental goals. It disintegrates further when we consider whether rural development measures should be targeted at certain groups, or at particular areas. In the same vein Davis[16] argues that there is need for a clearer consensus on the policy problems and priorities which specifically *rural* development initiatives should be addressing. There is also a rather confusing, at least to the uninitiated, set of rural development terminology: 'partnership', 'community', 'empowerment' and 'participation'. These are what Anthony Cohen[17] has called 'feel-good words'; they implicitly sound desirable and positive, and who can be against them? Yet, once we try to tease out what they mean, we discover that this is not at all simple, and usage of these terms frequently belies a less than well thought out conceptual framework and process.

As in most other regions throughout the EU, rural development, laden with all the perplexities outlined above, has taken a more central role in policy and practice in Northern Ireland. EU rural development programmes signal an attempt to move away from sectoral support measures (primarily agriculture) to a more area-based or territorial approach to development; rather than supporting a single industry in a rural area, the emphasis is shifting towards bringing the people of the area together to work out a more inclusive development plan. It is clear that the European Commission and the European Parliament anticipate, perhaps to different degrees, a shift in support policies from a sectoral to a more territorial policy framework. The fraught political nature of this shift is evident in the difference between the Cork Declaration[18] which placed great emphasis on rural development, and the finally agreed Agenda 2000 document, which more pointedly ties rural development to agricultural diversity. In a reformed system, the concern of policy would be less to support farmers per se but more to ensure the sustainable production of environmental and other public goods, together with investment directed towards the future prosperity of the wider rural population. Support may therefore be focused more on environmental measures and on rural development policies which develop the capacity of rural areas to support themselves.

The Cork Declaration begins with a lengthy preamble which commits the delegates 'to promote, in all possible ways, local capacity-building for sustainable developments in rural areas and, in particular, private and community-based initiatives which are well-integrated into global markets'. The Declaration proposes 'an integrated approach', aimed at 'reversing rural out-migration, combating poverty, stimulating employment and equality of opportunity, and responding to growing requests for more quality, health, safety, personal development and leisure, and improved rural well-being'. Moreover, rural development policy must be as decentralised as possible, based on partnership, participation and a 'bottom-up' approach. 'Rural development must be local and community-driven within a coherent European framework', building on the experience of the pilot LEADER programme. Agenda 2000 ties rural development to agriculture to a greater extent than the Cork Declaration. The changed funding arrangements for rural development, such that it is now funded from the European Agricultural Guidance and Guarantee Fund (EAGGF), represents on the one hand a logical marriage between structural agricultural change and rural development, but on the other hand there are fears that rural development will increasingly be narrowly understood as the diversification of farms.

Nonetheless, in both Northern Ireland and throughout the EU, policy statements have recently placed greater emphasis on enabling and empowering rural people to take greater control over their own destinies through 'bottom-up integrated rural development' approaches that owe much to earlier traditions of community development. Yet it is not clear that current practice is well-founded either empirically (does such rural development work? what are the lessons of past experience?) or theoretically (what are the theoretical foundations underlying it?).

In this review of rural development in Northern Ireland we focus on those programmes that emphasise participative structures, partly because, as outlined above, there is increasing EU emphasis on this type of programme. Objective 1 and 5b measures cannot be regarded as rural development programmes in this sense, as they are essentially top-down and with little emphasis on pre-development, capacity-building or innovation. However, it was Objective 1 status that qualified Northern Ireland for Community initiatives such as LEADER and INTERREG. While LEADER is generally understood as the main rural development programme, Northern Ireland also qualifies for INTERREG funding. Peculiar to the region is the rural development funding available from the International Fund for Ireland (IFI), and more recently, the Peace and Reconciliation Programme (PRP), which has a particular rural regeneration sub-programme. Both of these latter sources of funding are available because of the political situation, and have different goals to the LEADER programme. They are also, incidentally, worth more in monetary terms than LEADER.

In what follows we map the path of rural development in Northern Ireland since the mid 1980s. We then outline some of the main sources of funding and consider what we see as key issues arising, as seen through the lenses of rural development theory and practice. In particular there are five questions examined. First, the processes and goals of the various rural development initiatives, and how the latter may be achieved: is the goal economic regeneration, social cohesion, political stability or some combination?; how are social and civic goals weighed and supported relative to economic ones? Second, most rural development programmes now recognise the importance of a 'pre-development' aspect, or a period during which rural groups are assisted and prepared to participate in a territorial approach to development. The question of the time-scale for this aspect of development is often vague, as illustrated by reviews of rural development in Northern Ireland. Third, there is the question of legitimacy, ie the ways in which local government and elected representatives fit together with rural development partnerships. Fourth, are there fundamental underlying problems with the concept of territorial or area-based development? Finally, how do EU initiatives such as LEADER stand in relation to more mainstream programmes? These are five important questions for the future of rural dvelopment in the region and elsewhere. However, before attempting to examine these we begin by mapping out the history of rural development in the region and we then briefly outline the main programmes.

History of rural development

The emergence of rural development in Northern Ireland must be seen within an evolving EU policy framework. In the late 1980s, area-based programmes and 'bottom-up' development came to the fore in EU policy. A perceived failure of CAP and the advent of the SEM required a new strategy to develop lagging regions in order to secure economic and social cohesion; this thinking is set out in the EU Commission report 'The Future of Rural Society'.[19] Community Support Frameworks (CSFs)[20] were agreed with national governments. The Commission stipulated that programmes should be integrated across sectors, and that the preparation and implementation of plans and programmes should involve much greater regional and local participation.[21]

In Northern Ireland the question of rural disadvantage was already being raised. The Maher Report of the mid 1980s, and the Rural Action Project (RAP) clearly identified issues and areas of rural disadvantage, and the need for a political response. These initiatives also highlighted the lack of rural development structures outside agriculture in what was initially the only Objective 1 region in the United Kingdom. The EU rural development vision and strategy fitted well with these studies. While these events are examined in greater detail elsewhere,[22] there are a few points to note about early circumstances which influenced subsequent developments. It is interesting that the RAP was conducted under the auspices of the Department for Health and Social Services, the voluntary sector, and EU funding through the Second Poverty Programme. In other words, it was not initially born out of a rural focus, but was concerned with poverty. This strong anti-poverty focus and the action-research were clearly underpinned by a community development philosophy. Many of the key players in the RAP became key players in subsequent developments, and the RAP philosophy of community development could be clearly detected in the ethos of the ensuing Rural Development Council (RDC). An Inter-Departmental Committee on Rural Development was established in 1989 to advise government on the best way to tackle social and economic problems in the most deprived areas. As a result of this committee's report, an institutional apparatus to handle rural development was created. Rural development was underpinned by commitments to capacity building, community development and multi-sector regeneration projects in disadvantaged rural areas.

The first institutional change was that the Department of Agriculture for Northern Ireland (DANI) became the first ever government department to have responsibility for rural development. It established a Rural Development Division (RDD) with responsibility for developing and implementing policy, administering EU rural development initiatives and promoting awareness of needs in rural areas. Second, the RDD appointed rural area co-ordinators, dispersed throughout the region with responsibility for co-ordinating statutory responses to regeneration plans. In other words they represented the top-down approach to rural development, informing rural groups of the kinds of statutory measures and funding available. Third, the RDC was established in 1991. The RDC, a small public body funded by DANI, is managed by a council of 15 members representing a broad spectrum of rural interests. It was given two main roles. First, to provide all kinds of support to local groups; to help them form, organise, train, appraise needs and resources and formulate plans and project proposals. The RDC had a clear ethos of community development and had regional offices located in areas of disadvantage. The second role was to advise on all matters relating to rural development in Northern Ireland. This advice was seen as emanating from the development officers' close contact with community groups in rural areas, and represented the bottom-up link. Third, the Rural Community Network (RCN) was established in 1991. It was also part of the government's rural development initiative, part-funded by DANI, with further funding through voluntary trusts. It is an umbrella network for community groups and represents the needs and aspirations of rural communities.

What we have described is the *formal* institutional apparatus that developed to implement rural development. There are, however, a plethora of *informal* structures that have emerged. Many partnership boards are also actively involved in operationalising rural development programmes and projects, for example; district council Partnership Boards handle peace and reconciliation funding, Area-Based Strategic

Action Groups (ABSAGs) handle DANI rural deve
Local Action Groups (LAGs) handle LEADER fun
diminishing the importance of these organisations by cal
mal', rather we do so because of their more uncertain stat
rent tenuous sources of funding are terminated.

Rural development programmes

The plethora of complementary and overlapping EU-driven programmes is, in itself, somewhat bewildering; and it is clear that the political situation in Northern Ireland has also shaped the type and number of rural development programmes. Strictly speaking, Northern Ireland does not qualify as an EU Objective 1 region (the criterion being an income per head of 75 per cent or less of the EU average), but an exception was made because of political tensions. Categorised as Objective 1, the region qualified for the LEADER Community Initiative, a pilot programme for integrated rural development, intended to serve as a model for future practice. It is a partnership between the EU, national government and local action groups. The LEADER I programme, 1990–94, provided funding of £4 million. Unlike the rest of the EU, there was only one LAG for LEADER I; it was a formal organisation, the Rural Development Council. It funded 16 projects undertaken by non-profit, community-based companies in disadvantaged rural areas. The Rural Development Council itself questioned the efficacy of its role as the only LAG, given that one objective of LEADER is for local groups to formulate their own development plan for their area. Under the LEADER II (1995–99) programme there are 15 LAGs, and nine Other Collective Bodies (OCBs) engaging in rural development activities, who have bid for and received funding channeled through DANI. This time round, funding is not restricted to non-profit making bodies, and it can be used to finance activities outside disadvantaged areas. The LEADER II programme has funding of about £13 million.

Northern Ireland also qualified for the INTERREG I and II programmes. These aim to build up lagging regions along the border areas within the EU. INTERREG has considerably more funding than the LEADER programme; it is providing £125 million for all of Ireland; this covers all of the North excluding the Greater Belfast Area. It is channeled through the Department of Finance and Personnel, and as it deals with the border region, it has a particular impact on rural areas.

Alongside these EU rural programmes, Northern Ireland also receives substantial funding through the IFI, and more recently the PRP. The IFI was set up in 1986, its objective being to promote economic and social advance in Northern Ireland, and to encourage reconciliation and contact between the two communities. The PRP seeks to pursue its aims through economic and social development. Both the IFI and the PRP have rural regeneration sub-programmes; and have greater funding than LEADER which is probably the highest profile EU initiative.

There are smaller sources of funding made available through Northern Ireland Voluntary Trust (NIVT), DANI, RCN, and the RDC. In order not to complicate things we will not elaborate on these. The programmes we have outlined are sufficient to allow us to pose what we consider to be critical questions for integrated rural development practice at this juncture. Although primarily focused on Northern Ireland, the questions have wider relevance within the EU. So let us now consider some key issues in the practice of rural development.

The processes and goals of rural development

Many of the EU rural development programmes that have developed since the late 1980s emphasise the importance of the *process* of rural development, as well as the end point. There is a holistic view of development with emphasis on local participation, partnership, and greater inclusion and democracy as a result of subsidiarity. This resembles the community development approach fashionable in Asia, Africa and Latin America in the 1950s and 1960s: this was subsequently discarded because of a number of problems, many of which related to a lack of attention to the necessary pre-development work. For a fuller discussion of these issues see Shortall,[23] Varley[24] and Holdcroft.[25] The term 'rural development' implies a particular *style* of development as suggested by Matthews.[26] There is, of course, a rural or spatial dimension: this is characterised by an emphasis on local participation in the formulation and implementation of development objectives for an area, an attempt to include social as well as economic development, and a preference for developing indigenous skills. 'Area-based development' is another term which tries to capture the essence of this development approach.[27] It has come to the fore in Ireland since the late 1980s.

Rural development, area-based development, and a term used frequently in Northern Ireland, community development, all imply a style of development that attends to the *process* as well as the end *product*.

The importance of economic improvement as a goal of rural development is clear in all analyses of the subject. There is a great deal more confusion about social and civic, or community enhancement as a goal. More usually, the latter is seen as a process to a goal; frequently it is justified as a means to the goal of economic development, see for example Zeheri *et al*,[28] and Johnson and Rasker.[29] An evaluation of the RDC in the mid 1990s illustrated this conflict between community development and capacity building as a process and as a goal, and the difficulties for organisations when the value of each is not made clear at the outset of a programme. The evaluation refers to criticisms that there was too much emphasis on the community development 'process', and insufficient attention to the 'product' of social and economic regeneration. It states that 'an underlying assumption was that the capacity building work of the RDC would produce a "pool" of groups and proposals which could be supported by mainstream programmes'.[30] At the end of a three-year period, the review found the majority of the organisations to be at a very early/early stage of development, and as having a long way to go before they could hope to access and manage efficiently and effectively major funding for development.[31] The report notes that community development (in this instance meaning capacity building and animation) is seen to come first, and is not an end in itself but is expected to lead to economic and social regeneration.[32] The RDC assisted in the formation of 88 groups, and provided support for 176 community organisations. The majority of the groups placed stronger emphasis on social and community development than on economic development. Economic development aspirations were present but less pronounced.[33] The evaluation states that 'in relation to local self-help, many of the groups see themselves as providing a vital resource and addressing previously unmet needs in their community. While it is often purely social, it is very important to them'.[34] The current PLANET programme operated by the RDC illustrates similar results. Groups are accessing funds for pre-development and small economic projects, but fewer groups are applying for funding to implement larger economic initiatives. For many local groups community and social development is an end goal. This is not to suggest that they do not also recognise the importance of economic improvement. There is also evidence to suggest that those groups who undertake economic development may be different to those that undertake social and civic development.[35]

The priorities attached and commitment given at policy level to capacity building and animation, and therefore to social and civic development as a goal, as opposed to a means to economic development, needs to be more openly debated. In Northern Ireland there are also the added dimensions of cross-community activity and the combating of social exclusion. Interestingly, the rural economic development strand of the PRP in Northern Ireland states as its first objective; 'to promote the economic and thus social regeneration of the communities in the worst affected rural areas'. Here we see economic development preceding social regeneration. The idea of a linear process remains, however, simply the order is reversed. The review of DANI's rural development strategy presents a converse process: first, animation and capacity building (similar to the community development work carried out by RDC), followed by early stages of development, and finally self-sustaining development.[36] The programmes, therefore, display a certain confusion about what comes first, probably reflecting the limitations of a linear concept of the process. Interestingly, the IFI tacitly acknowledged this problem when it introduced its Communities in Action Programme in 1995. Prior to this, the IFI had primarily tried to encourage reconciliation through a focus on economic regeneration. Introducing the Communities in Action Programme, which has a social and civic focus, the IFI stated that while it had focused on economic regeneration activities in the past, it also recognised that the social and community development sectors have important roles to play in revitalising disadvantaged communities (Rural Action Project (NI), *Rural development: a challenge for the 1990s* (Derry, 1989)). It also said that 'given the nature and scale of deprivation experienced by these areas, people living in them are often unable to reap the benefits of economic development (Communities in Action pamphlet, IFI, 1995). The IFI have recognised that economic development alone is insufficient. A question remains, however, regarding the policy commitment to social and civic development goals, rather than social and civic development as part of a process towards economic development. We perceive a need for greater consensus on priorities and approaches.

Pre-development and time-scale

Pre-development is a phase when local groups are 'animated', that is, capacity is generated among local people to work purposefully in collective action.[37] A provision for animation is generally accepted as very important. Mannion points out that all of the actors, local government, central government departments as well as rural development groups need to be trained and prepared for development undertaken on a territorial basis.[38] Otherwise the success of the process is jeopardised from the beginning.

Pre-development, as the term implies, is usually presented as a stage that precedes development.[39, 40] There are some difficulties with this view of pre-development. Frequently a time-scale for pre-development is not specified. The RDC in Northern Ireland employed development workers with a brief of animation and capacity building. A review of the organisation pointed out that the time-scale required for the development model to work itself through in deprived rural communities was never stated. Other reviews, such as the mid-term evaluation of the LEADER II programme, and the RCN's evaluation of its role in the PRP, raise similar questions. How long does it take a community development process to develop into a process of successful social and economic regeneration? Is it possible to produce strong local groups and quality plans and proposals within a period of two to three years? Might the process of capacity building require a longer period, perhaps even 10 years in some areas?

It is unclear how long there is, or should be, a policy commitment to animation and capacity building. This question has particular resonance when we consider the PRP. The stated objective of the Rural Regeneration Sub Programme is: 'to promote peace and reconciliation in rural areas by encouraging activities which bring the communities in these areas together and by helping to develop the rural economy'. The amount of time it can take to build up a sense of community does not become obvious immediately. The two communities in Northern Ireland do not have a history of working together. Indeed, the opposite is the case; while sharing a geographical space, they live separate and distinct lives. Two types of youth clubs, two churches and church activities, two women's groups and so on is the norm in bounded rural areas. Anybody engaged in rural development immediately has to contend with the politics of space: to meet in the Orange Hall, or the Gaelic Athletics Association Hall is a loaded decision, and will exclude a certain group of people. There is little history of a shared, neutral space. Meeting places are tied up with politics and identity, and people do not use the one that does not 'belong' to them. The PRP is providing a means of doing things differently. The most palpable change is the discussion and awareness in rural areas that it is possible to act together. However, it is going to take a very long time. It is a fragile process, and setbacks are easy. What is the time commitment to this process? It is not stated. It is unclear for how long the Peace and Reconciliation Programme will be funded. There has been no considered discussion of the length of time needed for an effective process to take place.

Rather than pre-development being a stage that precedes development, there is an argument for it continuing alongside development. In other words, there is a role for animation and capacity building even after collective action has arisen. This role relates, for example, to the ability of animators to engage groups who may be slow to participate in the development process. Those who mobilised in a short initial period of time are likely to have relevant skills and experience of participation. Those who do not have a history of involvement, or relevant skills, will require more capacity building and continuing animation. This is clear in Northern Ireland where many women's groups and women need increased animation and capacity building to reach the stage that other actors in the local area have achieved more quickly. In 1999, concern is still expressed about the lack of involvement of women, small farmers and the long-term unemployed in rural development initiatives.[41] This issue is also relevant to differences between rural areas. Some areas have a greater history of local, collective action and this immediately places them in a better position to benefit from rural development programmes. In Northern Ireland this has a political dimension. Development workers have long noted the greater ease of initiating participatory development programmes in Catholic/Nationalist areas.[42] These areas have typically felt distrustful of the state, and have been more willing to undertake self-help activities and give voluntary labour. The Protestant/Unionist communities need greater animation and capacity building if they wish to participate in programmes on an equitable basis. The time-scale allowed for this might need to be even longer. Thus a question remains about the commitment to what might be a very lengthy process, with little visible 'output'.

Legitimacy, development partnerships and local governance

There are many rural development partnerships in Northern Ireland. For example, LEADER II requires partnerships, DANI has formed partnerships to work on area-based strategies, and partnerships exist to handle peace and reconciliation funds. Partnerships are mechanisms where form depends largely on the body responsible for the partnership arrangement. In other words, the make-up of the partnership depends on the guidelines of the relevant funding organisation or government body. So, for example, the Peace and Reconciliation Programme stipulates that the district council partnership boards which handle peace and reconciliation moneys must have a particular numerical balance of representatives from the private sector and the voluntary and community sector. The partnerships formed by DANI to work on area-based strategies have a different composition, stipulated by DANI. The LEADER LAGs have a different composition again. This illustrates one important aspect of partnerships: they are not uniform entities and representation of different groups is not automatic with the formation of a partnership; however, it is frequently built into a programme's guidelines. Their shape is thus often determined by the body initiating a rural development programme. Partnerships can be unsuccessful, tyrannical, or representative and egalitarian.[43, 44] It depends on the process of formation, the time-scale allowed and a great deal of work and effort.[45] The funding conditions which give rise to the formation of partnerships in rural areas has often meant that they are assembled relatively quickly. There are difficulties with the sudden, and largely unprepared, development of partnerships. Issues of representation arise. This is of particular relevance in Northern Ireland where the 'cross-community' representation of a partnership is often a key question, and one that sometimes determines funding – 'cross-community' being a colloquial euphemism for Catholics and Protestants.

It is obvious then, that while the aim of partnerships is to be inclusive and representative, they are not necessarily so. What then is the legitimacy of partnerships? Bryden considers the source of legitimacy of new groups and partnerships.[46] As he points out, the state is legitimate by virtue of its democratic structure. Yet can the state transfer this legitimacy to non-state bodies who are not themselves legitimised? 'What is "going on" when the state by-passes legitimate authorities (local elective authorities) in transferring power and responsibility to quasi autonomous, or autonomous, bodies like Local Enterprise Companies, *ad hoc* local groups, committees, etc?'[47] This question was also carefully deliberated in a recent rural development report in the Republic of Ireland.[48, 49] Both sets of authors had reservations about the role of local government in local development. Similar doubts exist in Northern Ireland where district councils raise fears of partisan strategies and lack of skills. Nonetheless, district councils are legitimate by virtue of their democratic structure, and are involved in some partnerships, though not in others. The establishment of partnerships inevitably raises questions about their relationship to local government, and their relative legitimacy. This has particular relevance in Northern Ireland, where close attention is paid to what provides mandate to a group who wish to represent people.

In addition, the power and effectiveness of new structures are weakened if there is not a clear channel linking them to government structures. It is crucial in the interests of effectiveness, and ultimately accountability, that within an institutional framework, roles are clear, and power is formal and legitimised. How new arrangements relate to existing government structures and procedures must be clear. This was illustrated in a recent review of part of the institutional apparatus established in Northern Ireland.[50] The RDC was set up with a brief of influencing and advising government on rural development policy. The evaluation, however, concludes that the RDC was restricted in its ability to fulfil this role because it was ill-defined and meant different things to different organisations, and the mechanisms for communicating policy advice to government were weak (p 3). Furthermore, the study concludes that the RDC lacked *formal* powers to exercise a function in development policies or strategies for disadvantaged rural areas (our emphasis). The institutional apparatus created in Northern Ireland to deal with rural development is impressive. What this review illustrates, however, is how the lack of clarity about formal powers, and how links with existing structures restrict effectiveness. It also leads to questions about the national commitment to and sustainability of rural development partnerships. If normal structures of governance continue to exist without engaging with the newly emerging partnerships, or without clearly established channels of communication, then partnerships occupy a very tenuous position.

The efficacy of an area-based approach

Much of the rural development programme in Northern Ireland is area-based, ie interventions and expenditures are centred on distinct spatial entities which are characterised as 'disadvantaged'. For example, the Rural Development Programme (1994–99)[51] is focused on five such areas.[52] The implicit assumption of this approach is that certain geographic areas can be differentially developed such that the 'development gap' between them and the wider region can be narrowed over time. The NESC Report argues strongly in favour of an area-based approach to rural and local development policy.[53] Although it presents little in the way of convincing evidence it concludes that, 'the experience of recent rural development initiatives ... shows that area-based programmes can promote rural development in ways which are not available to mainstream agencies' (p 104). This, the report argues, is because partnerships between the state, statutory, voluntary, local and community groups are effective vehicles for improved (targeted) policy design and implementation at the local area level.

Although we can see the fairly compelling administrative logic in the selective targeting of relatively small amounts of funding to geographic areas of perceived disadvantage, we believe that the efficacy of the area-based approach needs to be carefully considered. For example, what are the likely economic benefits to these areas from programme expenditures and what is the distribution of benefits? Kraybill argues that the boundaries of small sub-regional areas are much more open in economic terms than those of regional or national economies.[54] This can result in very substantial financial leakages from the area following capital or revenue injections, especially if the manufacturing and service base is already weak. Leakages can also occur as a result of education and training, which can result in the out-migration of young, educated workers from communities that lack competitive income and employment opportunities.[55]

Evaluating the effectiveness of area-based development initiatives in practice is a complex problem; and conclusive evidence is difficult to find. To a large extent the conclusions depend on the policy goals and priorities against which such initiatives are evaluated. At the simplest level the goals may be considered within the framework of the classic efficiency versus equity dichotomy. If overall economic efficiency in the use of national resources is given priority the benefits of area-based initiatives are probably dubious at best, but if equity is to be emphasised, a different picture emerges.

Perhaps the most objective criterion by which area-based initiatives have been evaluated is their ability to generate local employment. In any such evaluation it is essential to distinguish between programme-created and programmes-diverted employment. From the perspective of the development area both types of employment, of course, are positive. However, from a national or economy-wide perspective it is only the programme-created employment which contributes to overall national benefit. This national versus regional trade-off can pose a real dilemma for policy makers.

In a study of the employment generated by Mid Wales Development's factories between 1981 and 1985, Willis and Saunders took account of three distinct but related factors: (a) displacement effects, ie where the activities of aided firms within the area simply displaced those of existing firms within or outside the area; (b) replacement effects, ie where additional jobs in aided firms were filled by workers already in employment rather than the unemployed, thus failing to reduce the Exchequer's liability for social security and unemployment benefit; and (c) multiplier effects, ie the jobs created in non-aided firms within the area and elsewhere in the economy as a result of the additional inputs required by the aided firms and through the spending of wages by the additional workers in the aided firms.[56] They estimated that a total of 913 jobs in Mid Wales Development's assisted factories were additional, ie would not have existed without programme expenditure. These jobs represented 62 per cent of total employment in the firms concerned: looked at another way 38 per cent of the jobs would have existed without the aid (sometimes referred to as the deadweight effect). Of the 913 additional jobs they estimated that 676 had been diverted spatially from other areas of the United Kingdom in response to Mid Wales Development's incentives, ie only 237 or 26 per cent of additional jobs could be claimed as programme-created.

After taking account of displacement, replacement and multiplier effects they concluded that Mid Wales Development's employment initiatives had produced dubious efficiency gains for the UK economy as a whole, assuming a 10–year project life: the social costs of the programme had exceeded the social benefits at the national level. However, from a distributional and spatial perspective their conclusions were quite different: the area-based programme had been cost effective on public exchequer and social cost-benefit grounds. It was the benefits derived from jobs diverted into the region which had justified the programme. Although they identified an efficiency versus equity trade-off they were unable to offer guidance on what the likely magnitude of such a trade-off might be. Hence we return to the dilemma posed above, one which is all too common in development problems.

While there is much more we need to know about the efficacy of area-based development programmes, we believe it is possible to draw the following tentative conclusions. First, the area-based approach is an attractive administrative device for selectively targeting limited rural development budgets (usually small relative to mainstream programmes) to areas of greatest perceived economic and social need. Second, expenditure specifically in support of *rural* development within these areas must have clear, specific objectives which are differentiated from mainstream programmes and thus capable of demonstrating 'added value'. Third, the benefits to development areas of expenditure programmes may well be significantly reduced as a result of leakages from what are essentially small, very open economies: in some cases there might even be net resource losses if the areas are very fragile in economic and social terms. Fourth, area-based employment generation initiatives can probably be justified only in terms of the jobs diverted from other areas, ie through their contribution to greater spatial equity: in pure national exchequer terms there is reason to believe that they are not particularly good value for money. Fifth, environmental or locational goods may present unique development opportunities to certain areas; moreover the public good values of some of these resources may extend well beyond the local area. Finally, and perhaps unique to rural development, the area-based approach implicitly recognises the goal of spatial equity. This is to be set alongside the more traditional goal of economic and social equity as a policy goal: that is to say, *place* and its associated environmental and cultural landscape has a public value which justifies policy interventions. We believe these conclusions have relevance for rural policy makers and practitioners when framing area-based policies and actions.

The relationship to mainstream programmes

A final, outstanding issue is that of the relationship between integrated rural development programmes and the mainstream programmes, which dominate in expenditure terms, and which have become increasingly centralised in recent years. Commins and Keane show that in the Republic of Ireland (and we believe elsewhere) the policy framework is still 'distinctly and strongly sectoral' such that a number of measures for local area rural development have emerged in a compartmentalised form from individual sectoral perspectives.[57] Curtin and his colleagues suggest that 'the absence of an adequate mechanism for horizontal co-ordination of programmes and partnerships at the local level and vertical co-ordination between agencies at the local, regional and national levels is likely to result in a considerable degree of deadweight (activity which would have occurred anyway) and displacement of existing activity'.[58] They argue that local authorities should be made the core administrative organisation for co-ordinating local and rural development through partnerships of the public, private and voluntary sectors. Councils would thus become 'the focus for the horizontal co-ordination of local groups and the vertical links with national administration', while also providing permanence and stability.

As this suggests, apart from compartmentalisation, the other major weakness which follows from a failure to synergise with mainstream programmes is that integrated rural development initiatives may not survive after the initial funding period. Community development programmes are characterised by their temporary nature.[59] As Northern Ireland loses its Objective 1 status in the forthcoming round of funding, the future of LEADER initiatives starts to look more tenuous. As Shortall argues, 'if on the withdrawal of funding there is no significant change in how (governance structures) are organised, then what happened was not a genuine re-thinking and re-ordering on the basis of local and regional authority, but a short-term measure'.[60]

In summary, therefore, since the late 1980s, a tremendous amount of community activity has developed in Northern Ireland which is in no small part driven by the rural development programmes we have examined. There is an incredible energy and willingness to contribute voluntary labour on the part of many people living in rural areas. However, rural development policy and practice is confused, and the aims and objectives are still unclear. What exactly are the goals of rural development? How can we explain programmes that have different understandings of how rural development occurs? Is the development of new structures of governance part of the rural development agenda? Will rural development practice sit alongside agricultural measures in a divorced and segmented way?

A fundamental question remains about the efficacy and sustainability of a lot of the initiatives being carried out in the name of rural development. There is an abiding impression that much of the activity – as with agriculture – is grant-sustained. Is the capacity there in most rural communities to sustain initiatives if and when the funding is stepped down? Over 70 per cent of the rural development programme in Northern Ireland is funded from EU or IFI sources. It is not at all clear what the national approach and commitment to rural development in the region might be in the longer term. In the recent UK reviews of rural policy Northern Ireland was the only region which did not have a rural white paper.

A NEW DISPENSATION?

We conclude with an alternative, perhaps optimistic, scenario, which reflects some of the more radical ideas of Buckwell[61] and others, namely that rural development initiatives could become a much more significant vehicle for channelling funding into rural areas, largely through a restructuring of the CAP. There would be a major shift in emphasis away from direct payments to farmers towards a much greater level of funding for 'Environmental and Cultural Landscape Payments' and 'Rural Development Incentives': funding for these to come from major increases in the current CAP budgets for Agri-Environment measures and the Structural Funds respectively. Under this scenario the CAP would effectively become, by about 2008, a Common Agricultural and Rural Policy for Europe (CARPE). If this vision were to come to pass (which we would now doubt), many of the issues raised in this chapter and elsewhere in this book become even more crucial and a whole different set of questions arise: for example, about the ability of these new programmes to act as vehicles for significantly increased funding, the efficiency and distributional consequences for the rural economy and society, the effects on local and civic governance structures and so on. In practice, however, it would seem that political and bureaucratic structures will continue to frustrate any strategic shift of this magnitude in the policy framework; as evidenced in the Agenda 2000 papers and particularly the final agreement on CAP reform at the Berlin Council in March 1999.[62] We are forced to conclude that the brave liberal world lies some way off.

We have raised many basic questions and have offered some evidence and comment. Many of the issues can only be adequately answered by ongoing and systematic research and evaluation. Unfortunately, due to political imperatives, policy and practice can race ahead of the research and can be difficult to alter even when evidence is available. Yet evidence is important and can ultimately have an effect, as it did in the end (if only imperfectly) in the CAP reform process. We believe that agricultural and rural policies in the region, and elsewhere, must be informed by the research evidence and that this will help to ensure a co-ordinated and effective set of broadly-based policies in support of rural adjustment and change in the new millennium.

* There is a bewildering range of European terminology and acronyms which can be very difficult for the uninitiated to come to grips with. The Union itself has had three different titles. Initially known as the European Economic Community (EEC) it was then renamed the European Community (EC) and is now known as the European Union (EU). The chapter attempts to use the appropriate term for the time period under discussion.

NOTES

1. Commission of the European Communities, *The agricultural situation in the European Union* (Brussels/Luxembourg, 1996).
2. Department of Agriculture for Northern Ireland (DANI), *Statistical review of Northern Ireland agriculture, 1996*, (Belfast, 1997).
3. Department of Finance and Personnel, *Quarterly Economic Report (June)*, Economics Division, (1997).
4. Department of Agriculture for Northern Ireland (DANI), *Size and performance of the Northern Ireland food and drinks processing sector, 1994* (Belfast, 1996).
5. Department of Agriculture for Northern Ireland (DANI), *Statistical review of Northern Ireland agriculture.*
6. John Davis, *The competitiveness of the Northern Ireland dairy sector* (Belfast, 1991)
7. House of lords Select Committee on the European Communities, *The future of rural society* (London, 1990).
8. TF Stainer, *An analysis of economic trends in Northern Ireland agriculture since 1970* (Belfast, 1985).
9. P Caskie, J Davis, and C Papadas, *The impact of BSE on the economy of Northern Ireland* (Belfast, 1998).

10. J Davis, P Caskie, G Gilbreath, and M Wallace, *A socio-economic evaluation of the hill livestock compensatory allowances scheme* (Belfast, 1998).
11. JE Moss and SM Chilton, *A socio-economic evaluation of the Mourne mountains and Slieve Croob environmentally sensitive area scheme* (Belfast, 1997).
12. TF Stainer, 'The EU agri-monetary system', in *First Trust Economic Outlook and Business Review*, vol 12, 2, 1997, June.
13. TF Stainer, 'The EC's agri-monetary system illustrated in the context of cross-border trade in Ireland', in *Papers in Agricultural and Food Economics*, vol 1, DANI, (Belfast, 1988) pp 54–81.
14. J Davis, N Mack and A Kirke, 'New perspectives on farm household incomes, in *Journal of Rural Studies*, vol 13 (1997) pp 57–64.
15. Commission of the European Communities, *The future of rural society*, COM (88) 371, (Brussels, 1998).
16. J Davis, 'Rural adjustment and the research agenda', in *Agricultural Economics Society of Ireland Proceedings* (Dublin, 1994) pp 1–20.
17. A Cohen, (1985) *The symbolic construction of community* (London, 1985).
18. European Commission conference in Cork, 1996.
19. Commission of the European Communities, *The future of rural society* (Brussels, 1988), Commission (88) 601, Final/2.
20. These set out the basis for the disbursement of EC Structural Funds in the Community over the period 1989/93. The overall objective of these funds and other Community assistance under the CSF was to promote economic development to contribute to the raising of per capita incomes in lagging regions towards the Community average and to promote greater economic and social cohesion throughout the Community.
21. Michael Cuddy, 'Rural development in Ireland: an appraisal' in Tony Varley, Tom Boylan and Michael Cuddy (eds) *Rural crisis: perspectives on Irish development* (Galway, 1991).
22. Michael Murray and John Greer (eds) *Rural development in Ireland: a challenge for the 1990s* (Hampshire, 1993).
23. Sally Shortall, 'The Irish rural development paradigm: an exploratory analysis', in *The Economic and Social Review*, vol 25, no 3 (1994) pp 233–60.
24. Tony Varley, Rural development and combating poverty, Research Report no 2, Social Sciences Research Centre, (Galway, 1988).
25. LE Holdcroft, 'The rise and fall of community development in developing countries 1950–1965: a critical analysis and implications', in G Jones and M Rolls (eds), *Progress in rural extension and community development*, vol 1, (London, 1982).
26. A Matthews, 'Agricultural competitiveness and rural development', in JW O'Hagan (ed) *The economy of Ireland* (Dublin, 1995) pp 328–62.
27. Ibid, p 351.
28. Zeheri *et al*, Past activeness, solidarity, and local development efforts', in *Rural Sociology*, vol 59, no 2 (1994) pp 216–35.
29. J Johnson and R Rasker, 'The role of economic and quality of life values in rural business location', in *Journal of Rural Studies*, vol 11, no 4 (1995) pp 405–16.
30. Local and Regional Development Planning (LDRP), 'A review of the Rural Development Council', unpublished (1994) pp 9–10.
31. Ibid, pp 2–3.

32. Ibid, p 10.
33. Ibid, p 32.
34. Ibid, p 36.
35. J Bryden, RD Watson, C Storey and J van Alphen, *Community involvement and rural policy* (Edinburgh, 1996).
36. Department of Agriculture Northern Ireland (DANI), *The Northern Ireland Rural Development Programme: review of progress 1990–1996* (Belfast, 1996).
37. NESC, 'Rural development' in *New approaches to rural development*, report no 97, (Dublin, 1994) p 164.
38. J Mannion, 'Partnership, participation and capacity building: rural development bases on bottom-up strategies', in *LEADER Magazine*, no 12 (1996) pp 6–10.
39. P Commins and M Keane, 'Developing the rural economy: problems, programmes and prospects', in *New approaches to rural development*, NESC report no. 97 (Dublin, 1994).
40. NESC, 'Rural development'.
41. Department of Agriculture Northern Ireland (DANI), 'The rural development programme in Northern Ireland', preliminary discussion paper, 1999.
42. R McDonagh, 'Partnerships within Northern Ireland', in *Partnerships in action: the role of community development and partnership in Ireland* (Galway, 1996).
43. S Craig, *Making partnerships work* (Dublin, 1995).
44. Mannion, 'Partnership, participation and capacity building: rural development bases on bottom-up strategies'.
45. Craig, *Making partnerships work*.
46. J Bryden, 'Towards sustainable rural communities: from theory to action', in J Bryden (ed) *Towards sustainable rural communities* (University of Guelph, British Columbia, 1994) pp 211–35.
47. Ibid, p 233.
48. Commins and Keane, 'Developing the rural economy: problems, programmes and prospects'.
49. NESC, 'Rural development'.
50. LDRP, 'A review of the Rural Development Council'.
51. Department of Agriculture Northern Ireland (DANI), *Rural development strategy, 1994–99* (Belfast, 1994).
52. The Glens of Antrim and Rathlin Island; South Down and South Armagh; the western shores of Lough Neagh; the Sperrins; west Fermanagh.
53. NESC, 'Rural development'.
54. DS Kraybill, 'Towards computable general equilibrium methods in rural economic development', in Rowley *et al* (eds) *Rural development research* (Westport, Connecticut, 1996) pp 155–66.
55. KT McNamara and BJ Deaton, 'Education production and rural economic opportunity' in Rowley *et al* (eds) *Rural development research* (Westport, Connecticut, 1996) pp 17–28.
56. KG Willis and CM Saunders, 'The impact of a development agency on employment: resurrection discounted?', in *Applied Economics*, vol 20 (1998) pp 81–96.
57. Commins and Keane, 'Developing the rural economy: problems, programmes and prospects'.

58. C Curtin, T Haase and H Tovey, *Poverty in rural Ireland: a political economy approach* (Dublin, 1997).
59. Ibid.
60. Shortall, 'The Irish rural development paradigm: an exploratory analysis'.
61. A Buckwell, 'If ... agricultural economics in a brave liberal world', in *European Review of Agricultural Economics*, vol 24 (1997) pp 339–58.
62. Commission of the European Union: July 1997 Agenda 2000: for a stronger and wider Europe, Strasbourg/Brussels, (IP/97/660). The final Berlin Agreement in March 1999 represented a significant watering-down of the original reform proposals in Agenda 2000, and certainly did not elevate rural development to be the 'second pillar' of CAP, as the original papers had suggested. For details of the Berlin Agreement the reader is referred to European Commission DGVI Newsletter Special Edition, 11 March 1999, Agricultural Council, Political Agreement on CAP Reform.

Acronyms

ABSAGs	Area-Based Strategic Action Groups
ADM	Area Development Management
BSE	Bovine Spongiform Encephalopathy
CAP	Common Agricultural Policy
CARPE	Common Agricultural and Rural Policy for Europe
CB	County Borough
CJD	Creutzfeldt-Jakob's Disease
CRISP	Community Regeneration and Improvement Special Programme
CSFs	Community Support Frameworks
DANI	Department of Agriculture for Northern Ireland
EAGGF	European Agricultural Guidance and Guarantee Fund
EEC	European Economic Community
ERM	Exchange Rate Mechanism
EU	European Union
GDP	gross domestic product
HLCA	Hill Livestock Compensatory Allowances
IDCRD	Inter-Departmental Committee on Rural Development
IFI	International Fund for Ireland
LFAs	Less Favoured Areas
LAGs	Local Action Groups
LED	local economic development
MCAs	Monetary Compensatory Amounts
MIR	Minimum Income Requirement
NIVT	Northern Ireland Voluntary Trust
OCBs	Other Collective Bodies
OECD	Organisation for Economic Co-operation and Development
PRP	Peace and Reconciliation Programme
RAP	Rural Action Project
RD	Rural District
RDD	Rural Development Division
RDC	Rural Development Council
RCN	Rural Community Network
SEM	Single European Market
TSN	Targeting Social Need
UD	Urban District

Index